Spirits of the Passage

Spirits of the Passage

The Transatlantic Slave Trade in the Seventeenth Century

Text by MADELEINE BURNSIDE — *Edited by* ROSEMARIE ROBOTHAM
Foreword by CORNEL WEST

Produced by the Bernhardt Fudyma Design Group, Inc.
in association with the
Mel Fisher Maritime Heritage Society

SIMON &
SCHUSTER
EDITIONS

To the Ancestors

Calligraphy by Paul Shaw
Chapter opening photography by José Molina
End paper painting by Andrew Castrucci

SIMON & SCHUSTER EDITIONS
Rockefeller Center
1230 Avenue of the Americas
New York, NY 10020

SIMON & SCHUSTER EDITIONS and colophon are trademarks of Simon & Schuster Inc.

Designed by Craig Bernhardt, Bernhardt Fudyma Design Group, Inc.

Printed in Italy by A. Mondadori Editore

1   3   5   7   9   10   8   6   4   2

Library of Congress Cataloging-in-Publication Data

Burnside, Madeleine.

Spirits of the passage : the Transatlantic slave trade in the seventeenth century / text by Madeleine Burnside;
edited by Rosemarie Robotham; foreword by Cornel West.

p.   cm.

Includes index.

1. Slave trade—Africa—History—17th century.   I. Robotham, Rosemarie, date.   II. Title.

HT1322.B78   1997   96-43859
326'.09182'1—dc20   CIP

ISBN 0-684-81819-1

But they crossed, they survived. There is the epical splendour.
Multiply the rain's lances, multiply their ruin,
the grace born from subtraction as the hold's iron door

rolled over their eyes like pots left out in the rain
and the bolt rammed home its echo, the way that thunder
claps perpetuate their reverberation.

So there went the Ashanti one way, the Mandingo another,
the Ibo another, the Guinea. Now each man was a nation
in himself, without mother, father, brother.

—Derek Walcott, Omeros

Contents

SPIRITS OF THE PASSAGE

The Ignoble Paradox of Western Modernity

By Cornel West

The spiritual strivings of New World Africans began on the treacherous voyages of the transatlantic slave trade. These Dantesque journeys were the ignoble origins of Western modernity and the criminal foundations of American democracy. They constituted the *night* side of the Age of Enlightenment, the reality left unlit by the torch of natural reason. African slavery sits at the center of the grand epoch of equality, liberty, and fraternity, a center often concealed by modern myths of progress and liberation. And black doings and sufferings remain burdened by the unspeakable memories of the Middle Passage—the chamber of horrors enacted on slave ships like the *Henrietta Marie*.

Like other indescribable evils of the recent past, the centuries-long slave trade forces us to wrestle with levels of unjustified anguish and unmerited pain that are difficult to fathom. Most of us would prefer to turn our heads and hearts from this ghastly past and dream of a better future. Yet the pernicious effects and insidious consequences of New World slavery still linger in our perceptions and inform our sensibilities in regard to black people. The vicious legacy of institutionalized hatred of Africans is still with us (even if its raw forms are a bit out of fashion at the moment).

Slavery is nearly as old as human civilization itself, but when the *Henrietta Marie* first landed in Barbados on July 9, 1698, with 250 Africans aboard, the construct of "race" was hardly formulated. The African slave trade was sustained by profit-hungry elites of all kinds: Christian, Moslem, Jewish, European, Arab, African, and American. Yet the distinctive feature of New World slavery was its "racial" character. After a few decades of trans-racial slavery—that is, the enslavement of Africans by Europeans—this ancient form of subjugation became an exclusively black and white affair. This racialization of American slavery was rooted in economic calculations and psychocultural anxieties that targeted black bodies. Thus, the profitable sugar, tobacco, and cotton plantations of the New World were housed and husbanded by African labor, with the result that African men, women, and children defined the boundaries of European culture and civilization.

In fact, the human family was carved into modern "racial" pigeonholes—white, black, red, brown, yellow—in order to control, confine, discipline, and dishonor Africans. Racialized persons and racist practices were systemized and canonized principally owing to the financial interests and psychic needs that sustained the slave trade and New World slavery. The fundamental meaning of this white supremacist ideology is this: New World Africans enter European modernity cast as disposable pieces of property, as commodifiable bits of chattel slavery subject to arbitrary acts of violent punishment and vicious putdown. In short, legalized terror and institutionalized hatred, in the name of white supremacy and Western progress, rendered black peoples economically exploited, politically oppressed, and culturally degraded.

As Orlando Patterson noted in his magisterial work *Slavery and Social Death*, enslaved Africans experienced social annihilation. With no legal status, social standing, or public worth—indeed, no foothold in the human family—black people were natally alienated; that is, they had no claim to any of the rights that signified equality, liberty, or fraternity in European modernity. This meant, in part, that the glorious revolutions of 1776 in North America and 1789 in France were rooted in and based on the economic profits and psychic wages extracted from enslaved Africans. White supremacy is an integral component of European progress, with the evil of African slavery a precondition of progressive breakthroughs in the modern world.

The great paradox of Western modernity is that democracy flourished for Europeans, especially men of property, alongside the flowering of the transatlantic slave trade and New World slavery. Global capitalism and nascent nationalisms were predicated initially on terrors and horrors visited on enslaved Africans on the way to, or in, the New World. This tragic springboard of modernity, in which good and evil are inextricably interlocked, still plagues us. The repercussions and ramifications of this paradox still confine and circumscribe us—in our fantasies and dreams, our perceptions and practices—in these catastrophic times.

Yet the "natural" state of American society is to deny this paradox and downplay the grave consequences of its past and present reality. Instead, race is reduced to specks on our cultural lens to be cleansed in order to be "color-blind" (after more than three centuries of African slavery and seventy years of Jim Crow). Or it is recast as ethnicity so that we all become immigrants who rejoiced upon landing in America (even if black people's right to vote was delayed for nearly two hundred years after 1776). In other words, America's historical amnesia about black humiliation and black suffering is seen as a basic prerequisite for a better American future of racial harmony. Yet history—the past as history and the present as history—will not let us off so easily. The lofty claims of American exceptionalism that hold this country to be somehow outside the iron laws of history ring now more hollow than ever. No civilization fails to reap what it sows. No nation escapes the poison of its ignoble paradox.

The first death knell was heard in the barbaric Civil War in which over 600,000 human beings died by murder or disease. In this instance, the poison returned with a vengeance. And although the Abraham Lincoln–led Union won the war, the white supremacist South won the peace—after a grand but brief interlude of multiracial democratic experimentation. The second death knell was sounded in the turbulent sixties during which over 330 uprisings in 257 cities shook the foundations of American society. And although the Martin Luther King–led black freedom movement won precious civil and voting rights, conservative elites triumphed in the economic sphere. Hence joblessness and job ceilings still constrained most black Americans. Presently, the racially coded discourses about welfare reform, affirmative action, public schools, public health care, prisons, criminal punishment, suburbanization, and immigration still bespeak the weight of the paradox.

The great irony of black striving in America is that the ignoble paradox of modernity has yielded deep black allegiance to the promises of American democracy. The primeval screams and silent tears of enslaved Africans, the victims of American democracy, have been transfigured into the complex art of jazz, the most democratic of art forms. The terrors and horrors of black life have been fought against in the name of a fairer and freer American democracy. The best of the black freedom struggle—men and women like Ida B. Wells-Barnett, A. Philip Randolph, Fanny Lou Hamer, and Martin Luther King, Jr.—has been America at its best. And yet the promises of American democracy, under the gravity of its underlying paradox, remain unfulfilled for most black people in America.

In this sense, the horrible realities and unbearable memories evoked by the *Henrietta Marie* still haunt us. The American government—the mouthpiece of the American people—has not yet even acknowledged the impact of slavery on the present. It has erected no monuments, admitted no memory, made no reparations, accepted no responsibility for the lives lost, wasted, and stunted by the ugly legacy symbolized by the *Henrietta Marie*. The dominant American tradition of myopic denial, evasion, and avoidance of its root paradox still encourages us to turn our backs on the spirits of the Africans who suffered, unacknowledged, during and after the Middle Passage—and on the spirits of their descendants.

Thomas Jefferson trembled when he reflected on the price America may pay for its denial. Herman Melville wrote with heartfelt fear about the consequences in *Benito Cereno*. And Toni Morrison laid bare the human costs—for all of us—in *Beloved*. Can we, as a people and as individuals, muster the vision and courage to grapple honestly with this ignoble paradox of American democracy before we become as shipwrecked as the *Henrietta Marie*, overcome by lashing winds and rain in the deadly Florida straits, caught between the Dry Tortugas and the Marquesas Keys?

Spirits

By Rosemarie Robotham

One story in particular haunts me: A slave ship drops anchor in the colonies. The air on board this ship is unnaturally still but for the occasional cry of a sailor. No keening wails rise from the cargo hold where the black captives lie. No whimpers or sobs punctuate the crystalline morning. There are no moans of pain. On this ship, the Africans below deck are Igbos, a famously proud people from a region of West Africa that is now part of modern Nigeria.

The captain orders his crewmen to conceal as best they can the illness and sorrow that have sunk into the very marrow of these Africans during their long sea voyage. In the ensuing hours, the captives' bodies are washed and oiled, their sores dressed, and the men shaved in preparation for the slave markets. Then, at the barked instruction of the captain, the Africans, most of them men and boys, with a few women and young girls, emerge from the cargo hold, blinking in the sudden glare of the sun. Their oil-burnished skin catches the slanting light, but their gleaming blackness belies the cruel reality of their condition: Their chained ankles and shackled wrists, their pained grimaces and huddled postures offer stark evidence of their diseased and brutalized bodies.

And yet the European colonists who have gathered onshore to get a first look at the new arrivals recoil slightly, for they sense something different about these Africans. Despite their obvious physical discomforts, these blacks do not cower in fear but hold their heads aloft, chins thrust in the air. As they stumble onto the main deck, their eyes seem fixed on some distant memory; their bearing, even in the leg irons, is almost regal.

Now, a young woman emerges from the hold. I imagine her fierce flashing dark eyes, her bright black skin, her head wrapped in yards of colored fabric, her diminutive but muscular body clad in plain Osnaburgh cloth. Almost imperceptibly the rest of the slaves fall in step with this woman. She is their leader, a mystic perhaps, and they follow her as if with a predetermined accord.

As the African prisoners step from the ship onto the shore of the New World, they are pointed to a path that will lead them to the slave barracks to await auction. The young woman moves forward silently, the others behind her. No one understands what is happening at first, but then the woman's feet turn and enter the creek that leads to the sea. The waters swirl around her ankles, splash up her legs, close over her waist, cloak her shoulders. The other Africans follow her without a word, into the ocean, far out, where it is deep. The men follow her, the women and the children follow her, until, one by one, their sculpted black heads disappear below the horizon, and the surface of the Atlantic stitches together in their wake as if they were never there.

I am told that this story is true, that this silent revolt took place in the Georgia Sea Islands in 1803. Often while working on this book, the extraordinary image of so many solemn Igbos walking single file into the water would rise before me, and I would have to pause for a few moments and close my eyes. What vision of emancipation inspired these indomitable souls? What intimations of their future in the New World led this cargo of captive Africans to give their spirits to the sea?

Their final protest hovers in my imagination, their spirits dancing in the Atlantic, heroic and doomed. Later, I learned that the Igbos believed their spirits, guided by their ancestors, would travel home when they died as long as their heads were not separated from their bodies. So great was their belief and their longing to return to Africa that they walked with one will into the ocean as horrified slave merchants and planters watched their profits wash away to sea. For me, this story embodies not just the tragedy of the transatlantic slave trade—the loss of so many powerful spirits who might have helped build a village, heal a child, govern a city, create fine works of art, but who lie instead in the cold dark depths of the Atlantic Ocean—but also the epic courage of a people determined to wrest control of their destiny however they could.

Africans of the diaspora, descendants of those souls transported across worlds by the brutal human commerce, have always believed that the spirits of our ancestors are still there in the water, licking at the white sand shore of Caribbean islands, tugging at the rocky promontories of the American mainland, whispering our secrets, our sorrows, and our triumphs.

But what of the others, those who survived the forced journey only to be set to the task of building new nations in the Western world? In many ways they are the most powerful spirits of all by virtue of the astonishing fact that *they survived*. In the New World, they autographed their labors with their blood and watered fields of tobacco, sugar, and cotton with the rivers of their sweat.

Even now, we know so few of their stories, for most of them perished before they could share the fullness of their experience with the generations to come. Indeed, much of the material that survives about the slave trade was set down by whites: merchant sea captains on the African coast; plantation owners in the colonies; and, later, the abolitionists of Europe whose efforts would ultimately help bring the human trade to an end. Due in part to these abolitionists—who taught some blacks to read and write Western languages, and took down the oral histories of others—a few slave narratives have come down to us from that time.

Still, many millions of lives went undocumented, with the result that, as a people, Africans of the diaspora remain hungry for the personal stories that might shed light on how this long nightmarish passage of history could have occurred. In the fever to understand, we seek to gather up every new detail, carefully husbanding all the shards of the mosaic that will allow us to view the history whole.

This is what we find: The story of the slave trade is, finally, more than the story of how millions of Africans survived the abundant agonies of being ripped from their homelands and forced into bondage on foreign shores. It is more than the story of a single subjugated

race. Rather, it is about the world of human beings, some ennobled by suffering, others deeply corrupted by the role they played in sustaining the tragedy. It is the tale of men and women caught up in the rush of empire-building, people seduced by the desire for personal and economic dominance, people blinded by the idea that their race was supreme, people who, in the madness of it all, lost sight of their humanity and didn't know for centuries that it was missing at all.

The fact is, control and abuse and betrayal and anguish existed on all sides of the transatlantic slave trade. Back in the seventeenth century, no one group held complete power, just as no one group was monolithically suppressed. This book will endeavor to tell the story of the slave trade from all perspectives: African and European and American, through the experiences of both enslaver and enslaved. And it is a good time for the retelling, for now we are informed in our inquiry by the compelling testimony of a seventeenth-century survivor, an ancestral spirit, if you will, that has emerged from the sea.

She is called the *Henrietta Marie*. Three hundred years old, she lies in a watery grave off the coast of Key West, Florida, the earliest slave ship ever recovered and the only one to be fully identified, examined, recorded, and preserved in the Western world. From 1697 through the turn of the eighteenth century, the *Henrietta Marie* plied the waters of the transatlantic triangle—from London to the west coast of Africa, through the horror of the Middle Passage, to the colonies of the Americas, and finally back to Europe—to participate in the largest international business of her time. Through her recovery and the detailed reconstruction of her slaving voyages from such records as public archives, shipping logs, African narratives, seamen's journals, and the artifacts of the wreck itself, the transatlantic slave trade of the seventeenth century can for the first time be traced in concrete terms.

Spirits of the Passage represents the first visual chronicle of the early years of the slave trade, told in part from the decks and the cargo hold of a single merchant slaver. By serving as a touchstone throughout our inquiry, the floating world of the slave ship lends a rare intimacy and immediacy to the larger story of the trade at the time when transatlantic commerce, still in its relative infancy, was taking its final form.

The *Henrietta Marie* made two slaving voyages. The first one, destined for Barbados, completed its trade circuit and was judged a success by its investors. The second one, destined for Jamaica, ended in disaster. While both these voyages offer insights into a period when the transatlantic slave trade was newly burgeoning, the first voyage tells a more complete story, for it embodies all the complexities of the trade of human lives during the late 1600s. Thus, the chapters of this book will follow the three-cornered route of the *Henrietta Marie's* first voyage, examining through its prism the social and economic realities of three cultures that together permitted so appalling an enterprise to grow and thrive.

But if the first voyage illuminates the world of the *Henrietta Marie*, it is the ill-fated second journey that provides the window onto that time. When, in the year 1700, the merchant slaver struck a reef off the coast of Florida, sinking with all hands, she became a carefully preserved time capsule, a ghost of the late seventeenth century who would guard the horrific details of her history for almost three centuries. Some have said that the ship is the ancestors' gift to posterity, an invaluable archaeological record of the early transatlantic trade. Today, each artifact that the *Henrietta Marie* carried is heavy with meaning. The ubiquitous shackles—just short of one hundred pairs recovered from the site of the shipwreck—speak volumes about the restraints needed to subdue the Africans who were the quarry of the trade. Similarly, the superfluous cargo, broken ship parts, and crew's possessions, like the shackles themselves, provide a chilling context for the ghastly human commerce.

The lasting importance of the *Henrietta Marie* is this, then: It makes history tangible. Modern researchers can touch the ship's waterlogged timbers and watch the dark water's natural phosphorescence set the vessel's submerged cannons eerily aglow. We can appreciate the ornate designs on silver sugar spoons used by the ship's officers, and wince at rusty shackles that bound men, women, and children destined for the plantations that would harvest sugar for those spoons.

But when I consider our quest for the definitive story of the transatlantic trade, told through this one slave ship, I am struck by the audacity of our task, for the Atlantic is vast and all those who crossed its Middle Passage have a singular tale. And yet, we have no choice but to piece together the whole, examining each individual story for its hidden clues much as the archaeologists who combed the ocean floor at the wreck site attempted to do. As I picture them sifting through the water, scrutinizing each fragment they find, I am reminded of this line from "Frescoes of the New World," a Derek Walcott poem:

> . . . *we were like children*
> *emptying the Atlantic with an enamel cup.*

We, the inheritors of the brutal legacy of the *Henrietta Marie*, stand on our New World beach, that scarred enamel cup in our hands. Meticulously, we examine the contents of each cupful of sea water, trusting the spirits to speak to us, trusting the story to emerge. Perhaps, as the tale unfolds and we stretch our perceptions across the wide Atlantic to link the fates of three continents, we may at last move beyond the terrors and the angry racial conceptions that divide us, toward the deeper connections that can render us whole. If we choose, we can yet become a whole nation, a healed soul. So listen for the spirits of the ancestors. They can tell us in their sea voices how the story began. And perhaps, in the retelling, they can guide us home.

Chattel Slavery

The Rise of the Transatlantic Trade

A ship is at the center of this tale. She has waited three hundred years to reveal her story, her long sleep stirred only by the tireless currents that eddy around her resting place on the ocean floor. Impaled on a reef off the coast of Florida during a storm in the year 1700, she still holds within her wreckage the tangible objects of a horrifying trade. When she sank, she was a slave ship.

Originally built in France, she had not been destined for the slave trade but entered that life in the same way as many whom she would later transport in her cargo hold. She was a prisoner of war, a stout little merchantman and former privateer, captured during a military skirmish between France and England. When the ship, embattled and bruised, first limped into London's dingy port with her victorious crew of Englishmen around 1697, she found herself moored to a society in the throes of economic transition, a society that had, a century before, begun ferrying slave labor from the African continent to Spain's colonies in the Americas. As the seventeenth century drew to a close, the English were emerging as the world's premier slave merchants, and they displayed little ambivalence about the inhuman commerce in which they were involved. Indeed, they quickly became inured to the suffering of their African captives—men, women, and children bound for a lifetime of unforgiving labor and the lash of colonial masters in unfamiliar lands.

Princess Henriette Marie of France became the wife of Charles I of England. The king's heavy taxes and ardent Catholicism led to a civil war, at the end of which he was beheaded and Henriette, or Henrietta as the English called her, escaped to her native land. Loyalists eventually succeeded in placing her son, Charles II, on the English throne. (Sir Anthony van Dyck, Queen Henrietta Maria of England with Her Dwarf, *c. 1633.)*

This was the environment in which the captured ship would begin her new life. Named the *Henrietta Marie* by her English investors, she would be refitted as a merchant slaver and pressed into the service of the three-cornered trade between London, the west coast of Africa, and the American colonies. The *Henrietta Marie* was a solid little ship with some speed to her. Therein lay her value to the trade, for speed was the quality most cherished in slave ships since the mortality rate among both human cargo and crew rose exponentially with each day spent at sea.

In order to grasp the lasting significance of this humming trade, we must put a human face on it. The blanket consternation inspired by the millions of Africans forced aboard European sailing ships, the easy answers that result from a simplistic perception of "us" versus "them," "good" versus "bad," "victim" versus "predator," must be dispelled if we, the inheritors of the cultures and societies born of the transatlantic slave trade, are to move beyond the single most destructive legacy of that trade: racism.

The *Henrietta Marie* is such a face—not the face of one person but a portrait of a group of people bound together by their participation, willing and unwilling, in the transatlantic trade. Between 1697 and 1700 the *Henrietta Marie* carried over four hundred Africans in chains to the Caribbean. The significance of this particular ship is that her wrecked remains have been found thirty miles off the coast of Key West, Florida, on a reef that is now called New Ground. The *Henrietta Marie* is the only merchant slaver ever recovered that sank in the course of trade. She is also the oldest slave ship ever found and the only one to have been discovered and excavated in the Americas.

Surviving shipping records tell us that the *Henrietta Marie* made two voyages. On the first journey, the ship sailed to Africa in the fall of 1697 and then on to Barbados, where its cargo of slaves sold well. The voyage was completed in 1698 and profited its investors handsomely. Because its success can teach us much about the intricacies of the slave trade during the seventeenth century, we will examine that journey closely in the course of this inquiry. But our examination of that fruitful first voyage would be impossible were it not for the outcome of the *Henrietta Marie*'s second slaving venture.

This second voyage, undertaken in 1699, was a different story from the first. The ship left England with a cargo of manufactured goods that was typical of hundreds of other voyages of the time. She bore pewter tankards, flagons and bowls, and sacks of the ubiquitous trade beads that Europeans used as currency to buy everything from furs to Manhattan Island. Spirits in heavy glass bottles were also aboard, along with bolts of cloth and stock iron that could be forged into spearheads or farming tools. In addition, the ship carried weapons: blunderbusses, musket balls, and cutlasses. All these goods were traded in Africa for ivory, pepper, and slaves. On leaving Africa, the *Henrietta Marie* sailed to Jamaica where the captain sold the African captives and embarked on the voyage home. But, just a few days out, the ship was driven off course, probably by a hurricane, and was wrecked on New Ground Reef.

The *Henrietta Marie* went down in 1700, at the dawn of the transatlantic trade's second century. That date also represents the approximate halfway point of the history of the trade, despite the fact that the vast majority of Africans would not be transported to the Americas until after the mid-eighteenth century. Still, by 1700, slavery was already a well-established enterprise, even though the Middle Passage was not so frequently traveled as it would become, nor had it claimed as many lives as it would later.

So the story of the *Henrietta Marie* is the story of the trade just before it emerged as a full-blown world commerce. This one ship provides a window onto a particular moment in slavery's centuries-long, multilayered history. The insight it offers predates the more familiar nineteenth-century history of slavery in North America, providing a fresh context in which to explore the question of how millions of people were transported to the far side of the globe against their will.

Africa's Wealth

The story of the transatlantic slave trade begins with the Portuguese in the early 1430s. Prince Henrique of Portugal, who would become known throughout Europe as "The Navigator," urged his mariners to chart a new course to the unexplored shores of Africa and the Orient, allowing Portugal to trade for gold, silk, spices, ivory—and African slaves. Henrique was not the first European monarch to trade for sub-Saharan slaves, but he was the first to do so directly, without going through the Moors of North Africa, who in the mid-fifteenth century were still Europe's main procurer of all races of slaves.

Prince Henrique was determined to find a way around the Moors. Not only were their exorbitant fees a drain on Portugal's resources, but the prince felt that these middlemen distanced him from a wider world whose mysteries he longed to penetrate. Frustrated that his knowledge of that world was secondhand and frequently unreliable, Henrique gathered around him some of the most brilliant minds of his day. In a time of spreading xenophobia on the Iberian peninsula, the prince commissioned astronomers, cartographers, shipbuilders, and navigators of every race and creed in the hope that these visionaries would help him roll back the boundaries of ignorance by conquering the seas.

Ironically, this tale of daring, patriotism, and heroism was to have as its subtext the swift acceleration of human misery, although the far-reaching ramifications of Henrique's ambi-

Prince Henrique of Portugal, nicknamed "the Navigator" for his interest in maritime exploration, established a school for cartographers, explorers, and ships' pilots called The House of Winds. (Goncalves Nuno, The St. Vincent Polyptych, c. 1540. Museu Nacional de Arte Antigua, Lisbon, Portugal.)

tions would not be fully realized for another century or more. From the first, Africa was prominent in the Navigator's grand scheme, for that continent's goods and slaves were already well known in Europe. But the fees of hundreds of Moorish middlemen were written into the price of every trade commodity. Henrique reasoned that if his merchants could travel directly to sub-Saharan Africa, they could circumvent these burdensome costs of commerce and secure enormous wealth for Portugal.

Henrique's countrymen were essentially Atlantic voyagers. Not for them the oar-powered galleys of the Mediterranean. Like the other Atlantic nations, they favored sailing vessels: small, highly navigable, stoutly seaworthy. In this context Prince Henrique challenged his seafarers to find a direct route to sub-Saharan Africa and ultimately to Asia—not by following existing overland trails but by finding a new pathway across the sea.

But the journey was hazardous. Uncharted shoals, furious storms, inhospitable coastlines, and the animosity of the Arabs and Africans who inhabited the littoral caused many of Henrique's mariners to lose their lives. Still, each ship that returned brought new charts, and with each new voyage the Portuguese explorers pushed a little farther. New lands and new cultures beckoned them. Inspired by the promise of fantastic riches, they imagined returning home with cargos of gold, ivory, and spices—wealthy and lauded.

Although Africa's riches had been coveted in ancient times by the Romans, the continent's reputation for bounty reemerged in popular lore in 1324 when Mansa Mūsā, the Moslem ruler of the West African country of Mali, made a celebrated pilgrimage to Mecca, dispensing lavish gifts of gold as he went. He gave away so much gold in Cairo that the metal became devalued, and word of his wealth spread far and wide. For centuries afterward, Mansa Mūsā's image appeared on maps of the world as a symbol of Africa's vast treasure. The Moslem ruler was exactly the kind of ally that Portugal's Henrique now sought—rich, generous, and the head of a powerful kingdom—and, for a stake in Africa's wealth, Henrique was ready to deal with whatever political and religious realities presented themselves.

In actuality, Africa's wealth outstripped the myths. In ancient Ghana,[1] for example, gold was so plentiful that by the tenth century its distribution had to be strictly limited in order to maintain its value. This was achieved by keeping gold as a royal monopoly; all ingots belonged to the king. One storied ingot was so large that it weighed thirty pounds, and the

The World Context

A s the Moors breached the inhospitable Sahara to trade for African slaves, and Portuguese mariners pushed onward along the West African coast, bartering for handfuls of captives to be sold as bondspeople back in Europe, the rest of the world pursued its political, cultural, and economic affairs, often with little consciousness of, or concern for, the human plunder that was being initiated on the African continent. The following timeline is a selective sampling of world events related to those territories that played a part in the forced migration of more than fifteen million Africans to foreign shores.

1324

Mansa Mūsā, ruler of Mali, makes a famous pilgrimage to Mecca, leading an entourage of eighty thousand. He dispenses lavish gifts of gold and returns home with Moslem scholars and artisans who assist in the construction of local mosques. Word of African gold spreads throughout North Africa and Europe, the rulers of which begin to look covetously on the sub-Sahara. But they will not find riches in gold; instead, they will earn their fortunes in African slaves.

Christopher Columbus.

1444

The Portuguese import the first African slaves into the colony of Madeira, off the west coast of Morocco, to work their sugar plantations alongside slaves from eastern Europe and the Canary Islands.

1453

Constantinople is captured by the Turks, who close the slave ports of the Black Sea to western European ships. Western Europe's gradual shift to a dependence on African labor is due in part to the loss of its traditional sources of eastern European slaves.

Columbus landing on Hispaniola.

1492

In an action that foreshadowed the religious intolerance of the Spanish Inquisition, King Ferdinand and Queen Isabella of Spain drive out the last of the Moors, who have controlled the Iberian peninsula for seven centuries. Jews, too, were expelled or forced to convert to Catholicism. This same year Christopher Columbus crosses the Atlantic for the first time, establishing on the island of Hispaniola (now Haiti and the Dominican Republic), the first permanent European colony in the New World.

1494

Süleyman the Magnificent is born. He will rule the Ottoman Empire from 1520 through 1560, conquering Persia, the Balkans, Hungary, and North Africa. Under his aegis, the Turkish fleet becomes the most powerful in the Mediterranean, and at his death in 1566 the Ottoman Empire is the most powerful in the world.

1496

Askia the Great, Moslem ruler of the Songhai nation, is appointed caliph of western Sudan. He wages war to extend Songhai rule into central and western Africa, and presides over a thriving slave trade with Tripoli.

1513-16

Michelangelo sculpts The Dying Slave and The Rebel Slave, statues that depict European rather than African slaves.

Michelangelo's The Rebel Slave.

1514

After almost a decade of trying, Portuguese navigators finally reach China. A few years later they establish a trading port at Macao.

The world according to Copernicus.

1614
English settler John Rolfe of the Virginia colony marries Pocahontas, the daughter of an Algonquin chief.

1619
The first Africans are purchased by the Virginia colonists from a Dutch merchant slaver. They are treated as indentured servants.

Cortés meets Montezuma II.

The *Mayflower* sails to New World.

1519
The Spaniard Hernán Cortés invades Mexico with a small army. Entering Tenochtitlán, the capital of Aztec Mexico, he is received by Montezuma, its ruler. With Cortés are the first horses imported to the North American continent. By 1521, Cortés destroys the Aztec state, razing its central temple.

1527
The sack of Rome occurs when the Holy Roman Emperor's troops invade the Eternal City, burning, looting, murdering, and desecrating in a rampage that dwarfs the sacks of late antiquity.

1533
Elizabeth I of England is born. As queen she will initiate England's involvement in the transatlantic slave trade when she sponsors Sir John Hawkins in a 1562 trading mission to challenge Portugal's control over the transport of human cargo from West Africa to the Spanish colonies.

1535
The first modern diving bell is designed, initiating the technology that will ultimately make possible the recovery of shipwrecks such as the *Henrietta Marie*.

Early salvage using diving bell.

1543
Polish astronomer Nicolaus Copernicus's theory that the earth revolves around the sun (rather than the sun around the earth) is published posthumously. His discovery will not gain acceptance for more than a hundred years because it is considered heretical by the Catholic Church.

1548
The institution of slavery is well known in Italy when the Venetian painter Tintoretto paints *St. Mark Rescuing a Slave*.

1565
The Spanish import the first African slaves to the North American mainland. They arrive in St. Augustine, then the capital of Florida.

1575
Miguel de Cervantes, future author of *Don Quixote*, is captured by Barbary pirates and enslaved in Algeria. He makes several failed escape attempts, and is finally ransomed by family and friends five years later.

1603
The Tokugawa, the last of the shogunate warrior dynasties whose power exceeds that of the emperor, take control of Japan. During their reign (1603–1867), the Tokugawa will close Japan's borders, seeking to wipe out the Christian influence that has crept into the culture during a half-century of trade with the Portuguese.

1611
William Shakespeare's *The Tempest* is performed, based on an account of a contemporary shipwreck off the coast of what is now Bermuda. One of the major characters is Caliban, the slave of Prospero, a figure who represents a view of Native American slaves as domesticated savages.

1620
The *Mayflower* sets sail from England, carrying religious dissenters into exile. These Pilgrims, as they become known, land at Plymouth Rock, and a year later the governor of New England declares a day of thanksgiving to mark the Pilgrims' first harvest in America.

Iyeyasu of the Tokugawa shogunate dynasties.

1625

Charles I, England's Protestant king, marries Catholic French princess Henriette Marie, causing religious and civil unrest.

The Dutch purchase Manhattan in exchange for trade beads.

1626

Manhattan is sold by Native Americans to the Dutch for trade beads and other goods valued at 60 guilders, the equivalent of $24.

1631

The English begin to settle the Leeward Islands of the Caribbean, including St. Kitts, Antigua, and Montserrat. Eventually, they establish vast sugar plantations and import large numbers of African slaves to work them.

1665

The Great Plague of London begins. Before its end in the fall of 1665, it will claim seventy thousand lives.

1666

Most of the walled portion of London, a city congested by wooden buildings, is destroyed by the Great Fire of 1666. The Rebuilding Act of 1667 will specify that new structures be made of stone or brick, forever changing the character of the city.

Leather helmet used in Great Fire of London.

1671

Sir Henry Morgan, a notorious British buccaneer sworn to plunder Spain's ships and colonies, is made deputy governor of Jamaica by the English crown. His appointment legitimizes the freewheeling frontier quality of life in the English colonies.

1672

The Royal African Company is chartered to represent the commercial interests of the English crown, trading goods for slaves in West Africa and transporting those slaves for sale in the colonies of the New World.

Broadsheet on the Plague.

1680

Dodo becomes extinct.

1692

During the Salem witchcraft trials in Massachusetts, nineteen people are put to death by their fellow colonists.

1700

Massachusetts jurist and printer Samuel Sewall publishes the first North American antislavery tract, The Selling of Joseph—the same year that the Henrietta Marie, having delivered her cargo of slaves to Jamaica, is wrecked in a storm off the coast of Florida.

1715

Due to the thriving African slave trade, the first shipbuilding dockyard is opened in Liverpool, England.

1725

The slave population in the American colonies reaches 75,000.

1727

In America, the Quakers call for an end to the institution of slavery. Thirty years before, their church had banned the importation of slaves to the American mainland by members of the Society of Friends. The Society will become one of the most dedicated forces in the movement to abolish slavery.

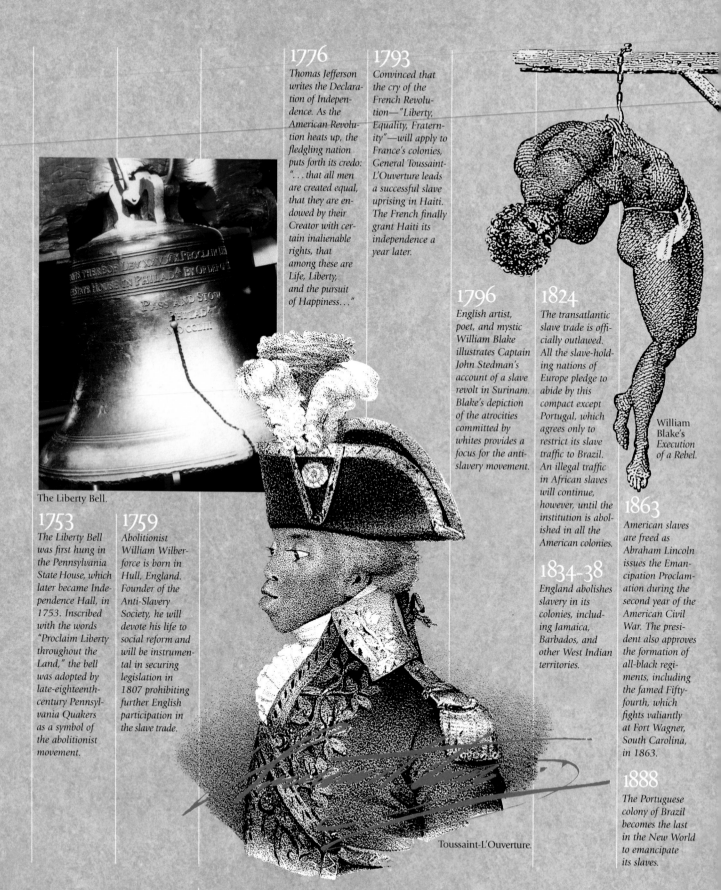

1776

Thomas Jefferson writes the Declaration of Independence. As the American Revolution heats up, the fledgling nation puts forth its credo: "...that all men are created equal, that they are endowed by their Creator with certain inalienable rights, that among these are Life, Liberty, and the pursuit of Happiness..."

1793

Convinced that the cry of the French Revolution—"Liberty, Equality, Fraternity"—will apply to France's colonies, General Toussaint-L'Ouverture leads a successful slave uprising in Haiti. The French finally grant Haiti its independence a year later.

1796

English artist, poet, and mystic William Blake illustrates Captain John Stedman's account of a slave revolt in Surinam. Blake's depiction of the atrocities committed by whites provides a focus for the anti-slavery movement.

1824

The transatlantic slave trade is officially outlawed. All the slave-holding nations of Europe pledge to abide by this compact except Portugal, which agrees only to restrict its slave traffic to Brazil. An illegal traffic in African slaves will continue, however, until the institution is abolished in all the American colonies.

William Blake's *Execution of a Rebel.*

The Liberty Bell.

1753

The Liberty Bell was first hung in the Pennsylvania State House, which later became Independence Hall, in 1753. Inscribed with the words "Proclaim Liberty throughout the Land," the bell was adopted by late-eighteenth-century Pennsylvania Quakers as a symbol of the abolitionist movement.

1759

Abolitionist William Wilberforce is born in Hull, England. Founder of the Anti-Slavery Society, he will devote his life to social reform and will be instrumental in securing legislation in 1807 prohibiting further English participation in the slave trade.

1834-38

England abolishes slavery in its colonies, including Jamaica, Barbados, and other West Indian territories.

1863

American slaves are freed as Abraham Lincoln issues the Emancipation Proclamation during the second year of the American Civil War. The president also approves the formation of all-black regiments, including the famed Fifty-fourth, which fights valiantly at Fort Wagner, South Carolina, in 1863.

1888

The Portuguese colony of Brazil becomes the last in the New World to emancipate its slaves.

Toussaint-L'Ouverture.

king, in a dazzling display of power, used it to tether his horse. Traders, however, were allowed only gold dust, although there was enough of that to make their wealth famous throughout the world.

Everyone wanted the gold. The Arabs who ruled North Africa and much of Spain traded salt for the prized metal and tried in vain to persuade the Africans to reveal the whereabouts of their mines. They frequently raided ancient Ghana, attempting to find the source of the gold, but they were never able to pinpoint its location. To the Europeans, the gold of Africa was as renowned as its source was mysterious. They knew only that the Moors had to cross the desolate Sahara to trade for it and that they charged accordingly. The overland route was not open to Europeans, for the Sahara was an arid wasteland ruled by fierce Berber tribes who were not about to abandon their long-standing ties with the Moors or to permit encroachment by the Europeans on Arab turf.

In approaching West Africa by sea, Prince Henrique's mariners sought to skirt the challenges of the Sahara completely and secure access to the wealth of Africa themselves. Gold would be particularly useful in bolstering Europe's sagging currencies, but exotic fabrics were always in demand; ivory, too, was considered a premier luxury by the European nobility and fetched high prices. The Portuguese were impressed not only with the size and quantity of African ivory but also with the delicate workmanship of the African artisans. Soon, enormous salt containers and other objects were being commissioned by European merchants on one voyage and picked up on another. In this manner, the beginnings of a direct trade were established. But before this amicable agreement was arrived at between two societies that knew little of each other, European seafarers engaged in the more traditional smash-and-grab approach: In 1441, two Portuguese ships seized twelve people from the west coast of Africa.

The Human Trade

For the Portuguese sea merchants, slaves would ultimately prove to be the most profitable form of commerce. Some historians suggest that the earliest seeds of the transatlantic slave trade were sown when the first Portuguese pulled ashore in West Africa. As the Africans approached the boat's strange-looking occupants with curiosity, the Portuguese sailors suddenly fell upon them, seizing the nearest of the onlookers and bundling them into a longboat to be ferried into the unknown. Of course, this happened only a few times before the Africans learned to conceal themselves when a European vessel was sighted or to launch the first attack. No doubt many of the first Portuguese ships lost along the coast fell prey to retaliating Africans. In a very short period, a stalemate was

Moor from the Barbary Coast. The great trading nations of the Mediterranean were familiar with Moorish merchants, including Arabs and Black Africans. (Cesare Vecellio, Degli habiti antichi e moderni, *Venice, 1590. Folger Shakespeare Library, Washington, D.C.)*

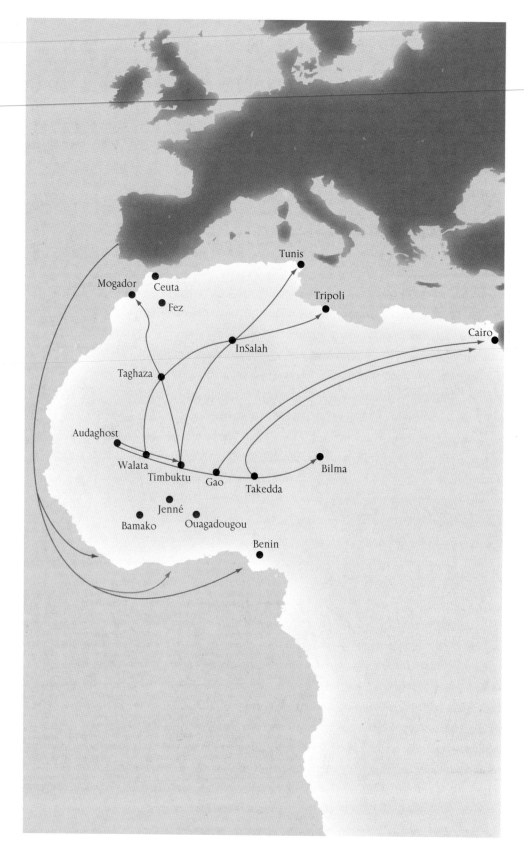

These overland trade routes from North Africa to the sub-Sahara were established over several centuries as Arabs crossed the desolate Sahara to trade for gold, bringing salt and other Mediterranean commodities to the kingdoms of West and Central Africa.

Mogador
Ceuta
Fez
Tunis
Tripoli
Cairo
InSalah
Taghaza
Audaghost
Walata
Timbuktu
Gao
Takedda
Bilma
Jenné
Bamako
Ouagadougou
Benin

reached, and the Portuguese realized that if they hoped to gain some share of Africa's wealth, they would have to establish formal trading ties with the Africans.

Between 1456 and 1462, Portugal sent an official diplomatic mission led by Diogo Gomes to open trade relations with West Africa's states. This encounter resulted in the successful exchange of goods and the peaceful purchase of slaves. Arabic became the *lingua franca* of trade for both the Europeans and Africans since both groups had long been accustomed to communicating with the Moors. Thus, a trading compact between Portugal and the West African states was entered into, and a truce of mutual benefit was declared.

In this context, the escalation of the human trade was all but inevitable. Slavery was an old custom in the Mediterranean, and by the mid-fifteenth century the Portuguese already held slaves in large numbers, though few were of African descent. The Africans, too, were no strangers to the idea of slavery. The institution had long existed on the continent, mostly as a way to deal with prisoners of war, debtors, and malefactors. In Africa, as in the Mediterranean, slavery was considered to be primarily a condition of servitude, more humane than indefinite imprisonment or killing outright. Now, with the new trading alliance between Europe and West Africa, the vast numbers of captives who had once been marched across the desert were diverted to the coast and herded aboard European vessels, particularly those of Portugal and Spain. This shift in trade resulted in an influx of sub-Saharan slaves into the countries of southern Europe, bringing new profits to European and African merchants alike.

But the trade would not benefit everyone. When the first captive Africans stepped aboard a Portuguese trading vessel, they embarked on a fateful journey that would be imitated thousands of times over the next four centuries. The agony of the Middle Passage—the sea voyage from West Africa to the burgeoning European colonies in the Americas—became notorious for the millions who died during its course. How many Africans traveled to the Americas in the reeking death ships of the Middle Passage? Conservative estimates range from 8 to 15 million, based on surviving customs records in both Europe and the Americas. More realistic projections run even higher, taking into account semi-legal trade ventures that were not documented, the widespread loss and damage of customs records, and the many countries in which no records were kept. Whatever estimate one accepts, the reckoning in human lives was staggering, almost incomprehensible.

The trade itself grew slowly. At first, African captives were sought after as replacements for eastern European slaves, for the fall of Constantinople to the Turks in 1453 had effectively blocked all access by western Europeans to their traditional slave markets in Russia and the Balkan states. Western Europe soon looked to Africa to fill its need for cheap labor. By 1500, roughly sixty years after the Portuguese reached the coast of Africa, five thousand Africans per year were exported as slaves. A hundred years later this number had almost doubled, and by

The legendary wealth of Mansa Mūsā seemed to know no bounds, and the inclusion of an African in Renaissance paintings of the Magi can be ascribed to his lavish gifts to those he encountered on his pilgrimage to Mecca. (Mecia de Villadeste, Detail of King Mansa Mūsā (Map of Europe and North Africa, from the atlas of Emperor Charles V, c. 1413. Bibliothèque Nationale, Paris.)

1700 the number had soared to thirty-six thousand. Over the centuries, the markets for buyers and sellers of African slaves would ebb and flow, influenced by shifts in African politics, improving maritime technology, and the development of the European colonies.

Nevertheless, there is about the trade the sense of an inexorable growth that, once begun, could barely be stopped. Africa would suffer an enormous depletion of its population, while the Americas would be bolstered by the forced immigration of a significant new race of people who would contribute their energies to the building of the New World alongside European settlers and native inhabitants.

Looking at these displaced Africans from the perspective of history, individual stories are obscured by the dry statistics, and each personal experience of servitude becomes lost in the mass. Terror, triumph, rebellion, compassion—all are subsumed by the overwhelming numbers, and the complexities of human misery are diminished. And yet, so many changes to the world as it existed were presaged in the sorrowing steps of those first victims of the transatlantic trade. The acceleration of the slave trade in the late fifteenth century would bring nothing less than a new economic world order. But it would also set in motion an unprecedented horror that would ultimately indict the institution of slavery itself. Slavery would finally be brought to an end in European countries and their colonies as a direct result of the struggles of Africans against their enslavement in the Americas, and the support and activism of those who empathized with their plight.

The Pirate Coast of Barbary

By the time Prince Henrique dispatched his fleet of mariners in search of new trade alliances for Portugal, slavery was already an ancient and widespread institution, frequently mentioned in the Bible and evident in the accounts of early historical documents. Slave labor is thought to have built the pyramids of Egypt, the Sudan, and South America; constructed the Seven Wonders of the World; and supported the glory that was classical Greece and the splendor that was ancient Rome. Human bondage took a variety of forms, depending on the society in which an enslaved person served. In some, a slave might eventually be freed and could rise to the ranks of the nobility; in others, he or she might live the life of a disposable pack animal.

After the fall of imperial Rome in A.D. 476, slavery declined in Europe until the Dark Ages. A resurgence came during the seventh century as various German tribes expanded eastward, capturing large numbers of people, among them the Slavic tribes of Middle Europe. The word "Slav" meant "people of culture superior to all others," and, indeed, the Slavs viewed anyone not of their own people as barbarians. Exported into bondage by their German captors, the Slavs ironically came to embody the very condition of being enslaved, and the words "Slav" and "slave" became synonymous in European languages.

Always a source of cheap labor, slavery was also an effective way to dispose of individuals deemed problematic; hence prisoners of war provided the greatest number of slaves in all cul-

Subject to a form of bound labor, medieval serfs are depicted here going about farming activities during the fall. Serfs did not belong to the lord of the manor personally but to the land itself so that a change in ownership barely affected the meager circumstances of these bondsmen. (The Limbourg Brothers, "October," Les Très Riches Heures du Duc de Berry, 1413–16. Musée Condé, Chantilly, France.)

tures. When invaders or defenders decided to give quarter, they often left numbers of people who would in all likelihood stage an uprising if left to their own devices. The larger the force conquered, the greater the potential problem—unless the prisoners could be politically and economically neutralized. Slavery provided such protection and was certainly a more humane approach than mass execution. Safest of all was the practice of selling slaves to other nations, trading them far from their native lands so that they had no hope of returning home. Abroad, the captives could be easily recognized as foreigners, and there they would have no underground or local community that might support them.

Slavery underwent another revival during the tenth century on the Mediterranean's southern coast, then called the Barbary Coast, when the militant spread of Islam brought with it a huge increase in the number of prisoners of war and thus of enslaved people. Not all of these captives were poorly treated. Indeed, the Arabs relied heavily on their slaves and sometimes gave them high responsibilities.

Accounts abound of enslaved Europeans who, deciding that they had no better alternative, "turned Turk," embracing Islam and seeking a career among the Arabs. The opportunities afforded a European within the Islamic empire were often better than those back home, hence the vast numbers of renegades from countries such as Corsica, off the west coast of Italy. Indeed, some of the most notorious pirates of the Barbary states—which included the Islamic nations of Algiers, Tunis, Tripoli, and Morocco—were, in fact, renegade Europeans, valued for their experience as sailors and promoted accordingly. Conversion to Islam, a vital step in turning Turk, was encouraged and would increase a European's opportunities and standing. Many were freed immediately after their conversion, although this was by no means automatic and frequently not desirable: A slave could achieve higher rank and a position of greater trust than a free man, who had to fend for himself. A slave might also benefit quite handsomely from the means and protection offered him by a benevolent master.

Among the many cases of European renegades who thrived on the Barbary Coast is that of a young Englishman, the son of a Bristol merchant, captured by Barbary pirates. After turning Turk, he rose to become the treasurer of the dey of Algiers. (Dey was the title given to the political rulers of the Barbary states.) So powerful did he become that in 1586 he offered to intercede on behalf of English slaves to make their ransom an easier process.[2]

Slavery under Islam was a complex matter, and for every story of a thriving renegade there are thousands who disappeared into the ranks of unknown captives, treated as draft animals, worked to death, and killed at their master's whim. Many of these unfortunate souls toiled as anonymous galley slaves.

The galley was the primary warship and mode of transportation in the Mediterranean during the Renaissance period. Galleys consumed enormous numbers of slaves, just as they had in ancient Rome. Life on the galleys proved short for anyone not in excellent condition; therefore galley slaves were usually selected for their vigor and strength. These oarsmen did not sit on benches to row; they worked standing and had to leap forward, throwing their whole weight behind the oar to propel the ship. The task required tremendous physical endurance in which the slaves were amply encouraged by the lash of an overseer.

Galley slaves had an average survival rate of only nine years, comparable to the notoriously low rate for sugar workers on the American plantations of the eighteenth century. But on the galleys, scurvy and generally poor diet may have been more significant factors in the high mortality rate than heart-bursting labor. While horrific abuses aboard galleys are the stuff of legends, in fact it was unusual for oarsmen to be worked continually. Rather, a skilled overseer would try to conserve the men's strength for those moments in which it was needed.

Even after the medieval period ended, European peasants continued to work for the lord of the manor much as their ancestors had done. They were no longer bonded serfs, however. Although they had few opportunities to pursue other livelihoods, they were nevertheless free to do so. (Wenzel Hollar, Peasant Plowing, c. 1650.)

When possible, the galley's lateen sails would be raised so that the men could rest until their efforts were required either to maneuver smartly or to press the ship's pace.

Prisoners of war and malefactors comprised the bulk of galley slave crews. In Christian countries, crimes against the state often carried a galley sentence, with seven years as a galley slave being the punishment for smuggling gold from Spain's colonies. For a fair number of these offenders, time aboard a galley would have been tantamount to a death sentence.

The ship's open design, which had changed little since the time of ancient Rome, and the large number of slaves required to man it made the galley a particularly attractive target for the Barbary pirates. Investing in piratical and privateering voyages proved profitable for both the Moors and the Christians, and many supposedly respectable merchants often dabbled in piracy. For some of the European traders, the distinction between their identities as a merchant or pirate might be one of opportunity. The Pisans and the Genoese, who exerted themselves in the trade with North Africa, were among the most successful pirates, and many of the people sold in Italian slave markets were acquired from this moonlighting activity.

As many as two hundred men might be required to man a galley. Frequently, commanders did not own enough slaves and were forced to hire additional hands from slave owners, a situation rewarding to the owners who not only received rental fees but shares of any prize, or goods, taken from a captured ship. Strictly speaking, the rented slave who manned the galley, and not the master, was due the share of the prize, but as this share had to be rendered to the master, even those slave owners who allowed their slaves to keep a small portion of the booty profited handsomely.[3]

By the fourteenth century, piracy was second only to the overland trade between the Moors and sub-Saharan Africa as the most common source of slaves. Even as trading treaties between European and Arab nations were being negotiated, predators on that trade were already sharpening their swords. For the Arabs, being a corsair, or privateer, was considered a noble profession since corsairs were essentially sea merchants sanctioned by the state. And yet the *rais*, or corsair captain, did not necessarily feel bound by his country's trade treaties, nor could his activities easily be controlled to enforce safe passage of foreign ships. Sailors and merchants, both Christian and Moslem, ran a constant risk of falling prey to pirates of the opposing faith. Many escaped or were ransomed, only to be captured and forced into slavery a second time.

At sea a cache of prisoners for ransom or sale was as good a haul as a cargo of goods. But pirate raids were not confined to ships. The Barbary corsairs took their largest numbers of prisoners on land. The younger of the Barbarossa brothers, one of the most infamous corsairs of the sixteenth century, brought five thousand captives back to Tunis from the Mediterranean island of Minorca alone. Land raids were staged in which so many people were captured that they could not all fit aboard the pirate ships and so had to be held in an encampment. As long as the captives remained in their native lands, their friends and relatives were allowed to come and ransom them.[4]

The Ransomed Children

Barbarossa and the Priest from Seville

The robust, red-bearded Barbarossa brothers, 'Arūj and Khayr ad-Dīn, were the two most infamous corsairs of all time. In the theater of the open sea, they proved as cunning as they were bold, each driven by an overweening piratical ambition that conveniently bolstered the sultan of the Ottoman Empire in his holy war against Christendom. As a consequence of their dedicated piracy between 1504, when 'Arūj first made his mark by commandeering two papal galleys, and 1546, when Khayr ad-Dīn finally succumbed to old age, the Barbarossa brothers were responsible for the capture and enslavement of hundreds of thousands of Christians who were forced to man the oars of Moslem galleys or serve Moorish masters in the states of Barbary.

Of Greek origin, the Barbarossa brothers soon joined forces with the Turkish corsairs and became the Mediterranean's most notorious pirates. (The Algerian Corsairs 'Arūj and Khayr ad-Dīn Barbarossa, from The Johnson General History of the Robberies, *1724, London.)*

Born in Greece and known to the Arabs simply as Barbarossa, Khayr ad-Dīn was the more ruthless of the two brothers. Striking in appearance, with dense brows and eyelashes, a bushy beard, and a headful of thick auburn hair, the younger Barbarossa possessed the unmistakable air of a man capable of savage acts. But his bearing also lent him a statesmanlike presence, which Khayr ad-Dīn capitalized on in his rise from seafaring outlaw to the highest ranks of Islam. His canniness, his remorseless style of war, and his political savvy assisted him in eluding his enemies and securing the support of powerful benefactors all his life, allowing him to thrive well into his nineties.

Barbarossa was fond of great displays, and he bought the continued benevolence of the sultan of Constantinople with gifts of looted treasure and Christian slaves. On one occasion, Khayr ad-Dīn donated to his imperial master two hundred slave boys in scarlet suits, each bearing a gold and silver bowl. He sent along another two hundred boys with bolts of fine cloth, and thirty more with monetary purses for the sultan.

If Khayr ad-Dīn's grand gestures typically involved enslaved Christians, one man, a Spanish priest from the town of Seville, was able to inspire a gesture of a different sort from the dreaded corsair. The priest, Fernando de Contreras, had founded several orphanages in his native country and had dedicated his life to teaching children. He first sought an audience with Barbarossa in 1532, expressing the wish that he be allowed to ransom the captive children of Seville. Barbarossa might well have dismissed the priest out of hand, for it was considered an act of great virtue to raise a Christian child

in the Islamic faith. But as it happened, Contreras had arrived on the corsair's doorstep in the middle of a severe drought, and faced with the distress of his vassals at the lack of rain, Barbarossa struck a deal with the priest. He would allow the Christian children to pray with the priest for rain, and if their prayers were answered, he would consent to their being ransomed.

The Algerians were bewildered by Barbarossa's willingness to negotiate with the priest, and they found the sight of so many Christians bowed in prayer peculiar indeed. After three days of almost constant prayer and spiritual preparation, the priest led the children in a solemn procession through the streets of Algiers. Each child held a lighted taper, their chorus of voices reciting the litany as they went. Then the miracle occurred. The heavens opened and rain— a thick, drenching rain like a waterfall— poured down on Algiers, soaking the children, extinguishing their tapers, and leaving the townspeople gasping. The downpour continued unabated for three days—as many days as the priest and children had spent in prayerful preparation. From that point on, Barbarossa was convinced that Contreras was a great *marabout*, a holy man capable of summoning the sacred spirits. True to his word, he allowed the priest to return to Spain with a shipload of ransomed children. Six more times in the years that followed, the priest from Seville returned to Algiers to intercede for enslaved children. And each time he came, Khayr ad-Dīn accepted Contreras's simple staff as a pledge against the three thousand ducats that he would send later as ransom money for the children of Seville.

In addition, those Barbary captains who were Christian renegades often used their vessels to pursue private acts of revenge against their former countries. Their familiarity with Europe—its territories, its people, and its fortifications—gave them an enormous advantage in mounting land raids to capture European prisoners for sale as slaves.

Once in North Africa, the prisoners were evaluated to determine whether or not they might raise a ransom. Those who were judged too poor were confined to rambling underground prisons called *bagnios*. There, men were displayed naked and forced to show their strength or athletic prowess by running, lifting, or jumping. Women were treated more carefully by the corsairs, who usually confined their female captives to special housing where they

could be examined privately. Although the women were usually displayed veiled, they often had to submit to prospective buyers reaching into their mouths to inspect their teeth, and the youngest among them had to endure the humiliation of being examined for virginity.

Sensual allure was always an aspect of the North African slave markets. While women might expect to enter a harem as a matter of course, young boys were also sought after in a society that did not divide itself along heterosexual and homosexual lines. Enslaved male concubines were held in the same households as female ones, and in equal numbers, and a corsair captain was usually accompanied by a male sexual partner on all his voyages. Women, too, sometimes took male slaves as lovers, though this was very risky for both sexes. A Christian man who slept with a Moslem woman faced being beheaded or burned alive, while the woman would be sewn up in a sack and thrown into the sea.[5]

An Algerian slave market in the seventeenth century. Western European slaves, often captured from merchant ships or coastal towns, dominated the slave markets of North Africa throughout the fifteenth and sixteenth centuries. (Dutch engraving, A Slave Market in Algiers, 1684.)

Initial slave auction sales were not final, for the dey had the right to buy any captive for the price that a private owner had paid. A slave who had been destined for domestic service might now find himself among the state-owned, or *beylik*, slaves, condemned to the galleys. For Christian slaves on a Moslem ship, this provided a possible opportunity for escape or rescue. While the labor would be arduous and possibly fatal, there was the strong likelihood of a hostile encounter with a Christian ship, and the chance that the Moslem ship might be overcome by the Christian pirates and the Christian slaves freed. Failing that, a slave might try to escape at one of the many Mediterranean ports where the galley stopped to replenish its supplies. For enslaved Europeans who declined to turn Turk, eluding bondage at a well-chosen seaport was usually the fastest way home.

A thirteenth-century slave market in Yemen. Slaves of all nations could be found in the great slave markets of North Africa, with the majority coming from eastern Europe and the Balkans. (A Slave Market in Zabid, Yemen, 1237. Bibliothèque Nationale, Paris.)

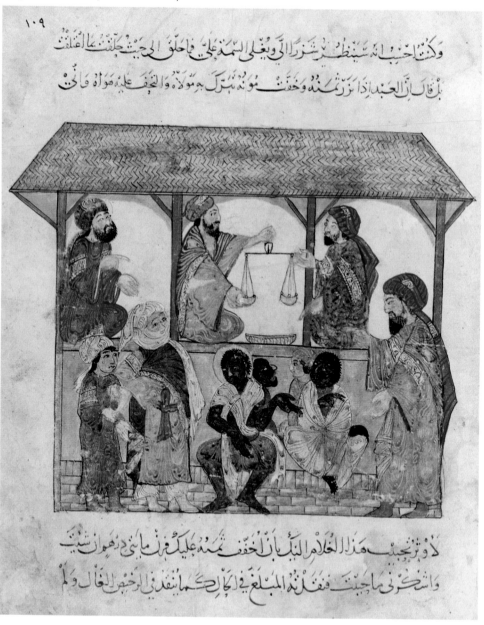

Sugar's First Slaves

Along with Europeans, sub-Saharan captives were also a strong presence in the North African markets, for merchants from Morocco regularly crossed the desert not only to buy gold but also slaves. After the Songhai nation of West Africa came to prominence under Sunni Ali during the late fifteenth century, the Songhai became a significant supplier of sub-Saharan slaves to North Africa.

Sunni Ali's brilliant successor, Askia the Great, led a campaign for dominance over neighboring states that vastly increased the wealth of the Songhai nation and resulted in a seemingly inexhaustible supply of prisoners accumulated through warfare and tributes offered to the king. The country's wealth gave its people the means to purchase the luxuries of Europe, almost all of which came to them through the Mediterranean basin. Venetian beads, fine cloth, and horses—the latter much in demand by the warring sub-Saharan kingdoms—were much sought-after commodities. Leo Africanus, a Spanish Moor who traveled widely in Africa during the early sixteenth century and was later enslaved in Italy, described transactions between Moors and Africans in which as many as fifteen or twenty slaves were traded for a single horse, a detail that is less astounding when one considers that warfare itself produced a surplus of prisoners, and therefore of slaves.[6]

Sub-Saharan slaves soon reached Europe through trade with the Arabs, and by the close of the fourteenth century approximately one thousand of them were being imported into Europe every year. They served as pages, assistants, laborers, and sailors, and some of them even traveled to the New World with early explorers.[7] Evidence of the African presence in Europe can be traced in the art of the Renaissance period. The German artist Albrecht Dürer sketched the portrait of an African servant entitled *Portrait of the Moorish Woman Katharina* in 1521. Farther south, the Spanish painter Diego Velázquez had an African slave apprenticed to him for many years. The subject of one of Velázquez's most famous portraits, Juan de Pareja, became a celebrated painter in his own right and was eventually freed by his master.

Because slaves were so highly valued in Europe, the Portuguese welcomed the advent of direct trade with sub-Saharan Africa. Some of Prince Henrique's explorers had recently settled the island of Madeira off the coast of Morocco, and the Portuguese colonists there had begun to grow sugar with extraordinary success. An emerging luxury in a world in which only honey had been available as a sweetener, sugar was an arduous crop to cultivate, and it did not attract voluntary labor, even from among the poorest of free men. Slave labor was the obvious answer to sugar's demands, and so slaves for the sugar harvest were soon being purchased in large quantities from the Arabs and Turks.

LEFT: *One of many Africans in Spain, Juan de Pareja began life as Velázquez's slave but also received training as an apprentice. He became a talented painter and Velázquez ultimately freed him. (Diego Rodríguez de Silva Velázquez,* Portrait of Juan de Pareja, *c. 1650. Metropolitan Museum of Art, New York.)*

ABOVE: *Albrecht Dürer was intrigued by the exotic and bought several pieces of carved African ivory. He also completed this sensitive study of an African woman, living far from her homeland. (Albrecht Dürer,* Portrait of the Moorish Woman Katharina, *1521. Uffizi Gallery, Florence, Italy.)*

Many of sugar's earliest slaves hailed from Russia and the Balkans—large, well-built men accustomed to hard labor. They had been put to work cutting cane in the fields of Sicily and Cyprus during the fourteenth century. When the island of Madeira was colonized by Portugal, it became the first outpost of sugar production in the Atlantic, and here, too, Europeans were sent to work as laborers, some enslaved, some free. But as sub-Saharan Africa became the new focus of Portugal's quest for cheap labor, Africans were imported to work alongside these white laborers, dying with them in the extreme heat, all mere fodder for the rapacious sugar harvest.

Queen Isabella and King Ferdinand of Spain. The marriage of these two powerful monarchs united Aragon and Castile, forming the basis of modern-day Spain. Together, Ferdinand and Isabella brought about enormous changes on the Iberian peninsula, expelling the Moors, the Jews, and other non-Catholics and supporting such empire-building endeavors as the colonization of the Americas. Enlightened in some aspects and repressive in others, Ferdinand and Isabella accepted slavery as a fact of life, for the institution was common in Spain. (LEFT, Artist unknown, Isabel la Católica, *c. 1500. Palacio Real, Madrid.* RIGHT, Países Bajos, Fernando el Católico de Aragon, *c. 1500. Kunsthistorisches Museum, Vienna.)*

By the late 1400s, Portugal's sources of Russian and Balkan slaves had dried up, cut off by the Turks of Constantinople who now stood between western Europe and their former slave ports on the Black Sea. At the same time, Africans had proven capable of withstanding Madeira's punishing heat, and so increasing numbers were shipped from the African mainland to chop cane. Soon, the majority of slaves in Madeira were sub-Saharans, and the brutal symbiosis of sugar and slavery that would be followed in the American colonies had been initiated.[8]

African slaves first arrived in the Americas as servants of the conquistadors. Their masters, who were part explorers and part soldiers of fortune, led the European invasion of the American continent during the Iberian land grabs of the sixteenth century. The African slaves who accompanied these conquistadors had far different lives from those endured by the slaves who came later to the colonies, when sugar was king. One account of an African slave called Estevan describes a life of trials mixed with the exhilaration of new experiences. Along with several Spanish crew members, including his master, Estevan was shipwrecked in 1518 off the coast of what is now Texas, but he and his companions survived with the help of local Indians. He was later required to guide an expedition through the Southwest, which he did with considerable ingenuity before he was finally killed by Zunis.

Elsewhere in the Americas, however, slavery was already being instituted in its more familiar form. Twenty-six years before Estevan's adventures, Christopher Columbus had arrived in the New World. His frustration at his inability to discover a major source of gold there was mitigated by the fact that he had found a whole new source of non-Christian people—potential slaves. In 1492, he brought a few Native Americans back to Spain with him, only to be disappointed when Queen Isabella announced that they were not to be enslaved. Since Columbus had claimed their native lands in the name of Spain, she pointed out, the Indians were subjects, not foreigners, and subjects could not be exploited in that way. But this royal decree was almost universally ignored, and by the time of Columbus's second voyage to the Americas in 1494, Native Americans were destined for the rigors of slavery.

This time, on his arrival in the Caribbean, Columbus did find gold, but in small quantities. Vexed by the tiny amount of the metal that seemed to be available, Columbus's men forced the Indians to start panning rivers, cultivating fields, and performing other tasks.

Then, preparing to return to Europe, Columbus captured sixteen hundred Taino Indians from the island of Hispaniola and selected more than a thousand of them to make the voyage back to Spain. About four hundred of the captured Tainos were allowed to go free—they fled in terror—and the rest were confined to the ship's hold or divided up among Columbus's crew to serve as personal slaves. Thus, the first crossing of the Middle Passage was not from Africa to the Americas but from the Caribbean to Europe, aboard Columbus's ships. A contemporary account of this voyage by Michele de Cuneo, an Italian adventurer and boyhood friend

European colonists brought Africans as slaves to the Americas to perform heavy labor. Here they can be seen mining and washing gold. (Sir Francis Drake, "Slaves Washing Gold Ore Under the Watchful Eye of a Spanish Overseer," from Natural History of the Indies, *MS3900, c.1590. Pierpont Morgan Library, New York.)*

of Columbus who traveled with him to the New World, reports that two hundred Indians died and were thrown into the sea, and half of those who survived were desperately ill and not expected to live.[9] This tragic journey foreshadowed the fate that millions of enslaved Africans would later suffer.

In its simplest terms, the transatlantic slave trade began because Native Americans did not make good slaves. Weakened by overwork and despair, huge populations were swiftly felled by European diseases to which they had no previous exposure. By 1520 native populations in the Caribbean had almost vanished. In Hispaniola alone the population declined from an estimated 3 million in 1494 to just twenty-eight thousand by 1549.[10] But this enormous loss of life did not persuade the Spanish colonists to reconsider the course of their actions. Rather, the next step seemed obvious to them: Africans must be brought in to perform the required tasks. Africans were imported to the Caribbean as early as 1512. As the native population declined, creating the need for more bodies to perform the backbreaking labor of establishing a new colonial infrastructure, the number of imported Africans steadily increased.

The first African slaves to arrive on the North American mainland were also brought there by the Spanish. These Africans arrived at St. Augustine, then the capital of Florida, in 1567,

Despite a royal decree from Queen Isabella to the contrary, the Spanish used Native Americans as their first slaves in the Americas, forcing them to work as miners, farmers, and even pack animals. (Theodore de Bry, Indians Taken as Slaves, 1590. Mariners' Museum, Newport News, Virginia.)

and were put to work as servants and laborers in the young colony. Even the English colonists, who were not accustomed to slave labor in their country of origin, soon experimented with slavery, buying twenty Africans who had arrived on a Dutch man-of-war in Jamestown in the Virginia colony in 1620. At the time, the English identified the Africans as "indentured servants," which implied that the Africans might expect to be freed after a certain period. Some of these Africans were in fact freed, and a few went on to establish thriving plantations of their own. But as history would demonstrate, this was generally the exception to an increasingly harsh rule.

A Latecomer to the Trade

The English were not as involved in the early evolution of the transatlantic slave trade as were Portugal, Spain, Italy, and the colonies of North America. The island's active role as a slave trader began with the ascendance of Elizabeth I to the English throne in 1558, and by the middle of the eighteenth century, England had become the world's primary slave-trading power.

Slavery did not exist in England when Elizabeth became queen, but she was familiar with the institution as it was practiced on distant shores. English merchant ships had been active in the Mediterranean since the first decades of the sixteenth century, and news had reached home of the many sailors who had fallen victim to attacks by Barbary pirates. By the time twenty-five-year-old Elizabeth came to the throne, hundreds of Englishmen were serving as slaves in North Africa. And as the island nation's seagoing ambitions grew, so did the number of English sailors who ventured to the Mediterranean, only to be captured by Barbary pirates and sold to Arab masters along the North African shore. By 1567 the number of Englishmen held as slaves in North Africa was sufficient cause for the bishop of London to petition Elizabeth's government to raise funds for their ransom.

As the most powerful Protestant monarch in Europe, Elizabeth was generally regarded as an enemy by Catholic powers, and was able to ignore some of the strictures placed on world trade by the Pope. Under her leadership England blossomed into a maritime mercantile empire and the beginnings of England's navy were established. (George Gower, Elizabeth I, The Armada Portrait, c. 1590. Marquess of Tavistock and Trustees of Bedford Estate, Woburn Abbey, Woburn, England.)

One might imagine that the enslavement of English people and the reports of their trials would have persuaded their countrymen to pause before engaging in so despicable a trade. But the practice of enslaving captives was by then so common that its legitimacy was barely questioned even when the practice itself was fought. In fact, their familiarity with slavery in general and African slavery in particular blunted rather than sharpened English sensibilities.

England's participation in the slave trade began with Sir John Hawkins, a privateer whose venture was sponsored by no less a personage than the queen of England herself. With profit as his motive, Hawkins set out in 1562 on the first of three voyages that were to transport Africans to Spain's colonies in the Americas. The Spanish were not allowed to trade with Africa themselves, for the Pope had "given" Africa to their Catholic rivals, the Portuguese, and Portugal was not willing to support Spain's empire-building objectives by ferrying slaves to its colonies.

Spain and England, too, were often political adversaries, but between these two nations brief periods of commercial neutrality sometimes occurred. While these were generally short-lived and always of dubious stability, it was during one such period that Hawkins seized the opportunity to deliver slaves to Spain's colonies. But since the Portuguese did not recognize England's right to establish its own trading alliances on the African continent, he had gone there in a spirit of entrepreneurship that bordered on piracy, intending to secure a valuable cargo one way or another. With the support of local political leaders, Hawkins joined in a war between states that netted him an adequate number of captives. His ship hold now full, he sailed from Africa to the Spanish colonies, where he was able to dispose of his human cargo, and return to England with a handsome profit for his main investor, the queen.

Elizabeth immediately funded another voyage for which slaves were to be among the first objects of trade, a bold directive since England's risk in the transatlantic slave trade of that time was enormous. Spain's colonies provided the only market, and occasionally, when simmering conflicts between Spain and England precipitously erupted, human cargos could not be sold in the Americas and had to be brought back to London and turned loose on its streets. Indeed, England's African population was becoming significant enough to draw comment from Elizabeth herself, who complained that its numbers were growing among the impoverished classes. But no thought was given to returning these uprooted Africans to their homeland.

Even as Hawkins and other English privateers were making inroads in the transatlantic slave trade, Queen Elizabeth was seeking to establish more official trade links with Africa. By the 1570s, in addition to the slave business, England was engaged in buying Moroccan sugar, an increasingly popular taste among the English, and saltpeter, which the queen desperately needed to make gunpowder for her armies. In 1581 the English sought to organize their shipping and trading interests, and the Levant Company was formed. Safe conduct for the Levant Company's ships was promised by the dey of Algiers, but the Barbary pirates did not feel the need to observe it; from time to time English vessels were still attacked in the Mediterranean and their crews captured. Elizabeth complained to the dey about the dangers her sailors faced at the

While attempting to trade for African gold in 1562, Sir John Hawkins realized that slaves could be a more profitable cargo. He soon began to lead slaving expeditions with the blessing of his most notable investor, Elizabeth I, queen of England. (English School, Sir John Hawkins, 1581. National Maritime Museum, Greenwich, England.)

hands of the Barbary pirates. But an alliance with the Islamic nations of the Barbary Coast was crucial to Elizabeth, since England's only source of saltpeter was the Moors. And so, despite her displeasure at the continuing raids on her ships by Mediterranean pirates, the queen did not halt the North African trade.

England sent cloth, tin, and other goods to Morocco, and English merchants and artisans as well. Captain John Smith, who had once been enslaved in North Africa but is today more renowned as one of the original settlers of the Virginia colony, mentions goldsmiths, plumbers, carvers, and watchmakers in his journals. Al-Mansūr, the sharif of Fez in Morocco, was particularly interested in the latter, and he employed two English watchmakers to maintain his collection of navigational and other scientific instruments. Free Englishmen were also engaged in the production of Moroccan saltpeter and sugar.

England held a particular advantage over other European countries in the North African trade since Europe's Catholic monarchs had jointly committed not to sell the North Africans anything that could be used for warfare. Elizabeth, the Protestant queen, was not so constrained. When the Moors requested weapons to defend their ships and their country—and to continue their intermittent raiding of Spanish ships—the English secretly supplied the arms, including cannonballs and muskets. They also sent timber for galleys and shipwrights to aid Moroccan shipbuilding, an action that directly benefited the Barbary pirates themselves. This secret trade survived for only a brief duration, however—Philip of Spain fought too many battles with the Moors in which his enemies were armed with English weapons to remain deceived for long. But his heightened animosity toward England only increased Elizabeth's need for gunpowder, thus strengthening her trade alliance with the Moors.

The North Africans banked on England's enmity with Spain and fueled their rivalry however they could. At one point, in 1600, a Moroccan ambassador even visited Elizabeth in secrecy and proposed that she and al-Mansūr attack Spanish holdings in both the Old and New Worlds and divide the spoils between them. Whatever Elizabeth's ambitions, she had no delusions about her country's ability to engage in a conflict that would no doubt escalate into full-scale war, and so she politely declined the Moroccan ambassador's offer. But she delivered the rejection as mildly as possible, taking pains to ensure that her primary source of saltpeter did not dry up.

The queen played her cards discreetly, for no doubt she had another unspoken reason for not engaging in open warfare with Spain. Even as the Moroccan ambassador was taking his leave, the English were escalating their participation in the transatlantic slave trade. In the decades to come, increasing numbers of English ships, many of them under the auspices of the crown, would cross the Atlantic ferrying African captives to be sold as slaves in Spain's American colonies.

Thus Europe, Africa, and the colonies of the Americas came to comprise the three corners of a commercial route that would finally become infamous as "the Triangle Trade." This cruel transatlantic commerce did not arise in a vacuum. Instead, as we have seen, the social and economic circumstances surrounding its development led with fatal logic to the largest forced migration in human history. Obscured by this horror is the reality that the vast numbers of Africans who endured the Middle Passage were casualties of only one chapter in the larger history of slavery. Perhaps this is ultimately the most astonishing fact of all—the realization that the transatlantic slave trade was only one brutal passage in slavery's long and dehumanizing march.

In 1600, the Moorish nobleman Abdul Guahid was sent by the king of Morocco along with other nobles and their slaves to the court of Elizabeth of England. The mission of this embassy was to secure a treaty against their common enemy, Catholic Spain. (English School, Portrait of Abdul Guahid, Age 42, 1600. *Barber Institute, University of Birmingham, England.)*

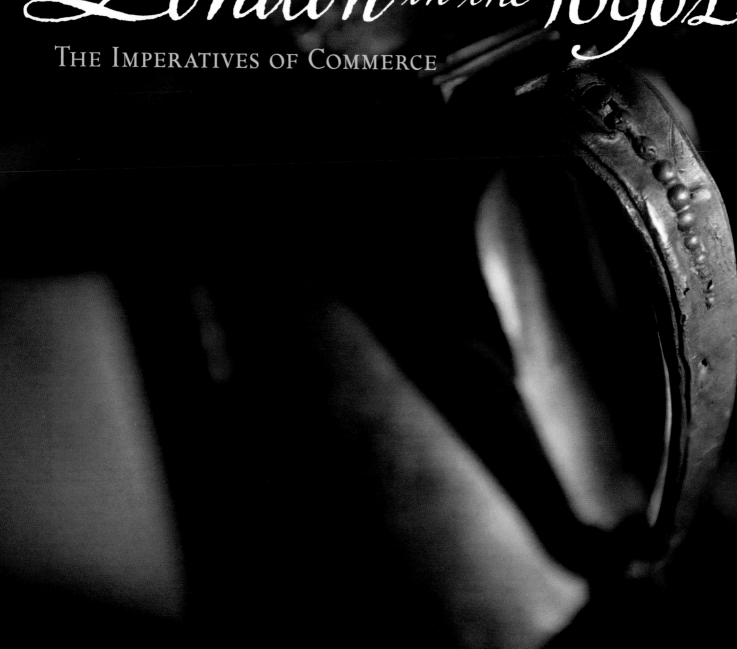

London *in the* 1690s

THE IMPERATIVES OF COMMERCE

Throughout the spring of 1697, carpenters, cordwainers, sailmakers, coopers, and even schoolchildren, who earned a few pennies picking oakum from the old ropes of ships, labored in the dockyards of London, readying a new merchant slaver for the Triangle Trade. Constructed of wood, fastened together by iron spikes, her rigging secured by hempen rope, the ship was a stalwart little vessel, about 120 tons burden with a sixty-foot keel. A consortium of London investors had purchased her at an official navy auction—prizes of war such as she was were regularly sold off to help support the Royal Navy's costs—intending to remake her as a slaver.

To this end, the vessel's hull had been scraped clean of barnacles and covered with an additional layer of planking to protect against the wood-boring teredo worm that thrived in the warm waters of the Tropics. The tiny mollusks had been known to eat their way clean through the hulls of ships, so bovine hair had been stuffed between the two layers of planking as a further deterrent to the borers.

Other refinements had been made as well. The ship's galley had been enlarged to accommodate a capacious single-burner cookstove capable of preparing mammoth pots of gruel. Up on the main deck, the ropes of the ship's rigging had been completely retarred, its rotten lines replaced. A variety of anchors had been stored, a fresh coat of paint had been applied, and a new name—the *Henrietta Marie*—had been carved into a panel. The ship's investors had

The ship's bell told researchers the name and date of the merchant slaver Henrietta Marie.

chosen to rechristen her after a seventeenth-century French princess who had married England's King Charles I; the name that would indicate both the ship's French origin and her British allegiance. As a special mark of pride, a bronze bell would also be forged. It would bear the ship's name and a date: "*Henrietta Marie*, 1699."

But even after her refitting was complete, the *Henrietta Marie* was forced to linger in port awaiting the final resolution of King William's War, the very skirmish in which she is thought to have been captured. Her investors would not have to wait too long, however; in September 1697 the Treaty of Ryswick finally brought the Anglo-French conflict to a close. London was abuzz with excitement, for the political stalemate that had crippled overseas trade for eight years was finally broken. The city celebrated wildly, its citizens parading through the streets or dressing themselves in glitter and finery for balls and masquerades. Fireworks exploded in the evening sky, and everywhere wine flowed freely from public water pumps.

On November 2, 1697, the London *Post-Boy* reported that the English Channel was now clear of enemy vessels, and "our ships can go and come without the least molestation." Less than a fortnight later, the *Henrietta Marie* slipped her moorings on the Thames and glided downriver to the channel, bound for the slave coast of Africa.

All around Europe similar journeys were taking place. Nantes, La Rochelle, and Marseilles were the great slave ports of France; other voyagers left from harbors in Denmark, Sweden, Holland, and Portugal. Now, as the seventeenth century entered its twilight, the slave trade was about to be transformed from a minor industry into the largest involuntary migration of people in the history of the world.

As one of the agents of this transformation, the *Henrietta Marie* was typical of scores of other English slaving vessels. But the fate of this ship would turn out to be unique, for, by virtue of her untimely demise and her long preservation on the ocean floor, the *Henrietta Marie* would offer unique insights into the nature of the transatlantic slave trade during the

The English slave ship Henrietta Marie, *c. 1699. Small but sturdy, the merchantman was approximately sixty feet in length and was manned by a crew of fifteen. (Reconstruction of the* Henrietta Marie, *Peter Copeland, 1996.)*

Two cooking stoves were found at the Henrietta Marie *wreck site. This, the largest, was probably used to feed the African captives and the crew. It is made of copper and would have been surrounded by bricks to prevent a fire from spreading. Its chamber would have been filled with wood or coal and a large cauldron would have been set on top of its single "burner." (Collection of James Willesley.)*

French ironworks in the area of Normandy and Brittany would have supplied the Henrietta Marie's *anchors. (Denis Diderot, "Forging an Anchor," L'Encyclopédie, Vol. 7, Plate 104, Paris, 1763.)*

early period of its evolution. The recovery of the ship's wrecked timbers, rusty chains, unsold cargo, and, in particular, her bell,[1] would send researchers scurrying for new answers to the enduring questions of the slave trade: What forces funded it, who launched it, and what events could have produced a social climate in which trading in human beings became an acceptable, even gentlemanly form of commerce? The answers to these questions, at least with regard to England's participation in the trade, can be discerned through careful examination of the societies and individuals—in England, Africa, and the Americas—associated with this one slave ship. Indeed, the key to understanding the complex mechanism that was the Triangle Trade lies in our first comprehending the political and social arrangements out of which this commerce grew.

London itself provides the first clues. A bustling metropolis of about a quarter of a million people, it was the largest city in Europe—larger than Paris, which was still emerging as the center of a unified France, and larger than Amsterdam, which enjoyed the highest standard of living in Europe during the late seventeenth century. Originally built as a military stronghold and commercial entrepôt by the invading forces of the Roman army in A.D. 43, London in the

Howland Great Dock, begun in 1695, covered ten acres and could accommodate 120 large merchant ships. The pride of early eighteenth-century engineering, it was protected from the tides by a lock and from the wind by the surrounding planting of trees. For more than a century it was London's largest dock and it remained in use throughout the nineteenth century. (Howland Great Dock, c. 1720. National Maritime Museum, Greenwich, England.)

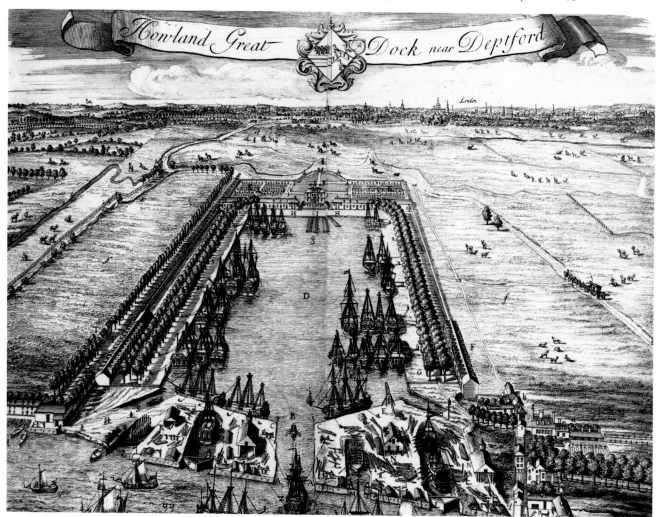

1690s stretched for five miles and twenty yards from east to west and two and a quarter miles from north to south.[2]

The close of the seventeenth century was a particularly eventful period in the life of the city. King William and Queen Mary had recently succeeded to the English throne, crowned as joint monarchs in 1689. Mary II had been the rightful heir; William III, a Dutch prince before his marriage to Mary, had had to wrangle with Parliament to make sure that he was given equal power. The Anglo-French war, in fact, had been fought in part to defend the legitimacy of William's crown. Meanwhile, French Protestants, known as Huguenots, flocked to London in enormous numbers after 1685 when the French monarchy revoked the Edict of Nantes, which had protected their religious freedom.

In the realm of arts and letters in London, Jonathan Swift, author of *Gulliver's Travels*, had already penned several scathing social commentaries by the late century; his younger contemporary Daniel Defoe was only just beginning to write, but Defoe's *Robinson Crusoe*, published in 1718, would reflect the misfortunes and triumphs of an English adventurer and his encounters with international slavery during the late seventeenth century.

If London was a city in political and social upheaval, momentous advances were taking place in the arenas of philosophy and science, intellectual leaps that would turn out to be the precursors to the next century's Enlightenment. Sir Isaac Newton had already written his *Principia* defining the laws of motion and had conceived a new form of mathematics known as calculus. The Royal Society of London, created to promote the study of mathematics and the natural sciences, had been incorporated in 1662. One of its founders, the great architect Sir Christopher Wren, had recently been appointed surveyor general of the city and was working on the first of his proposed designs for the reconstruction of St. Paul's Cathedral, which had been ravaged by fire. In 1690 the philosopher John Locke put forth his theory of empiricism, which included the notion that all persons are born good and equal, their minds a tabula rasa on which the experiences of the world create indelible marks.

Almost a century later, John Locke's idea would become the guiding principle of a fledgling nation called the United States of America. In the context of the transatlantic slave trade, the irony cut deeply. Enlightenment thinkers such as John Locke in England and, later, Thomas Jefferson in America were convinced that Europe had finally shaken off centuries of darkness

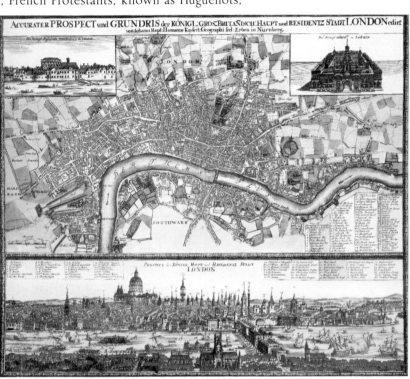

In the aftermath of London's Great Fire, disputes over property and street boundaries were settled by arbitration and officials had to resort to rough maps and surviving deeds. Among the first projects undertaken by the city fathers after the fire was the mapping of all the rebuilt areas. (Johann B. Homann, Aerial Map of London and View Across the Thames from South Bank with St. Paul's and London Bridge, *c. 1730. British Library, London.)*

and was moving into an era enlightened by scientific inquiry, reason, and a respect for human potential. However, even among such "enlightened" thinkers, the notion of an individual's innate goodness and fundamental equality seems never to have extended to those taken to the Americas as slaves.

This was the contemporary reality of the merchants who would direct the slaving voyages of the *Henrietta Marie*. On the surface, London appeared to be in a period of commercial prosperity and creative growth. But the deeper reality of the city was far more complicated. Indeed, London at the time of the *Henrietta Marie* was a city in the difficult throes of rebirth, a town forced to reinvent itself in the aftermath of two horrific disasters.

The Reckoning

In nature and scope the catastrophes had been almost apocalyptic. The first reckoning came with the fresh outbreak of the Black Death, or bubonic plague, in 1665. The people of London had long lived in terror of the plague, which came over its victims with unmistakable fits of sneezing, followed by the eruption of black pustules all over the body (hence the moniker "Black Death"). The bubonic plague had actually been petering out during the mid-seventeenth century—its most recent episode had been halted by the deep frost of the winter of 1664—but, as Plague Year 1665 would demonstrate, the Black Death could still cause large pockets of devastation.

Londoners knew very little about how exactly the plague was spread; they knew only that it appeared to be highly transmittable. The famous diarist Samuel Pepys wrote that he feared going to London's financial center, the Royal Exchange, for he knew that he would run into people in the contagious stage of the disease. The well-to-do fled town, observing that the disease spread fastest in large congested cities. Their erstwhile servants, now dismissed, were forced to find jobs as corpse carriers or roamed the city in armed gangs, robbing and looting. Pepys walked the streets of plague-torn London and was saddened by the sight of the afflicted huddled on street corners begging for alms.[3] Shopkeepers went bankrupt for lack of customers, and factories closed down because barge workers from the north of England were too afraid of contracting the disease to deliver the coal needed to run them. Graveyards overflowed, and drunken gravediggers worked around the clock until they, too, fell ill. By July 1665, the weekly death toll was more than one thousand, and by August the number had risen to two thousand.

Pepys, a dedicated civil servant who would later become secretary of the Royal Navy, a member of Parliament, and president of the Royal Society, was called in to help make plans to contain the contagion in Greenwich on the outskirts of London. "Among the stories," he later wrote, "one was very passionate methought...a complaint brought against a man in the town for taking a child from London from an infected house. Ald[erman]Hooker told us it was the child of a very able citizen in Gracious street, a sadler, who buried all the rest of his children

Samuel Pepys is probably the most famous diarist of all time, and we know from his writings that the slave trade impinged upon his life. It is typical of this early period in the trade that while he treated the free Africans he met in London as equals, he also helped a friend recapture a runaway slave and was shocked by the slave's "ingratitude" at being brought to England. (John Hayls, Portrait of Samuel Pepys, *1666.)*

of the plague; and himself and wife now being shut up, and in despair of escaping, did desire only to save the life of this little child; and so prevailed to have it received stark naked into the arms of a friend, who brought it (having put it into fresh clothes) to Greenwich; where, upon hearing the story, we did agree it should be permitted to be received and kept in the town."[4]

This act of mercy aside, the Lord Mayor of London soon announced harsh measures to control the spread of infection: Visitors who were staying with friends and relatives in London households must leave the city immediately, and any house harboring a person diagnosed with the plague was to be marked with a red cross. Such red crosses proliferated throughout

the city, and sometimes the sick and dying crept out of their homes to add the inscription "Lord have mercy upon us."[5]

With the ugly humor of the doomed, the hopelessly ill would lean out of their windows and try to breathe on passersby.[6] On the mostly deserted streets of London, death-cart drivers collapsed at their reins, leaving their horses to wander aimlessly about the city until some brave soul took charge of them. Not until autumn, when the weather once more turned cold, did the plague finally begin to abate. But by then, seventy thousand lives had been lost, and wary Londoners looked with fear on their neighbors and friends. In an

Death appeared to triumph over Londoners during the plague years. This woodcut shows their plight, as they fled contagion in the city only to be rejected by terrified countryfolk. (Lord, Have Mercy on London, contemporary English woodcut of the Great Plague of 1665.)

attempt at fumigation far more effective than anyone knew, fires burned in the streets of London as gradually the citizens returned.

But the city's troubles were far from over. The fires that dotted the city in the latter months of 1665 unwittingly foreshadowed a second disaster. In Tudor London, wooden houses were built so close together that the inhabitants could shake hands with their neighbors just by reaching out their second-story windows. Thus, when a careless cook in Farriner's Bakery on Pudding Lane accidentally started a fire on September 1, 1666, it intensified with dramatic results.

Samuel Pepys provided one of the most gripping descriptions of the fire. The first night, he traveled up and down the Thames in his boat and watched as houses, inns, churches, even buildings made of stone, succumbed to the blaze. Cries of terror mingled with the loud hiss of flames, and everywhere the people of London were hurriedly grabbing what they could of their possessions and running for their lives.

The blaze showed no signs of diminishing. "With one's face in the wind you were almost burned with a shower of Firedrops," Pepys wrote, "…and in Corners and upon steeples and between churches and houses, as far as we could see up the hill of the City, [is] a most horrid malicious bloody flame, not like the flame of an ordinary fire."[7]

The following day the firefighters began blowing up the houses closest to the Tower of London in order to stop the fire's spread. Pepys and his family, like the rest of London, gathered up their belongings and fled to safety. But despite the best efforts of the firefighters, the blaze raged for five more days, until September 6, when the last isolated flames were finally extinguished.

Amid the smoldering rubble, thousands of Londoners roamed—homeless, jobless, and filled with despair. The Great Fire of 1666 had devoured many of the city's oldest structures, leveling the town to a degree never seen before and not to be seen again until the Blitz of World War II. With a paranoia that has a modern ring, Londoners at first suspected terrorism as the original cause of the fire, but these fears were dismissed as the disaster became so generalized. Fire had destroyed a large portion of the medieval Guildhall, the center of London's civic government, as well as the Royal Exchange, which housed the city's stock exchange and financial center. London Bridge, which at that time had dwellings and shops nestled along its entire length, had been aflame from one end to the other, and the world-famous St. Paul's Cathedral had burned to the ground. In all, the fire had razed nearly four hundred acres within

Fine new buildings made from stone and other fireproof materials made London one of the most modern cities of the eighteenth century. (General View of London, eighteenth century. Musée Tavelet-Delacour, Pontoise, France.)

the city and sixty-three acres on its outskirts. Eighty-seven churches and thirteen hundred houses had been destroyed, but, amazingly, only nine people had perished in the inferno, including the maid of the baker in whose house the fire had started.

Up from the Ashes

Although London could not yet know it, the fire would turn out to be its salvation. The mighty conflagration had consumed not only the living quarters of people infected with the plague but also London's vast population of rats. In fact, it had been the city's hundreds of thousands of rats that had carried the fleas whose bite had caused the inexorable spread of the plague. But as the Great Fire raged throughout London, the roosts of the underclasses, the dwellings of shopkeepers, and the mansions of the wealthy—all with their infestations of rats—fell together in a cleansing pyre.

In the wake of this physical and economic disaster, London would be rebuilt, and the new city would boast broad avenues, redbrick pavements, improved sanitation, and fine houses constructed of fire-resistant materials. Within five years, most of London's large private houses, shopping areas, and the Royal Exchange had been reestablished. During the next half-century, architect Sir Christopher Wren would oversee the construction of a magnificent new cathedral on the site of the old St. Paul's.

Like all great disasters, the Great Fire of London had spawned its share of visionaries, opportunists, and entrepreneurs. Architects and designers were given expansive tracts within which to create their best work, and everything from grand churches to modest cottages to simple shop fronts was being reconsidered in terms of permanency, investment, and the facil-

The pewterer's workshop was generally manned by a master and his apprentices. (Denis Diderot, "The Pewterer's Workshop," L'Encyclopédie, Vol. 1, Plate 197, Paris, 1763.)

itation of commerce. These radical improvements had the effect of moving medieval London decisively into the modern age. Individual involvement in commerce of all kinds was a fundamental aspect of this transformation, prompting Napoleon Bonaparte to refer scornfully to England a century later as "a nation of shopkeepers."

During the final decade of the seventeenth century, the city of London was free of plague and vigilant about fire, its dwellings clean and safe. And although the bubonic plague might occasionally erupt in pockets of the city, it would never again bring the devastation that it had in 1665. But despite the city's evident pomp and shine, its appearance of activity and progress, the people of London remained haunted by bitter memories. The city had been forced to reckon with nature's most violent uncertainties—and its citizens still harbored the scars.

The Way of the Guilds

In 1698, the year of the *Henrietta Marie*'s first voyage, international commerce in London was still in its relative infancy. Democracy was yet a vague notion, and an individual's right to personal freedom was a new idea that had yet to be explored. Although the stage was already being set for a period of enormous growth that would later be known as the Industrial Revolution, none of its sweeping changes had yet occurred. Still, the city was in a period of comparative wealth, with a standard of living that was by then second only to Amsterdam. Ironically, this economic boom was due in part to the thinning of the population by the plague, which made jobs available to all those who sought them. As a result, those with scant economic means were not quite as destitute as they had been for much of the previous century, nor were their lives as wretched as they would become during the next when the impoverished classes would be forced to scramble for survival in dreary and dilapidated tenements. But in London in the late 1690s, the poor were still able to pay rent, put food on the table, and even have a few pennies left over to spend on drink.

During this period, the wealthy still possessed a genteel sense of *noblesse oblige*, which not only impelled them to provide relief to the less fortunate through handouts of money and food but also prompted them to agitate for social change, resulting in improved education, job-related training, and communal services for the poor. Although the form this charity took might seem patronizing to our modern sensibilities, it was not viewed as such by its recipients, many of whom would otherwise have been condemned to the most pernicious effects of poverty.

Even before the Great Fire, two very different hubs of activity had been evident in London. The newer of these was known as "the West End," centered in Westminster and clustered around the central court at St. James's Palace. Here, London's aristocrats had built their large mansions. On the opposite side of town was the area of the original settlement of London, still known as "the City." This was the center of commerce and trade, encompassing both the Royal Exchange and the London docks. It was in this part of London that *Henrietta Marie*'s cargo would have been bought and sold, among the pewterers' shops, the ironmongers, and the wholesalers, all of whom belonged to professional companies, or guilds.

The city and its commerce were largely controlled by these business organizations, the direct descendants of medieval guilds. The mayor himself conducted his affairs from the Guildhall, which controlled not only the administration of the city but its trade activities as well. The Guildhall was, as its name suggests, the headquarters of London's guild system, acting as its archive, court, and ultimate ruling body.

Scattered about the Guildhall were the guilds themselves, each one comprised of a group of artisans and businessmen engaged in a common trade. The guilds defined themselves accord-

Inſtruĉtions for the Apprentices, in the City of *LONDON*.

YOu ſhall conſtantly and devoutly on your knees, every day, ſerve God Morning and Evening, and make Conſcience in the due hearing of the Word Preached, and endeavour the right practice thereof in your Life and Converſation: You ſhall do diligent and faithful Service to your Maſter for the time of your Apprenticeſhip, and deal truly in what you ſhall be truſted: You ſhall often Read over the Covenants of your Indenture, and ſee and endeavour your ſelf to perform the ſame to the uttermoſt of your power: You ſhall avoid all evil Company, and all Occaſions which may tend or draw you to the ſame, and make ſpeedy return when you ſhall be ſent on your Maſters or Miſtreſſes Errands: You ſhall avoid Idleneſs, and ever be employed, either in God's Service, or about your Maſter's Buſineſs: You ſhall be of fair, gentle, and lowly Speech and Behaviour to all Men, and eſpecially to your Governours. And according to your Carriage, expect your Reward, for Good or Ill, from God and your Friends.

Apprentices were bound to their masters for a period of five to seven years, during which time they were dependent for everything from food and clothing to rules of behavior. This pamphlet, while not itself a contract, was issued by the London guilds and outlines what was expected of an apprentice during his or her term of service. Failure to conform to these standards could result in punishment or early dismissal. (Instructions to Apprentices, c. 1750. Worshipful Company of Pewterers, London.)

ing to their product, from the various kinds of metalworkers to weavers, dyers, and whole-salers. These groupings, almost exclusively male, operated in a preindustrial tradition that was common in all European cultures of the seventeenth century, and could also be found else-where. Indeed, very similar guilds had been established in the West African states of Benin and Sierra Leone long before the arrival of the Europeans in sub-Saharan Africa. In Europe, as in Africa, these guilds dated from before the twelfth century and reached their apogee in the four-teenth and fifteenth centuries when many new trade companies were added.

Typically, a guild established manufacturing standards for its particular trade, awarding the "freedom" to practice that trade to those who met these benchmarks. The upper echelons of each guild were composed of "liverymen," the only mem-bers entitled to wear the guild's uniform. Liverymen were the employers and teachers of the freemen, journeymen, and apprentices who composed the hier-archy of the rank and file. They trained young people to conform to the guild's standards, censoring or ostracizing those who failed.

Entry into a guild could be obtained either by having a father who was already a member, by buying the privilege outright, or by apprenticeship, which involved several years' training, often in restrictive circumstances. Because gaining the freedom to practice a trade was so valuable, parents had to pay master craftsmen a fee to take their children on as apprentices, sometimes as much as several hundred pounds, depending on the return that could be expected by one who learned the trade. In London, youths ordi-narily became apprenticed at about fourteen years of age, and this apprenticeship period was likely to entail far more than straightfor-ward instruction in a trade. A formal contract was drawn up that bound the child to his master for seven years, during which the youth would live in the master's household and perform whatever tasks were asked of him in exchange for food, clothing, shelter, and pocket money.

The best masters gave technical training and regarded their apprentices almost as family members. The worst treated them as servants or pack animals, teaching them noth-ing but the miseries of being at the beck and call of a cruel master. Although the more com-mon experience fell somewhere between the two, overwork, poor food, and lack of real training were frequent complaints in the journals of those who recorded their apprenticeship experiences, and terms such as "restraint," "drudgery," and even "slavery" were liberally used.

The Apprentice's Lot

Sir John Fryer is a case in point. A successful pewterer who later became lord mayor of London, Fryer was apprenticed in 1685 at the age of fourteen. His term of indenture was not a happy one, for he was driven to extremes by a drunken and ill-tempered master. "My dear Mother had not inured me to any hard labor," Fryer reflected in his journal of that time, "and which was worse, in my infancy, I had been cured of a Rupture [hernia], and I found such carrying of burdens strained that part of me and did me much hurt; my Master being of a very near temper in his house and put me to doing the servile part of the trade…

Apprentices were bound laborers who accepted this situation in order to learn a lucrative trade. Here, the master peeks from behind the door as his two apprentices, one diligent, the other less so, work at their looms. The master carries a stout stick in his hand and will not hesitate to use it on an apprentice who appears idle. (William Hogarth, Plate I: "The Fellow 'Prentices at Their Looms," Industry and Idleness, 1747. Lewis Walpole Library, Farmington, Connecticut.)

Few options were open to an apprentice who did not get along with his master, although the dangerous life of a sailor was one possibility. In this Hogarth print, the lazy apprentice we met in the earlier image listens to the tall tales of an old hand. While the boy's mother weeps, another sailor teases the boy's shoulder with a frayed rope's end, a short whip commonly used to coerce seamen who did not work quickly enough to satisfy their superiors. (William Hogarth, Plate 5: "The Idle 'Prentice Turned Away and Sent to Sea," Industry and Idleness, 1747. Lewis Walpole Library, Farmington, Connecticut.)

and other such like things not commonly done by other apprentices and some other things which I forbeare to relate; these things as well as my severe confinement were irksome to me." But Fryer was well aware that an apprentice could severely blight his prospects by leaving a master before the full term of indenture had been served. And so he persevered. "I had some thotts of quitting such servitude," he admitted, "but then I considered my mother haveing only me should I ruin myself it would be a sore affliction to her."[8]

Fryer's experience was not an isolated one. Most masters, reasoning that they were providing their apprentices with an education, placed their charges under strict restraints, supposedly for their own good but more often for the benefit of the master. Apprentices were forbidden to frequent taverns or theaters, to gamble or fornicate, to answer curtly to their masters and mistresses, or to flout a host of other even pettier regulations. Apprentices were also not allowed to leave the house without permission, and then only for a prestated period, on pain of punishment or, worse, dismissal. In the case of the latter, they would have to start all over again with a new master, if indeed any would take them.

Running away was, as John Fryer understood, a truly desperate option for an apprentice. One's hope for a career in the trades might be forever dashed, and imprisonment or fines might be imposed on the apprentice who was deemed in breach of his contract. In many respects, household servants were less constrained than apprentices. Pepys mentioned that during the Great Fire one of his servants left and went to her mother's instead of staying to help the Pepys family pack. When Pepys's wife went to complain, the girl's mother retorted that her daughter was "not a prentice girl, to ask leave every time she goes abroad."[9] His wife fired the girl, but this troubled Pepys who knew that there were no real grounds for doing so.

Young women were seldom apprenticed in the same trades as men, but within the male-dominated professions they could be taken on by the wife of a craftsman to learn domestic duties. Female apprentices, bound by contract to their masters just as their male counterparts were, had little defense against aggressive seduction or rape by the master, his sons, or male apprentices. Compounding their predicament was the fact that both male and female apprentices could be beaten for any offense, but a female apprentice who became pregnant, even through rape, might also lose her job and would probably find no other alternative than to become a prostitute.

Despite the common abuse of apprentices, at the turn of the eighteenth century and well into it, the strongest guilds were able to retain their influence in the areas of manufacturing and commerce. But the guild system was changing. Masters with smaller incomes found it cheaper to hire a series of servants than to commit to training apprentices. At the same time, new trades were forming their own guilds, so that by the turn of the century, professional companies were no longer limited to artisans. The guild system was being forced to accommodate shifts in economics and fashion, but by refocusing its areas of responsibility and opening its doors to other business concerns such as wholesaling, it was able to expand its membership and sphere of influence, and maintain its role in London's hierarchy of power.

Africans in London
Shadow Lives

During the early centuries of the slave trade, in those times when simmering conflicts between England and the other European nations precipitously erupted, human cargos could not be sold in the colonies and had to be brought back to London. There, the captive Africans were released from their chains and turned loose in a chilly, bewildering city. Since slavery was not practiced in London, these Africans, once bound for a life of enslavement, were now technically free, but their fate in such a profoundly unfamiliar setting was uncertain at best. Some of the stranded Africans found work in wealthy households. Others not so favored had to fend for themselves on the streets of London, picking up whatever odd jobs they could, foraging for food, or relying on the largess of churches and guilds for their meager existence. And others still, exploiting skills they may have picked up on their Atlantic crossings, returned to sea to serve on European merchant ships.

One young servant called Mingo was perhaps among the more fortunate blacks in London. Since boyhood he had been employed by the most famous naval architect of the seventeenth century, Sir William Pett. Like so many other African Londoners who cast the faintest shadows in formal historical texts, Mingo was probably English by birth but certainly not by descent. Left out of the history books, Mingo and a few other Africans are only visible to us through personal documents of the time, most notably Samuel Pepys's diary.

Raised as a servant, Mingo became well known in London's fashionable circles. His life was perhaps less oppressive than it might have been, for he spoke English fluently and knew how make himself a valued and trusted assistant of important people. He ran errands, received some formal schooling, and even struck up an affectionate friendship with his master's parrot, a famously

While England was not usually the intended destination for a slaver's cargo, Africans often found themselves in London, some abandoned at the end of an unsuccessful voyage, others brought home to serve merchants and colonials. Africans in London were treated under the same conventions that bound European servants. (Johann Zoffany, The Family of Sir William Young, detail, c. 1766. Walker Art Gallery, National Museums and Galleries at Merseyside, England.)

intelligent African Grey. One can imagine the two Africans stranded in London's fickle climate, the boy and the bird, both of them exiles from a vastly different world. But judging from Pepys's diary, the young African made the best of his situation.

Africans were a common sight in London from the earliest years of the slave trade, and by the mid-eighteenth century it was considered fashionable to be served by a black page, such as the young boy on the right. (William Hogarth, Plate 5: A Harlot's Progress, 1731. Lewis Walpole Library, Farmington, Connecticut.)

Pepys, who seems always to have noticed other people's servants, makes special mention of Mingo, and also of Jack, the African servant of Sir William Penn, commissioner of the Navy. But Pepys was particularly impressed by Mingo, whose sense of humor and skillful dancing he records.* While Mingo's attributes may not seem significant today, the ability to perform was a highly desirable trait in an age when people were expected to entertain one another. One friend of Pepys even went as far as to dismiss his young servant because he was bad company, for although servants were not equals, they were expected to be at least friendly, sympathetic companions.

Pepys reports that during long social evenings, after the masters grew tired of providing their own entertainment, the servants were bid to dance, including "W. Batalier's blackmore and blackmore maid."† Eventually one of Batalier's "blackmores," Doll, became Pepys's cook, "who dresses our meat mighty well, and we are mightily pleased with her."‡

By the turn of the eighteenth century, it had become the vogue in London to have a black servant. The practice of employing a young boy as a page had long been common, but now to have a young black boy act in such a capacity grew more popular. The artist William Hogarth documents this fad in his print series, *A Harlot's Progress*, in which the young female protagonist at the height of her success is shown kicking over an elegant table in the house that her much older lover has furnished for her. Her page, an African of perhaps ten years of age, looks on in fear. He is depicted as an exotic creature, dressed in the standard costume of the day but wearing a turban to denote his real or imagined Moslem heritage.

Samuel Pepys saw one such child under far more chilling circumstances. A guest of Sir Robert Vyner, a goldsmith and banker, he records how Vyner "showed us all his house and grounds." Among the curiosities of the house was "a dead black boy that...had died of a consumption; and being dead, he caused him to be dried in an Oven, and [he] lies entire in a box."§ So grisly a fate could only have befallen one who existed on the remotest fringes of his society, a child considered an exotic trophy rather than a human permanently exiled from his native land.

Thus, even though the percentage of London's population that was apprenticed went into decline, those who aspired to wield commercial power in London were still obliged to achieve the "freedom" to practice the trade of a recognized guild.[10]

The Birth of Western Racism

By the end of the seventeenth century, with fewer young men and women making their way through the apprenticeship system, the social and economic gap between rich and poor in London began to widen, and the lot of the latter deteriorated dramatically. Only a half-century later, English society would be marked by a generalized disdain toward those whose lives were gripped by poverty. During the subsequent centuries of the slave trade, this tide of contempt for the poor would inform the treatment of slaves as closely as any prejudice against a stranger's skin color or land of origin.

Consider the arrangement of social classes in London during this period, particularly the nature of the relationship between the apprentice and his master. In a sense, European society in general, and English society in particular, exhibited a social arrangement that would be echoed in the colonies of the New World. In both settings there was an all-powerful master and an underclass of people whose lot was to serve him and his family. This underclass—the apprentices in London, the slaves in the colonies—labored virtually without personal rights or individual freedoms, and, more often than not, with little consideration of their basic humanity.

It would be disingenuous to suggest, however, that the apprenticeship system and slavery were analogous social institutions. Apprentices were, in effect, contracted labor, while slaves were human chattel, their very bodies the property of the master. In addition, apprentices had much to gain by enduring even the harshest treatment from their masters, and their term of indenture to the master craftsman was for a finite period of time. Slaves were not so fortunate. They faced a lifetime at the mercy of their owners, and they could only pray that fate would spare them from the most brutal and sadistic circumstances. Still, the comparison of the two states of labor is, in one regard, a valid one, for the attitude of slave masters toward their human chattel during the seventeenth century owed much to the manner in which apprentices were viewed and treated by their masters back home. Further, the colonial slave masters themselves were frequently survivors of the apprenticeship system, and no doubt many had developed their attitudes toward bonded labor during that difficult passage of their lives. But rather than impart an empathy for human suffering, harsh treatment as an apprentice seemed to inure the European slave owner to the emotional and physical anguish felt by the Africans.

Of course, slavery and racism are inextricably linked to the twentieth-century mind. And yet the transatlantic slave trade began less as a result of racism than of economic opportunism. Racist sentiment, however, was the justification for the slavery that emerged at the height of the transatlantic trade, particularly in the nineteenth century, when the brutality of the institution as it was practiced in the New World was becoming more widely criticized. The roots of this racism were buried deep in the enslavers' belief in the fundamental "rightness," and indeed the superiority, of their own culture. Such ethnocentric feeling was evident even in Africa, where one kingdom might consider itself politically and culturally more evolved than a rival state. But when the element of race entered the equation of slavery, as it did in the transatlantic trade, the ethnocentrism of the enslavers quickly redefined itself to include a belief in their racial superiority as well.

Thus, as Native American and later African populations were overpowered, mistreated, and finally murdered in the Americas, the aggressors shielded themselves from the full comprehension of their brutality by rationalizing that the slaves were ignorant heathens who were somehow less human than themselves and who need not be accorded the same consideration as Christian whites. In time, the vast majority of those involved in the slave trade would choose to quiet the rumblings of conscience through such cultural and racial stereotyping, so much so that when the official Constitution of the United States of America was ratified in 1887, a black slave was counted as only three-fifths of a person—two-fifths less of a human being than his white master.

Although Robinson Crusoe *is best remembered as the tale of a man marooned on a desert island, the story hinges at every turn on the experience of the slave trade. (Daniel Defoe, scenes from French edition of* Robinson Crusoe, *c. 1730.)*

Early intimations of such rationalizations can be traced in the writings of seventeenth-century slave traders such as Jean Barbot, a Frenchman turned English ship's officer whose journals provide the elaborate detail about the slave trade that Pepys's journals provide about everyday life in London. Barbot mollified his qualms about the atrocities of slavery by cleaving to the belief that the African slaves would be better off in the New World where they would have the benefit of a Christian baptism. Barbot did not go so far as to suggest that he found the Africans racially inferior, which is the true basis of racism, only that their religious practices were less enlightened than his own.

In fact, at the time of the *Henrietta Marie*, racist justifications for slavery were not yet widespread. They were hardly necessary. European society itself was characterized by enough desperation to motivate violence, brutality, and personal disdain for those who could be preyed upon, whatever their race. In this milieu, hardship itself—even the ordeal of human bondage—was unremarkable.

Daniel Defoe's *Robinson Crusoe* illustrates many of the issues and attitudes surrounding the institution of slavery during the seventeenth century. Defoe relates the misfortunes of his hero, Robinson Crusoe, in a manner that suggests his plight is only rendered unusual by his survival of every disaster. Interestingly, Crusoe's career is linked with slavery at every turn, suggesting just how commonplace the institution of human bondage had already become. His first commercial voyages are to Africa, where he trades for gold and observes the trade in slaves. When next he ventures toward Guinea, he is captured by Sallee raiders and held as a slave himself. Dismayed by his sudden reversal of fortune, Crusoe nonetheless never questions the morality of his condition. Slavery is simply a fact of seventeenth-century life, and Crusoe intends to escape it. He eventually does achieve his freedom, taking with him a young Moorish boy named Xury. Crusoe offers Xury a choice: He can go with him as a servant and companion or swim to shore and take his chances. Xury promises to follow Crusoe forever.

After various adventures along the African coast, including one in which the man and the boy are saved from starvation by friendly Africans, they are picked up by a Portuguese slave trader on his way to Brazil. The trader is depicted as a kind and honest man, willing to take Crusoe with him at no charge since he himself would hope to be rescued from similar circumstances in the same way. But the young Moor, Xury, suddenly becomes a commodity when the captain offers Crusoe money for him. At first Crusoe is unwilling to sell his faithful companion, but the captain promises to free Xury after ten years "if he turned Christian." This convinces Crusoe: "Upon this and Xury saying he was willing to go to him, I let the captain have him."[11] Xury evidently has no great expectations of his future, and although Crusoe frequently regrets selling him, it is not because he recognizes the betrayal but rather because he needs a servant—a role soon filled by Friday, a Native American.

Even in the literature of the time, the ethnocentrism that would, in hindsight, turn out to be the precursor of full-blown racist sentiment was being expressed. In *Robinson Crusoe*, those of like culture subjugate those who are racially and culturally different from themselves. Thus, the Africans enslave the European Crusoe and the young Moor, Xury; Crusoe makes a servant

After many years of isolation, Robinson Crusoe was rescued and returned home at last. However, Crusoe realized that his long-time servant, Friday, would not be sufficiently sophisticated to meet his needs in Europe. He did not free Friday, but purchased a new slave in Portugal on his way to England. (Daniel Defoe, scenes from French edition of Robinson Crusoe, c. 1730.)

of Xury and, later, of the Native American, Friday; the Portuguese slave trader spares Crusoe but pays him money in order to enslave the swarthier-skinned Xury.

The New Feudal Lords

Among the English, seventeenth-century attitudes toward enslaved peoples were forged in the atmosphere of economic insecurity that had gripped much of England immediately following the Fire and the Plague. In late-seventeenth-century London, the middle class hardly existed, and those who inhabited the netherworld between rich and poor were still fighting for security. Unlike the aristocracy, whose wealth was based on landholdings that had been passed down to them from feudal days, those who aspired to the merchant class knew that neither their name nor their paternity would gain them any advantage; money was their only protection. As they watched the destitute disappear into disease, despair, and death, they endured apprenticeships and clawed their way to the trading and manufacturing fortunes that would stabilize their lives and those of their immediate families. In the attitudes of these newly wealthy citizens, and in their treatment of those who served them, England's perception of the transatlantic slave trade would ultimately be crystallized.

The merchants who invested in slaving voyages and the colonial plantation owners whose continuous demand for bonded labor fueled the slave trade were not usually drawn from the ranks of the old aristocracy but from the bourgeoisie, the new money, who saw the transatlantic trade as an opportunity to break out of their role as manufacturers and shopkeepers and to reproduce the feudal model—a lord and his serfs—in a new context. Such a re-creation of feudalism had little chance of success in Europe where the best lands were already taken and, despite the relentless drudgery of peasants' lives, some individual rights had already been won. But the colonies of the Americas were ideal for a new feudal model. Grasping the possibilities, members of Europe's new money elite were quick to purchase and develop their own plantations in the colonies, positioning themselves to benefit from a highly profitable cycle in which manufactured goods from Europe were sent to Africa, where they were traded for raw materials and human cargo. The humans were then sold in the Americas for more raw materials and cash, which flowed back into England, initiating another cycle.

For these lords of commerce, ownership of the ships that traveled this triangular route proved the most effective hedge against financial risk. Profits and losses could be spread among several ships, and the owners could control the choice of captains for each voyage. Indeed, the nature of the whole transatlantic enterprise suited the wealthy over the small investor, and many of the smaller speculators in the trade saw their fortunes destroyed by a single slaving venture that failed. Those who could afford to sponsor a significant number of slaving voyages, however, could expect their fortunes to grow.

Foreign trade was becoming a highly organized business in London at this time. Commerce with other European countries was already well established, and trade with Europe's new colonies or with uncolonized lands on distant continents now required a more sophisticated level of government administration. The guild system represented one widely embraced model of professional association, and the new companies that sprang up to facilitate the increasingly profitable slave trade were quick to adopt this approach of pooling resources for a common goal. Thus, the East India Company was formed in 1663, and with it its less successful rival, the Royal African Company. The East India Company controlled English shipping in India proper; it also conducted trade in East Africa and a number of Asian countries. The Royal African Company specialized in the trade with Africa and the West Indies, and sought to dominate the slave trade. The Royal African Company lacked the efficiency of its East Indian counterpart, however, and planters complained that its ships were unable to keep up with the African demand for European goods or the colonists' demand for African slaves.

A new class of sea merchants known as interlopers, or "separate" traders because they were not part of the government-endorsed shipping companies, arose to fill this void. For many years these merchant ships hovered at the edges of Africa's best markets, picking up what cargo they could. Eventually they proved so much more successful than their officially endorsed counterpart that their ventures were made legal, no doubt as a result of pressure from London politicians and merchants who had investments in the colonies. Soon businessmen were forming their own consortia and funding their own slaving fleets to take advantage of this easing of trade laws. The activities of the separate traders expanded rapidly, and they soon controlled some of the most promising African markets.

The *Henrietta Marie* was probably owned by one such consortium of separate traders, merchants who had already backed several slaving voyages and who were well acquainted with the Triangle Trade's potential profits. Thomas Starke, the ship's chief investor, was a wealthy man thanks to the slave trade, which kept his five tobacco plantations in Virginia well stocked with the cheapest labor possible. And Starke protected his profits. Known to be a litigious man, he had more than once sued his captains for taking insufficient care of his merchandise.

Starke, who in 1697 consigned more than £18 worth of bugle beads to the *Henrietta Marie*, was part owner of several other slaving vessels, including the *Eagle, Concord, Endeavor*, and *Africa Galley*. He conducted business from his counting house in Mincing Lane—the entire street had been rebuilt after the Great Fire—a few doors away from the hall of the Clothworkers' Company and just a short walk from the financial hub of the Royal Exchange. Born near Ipswich in East Anglia in 1649, Starke had begun his career as an attorney and had spent some time in the British colony of Virginia.[12] In 1677, he had returned to England and embarked on a career as a merchant, trading various goods in return for tobacco from Maryland and Virginia. He soon expanded from this two-way interchange to the more elaborate commerce of the slave trade. Among his business associates were Micajah Perry, a slave trader and the government agent for Virginia, and a younger man by the name of Gilbert Heathcote, who was the richest commoner in England.

Heathcote had helped found the Bank of England in 1694 to assume King William III's burden of debt accumulated in the ongoing war with France. He had begun his career as a wine importer, soon enlarging his interests to include other merchandise. But Heathcote was a famous penny-pincher, and when in 1697 he and Thomas Starke dispatched their jointly owned merchant slaver, the *Eagle*, on an interloping voyage to Bandy, near New Calabar, disaster struck. Due to inadequate provisioning, the *Eagle* was not able to deliver its human cargo to North America but was forced to make a hurried landfall in Brazil. Starke was furious with himself, for he had tolerated his partner's parsimony, which had resulted in the loss of human merchandise, a not atypical story of the trade. Heathcote,

Coat of arms of the Tournay family. Anthony Tournay was a major investor in the Henrietta Marie. *(Guildhall, London.)*

however, was not an investor in the *Henrietta Marie*, which was preparing to sail for Africa, and Starke trusted that it would escape the effects of such overzealous frugality and reach Barbados on schedule.[13]

Starke's experience and success in the trade would have had a considerable influence on the *Henrietta Marie*'s other investors. Perhaps he selected the ship's African destination, New Calabar, a location along the Bight of Guinea that would have been familiar to many of England's free traders. Even though New Calabar was generally acknowledged to be a disease-ridden area, dangerous for Europeans and enslaved Africans alike, the supply of human cargo there seemed inexhaustible. Starke knew the value of slaves not only as cargo but also as labor. He had complained bitterly when England's war with France interrupted the slave trade, leaving his five Virginia plantations shorthanded.[14]

Another major investor in the voyage was Anthony Tournay, a London merchant in his late forties. Tournay dealt in iron and delivered thirty-three tons of it to the *Henrietta Marie*, a value equal to $265,000 in U.S. currency today.[15] In temperament Tournay was a very different man from the quick-tempered Starke. He lived well, drove a splendid carriage, and resided in a fine house on Thames Street. He also made a point of sharing what he had, giving alms to the poor, even going so far as to have a special door built at the back of his house through which to do so.

Son of a wealthy lawyer, Tournay was the scion of a Lincolnshire family that could trace its origins back to the eleventh century. He did not follow his father into the law but was apprenticed to Edwin Ball, a merchant adventurer and, like Tournay, a member of the Skinner's Guild. Tournay's wealth, however, was not from furs; in England, such ostentation had gone out of vogue. Tournay had profited hugely during the war with France, becoming one of the major suppliers of iron hoops for barrels to the Royal Navy. He probably also supplied the iron accouterments of slavery such as the shackles found aboard the *Henrietta Marie*. Since the Skinner's Hall was the meeting place of the East India Company during the 1690s, Tourney would have been well placed to anticipate the commodities of trade that were in keenest demand. As a testament to his success, he was elected master of the Skinner's Guild in 1700.

Squalls at Sea

An Account by Jean Barbot

This starkly poetic eyewitness account, written circa 1700 by Jean Barbot, a French Huguenot who served for many years aboard English slave ships, describes the terrifying nature of storms at sea and the fear they could strike in the hearts of hardened seamen:

I was one day surprised by a squall so severe that although we had brailed our sails, preparatory to furling them, and although the ship was very large, it was pushed over until the deck was almost in the water. This by itself makes those who are not accustomed to it tremble, and it might be said, when you see this, that all nature is confounded or that the elements are at war. A little black cloud forms gradually on the horizon in the direction of the approach. The air darkens by degrees, large clouds are seen rolling forward, and in less than no time the whole extent of the sky becomes so dark and so shot through with lightening, that you become terrified at what is in store. The sea, borrowing the color of the sky above, takes on a mourning aspect. The wind drops, the waves are subdued, everywhere there is a deep foreboding. At last, the storm breaks, lightening pierces the sky in a thousand different shapes, everywhere there are snakes and zigzags of fire. The thunder rolls, with a loud, deafening, frightening noise. The wind gets up, little by little, finally bringing with it torrential rain, augmenting the violence in a strange way, so that in an instant you seem as if entombed between the various elements, which appear to dissolve into each other and to unite, in order to send to the bottom any vessels they encounter in these localities. The wind shrills. The sea rises, it roars to increase the horror, and the foam on the waves takes on the color of the flashes of the lightening above, redoubling the fear and dread of the seamen. Aboard ship, you hear only the confused cries of the sailors, as they carry out their tasks, shouting from up aloft to those below, and the latter replying—this, together with the whistling of the rigging and the creaking of the ship, added to the noise of the storm and the thunder, and the roaring of the sea, only inspires fear and creates a paralysis of dread. Sometimes you are five or six hours in this condition, without knowing whether you are alive or dead....[11]

Despite the fact that so many ships were lost at sea—wrecked by storms or driven onto uncharted sandbanks and reefs—the maritime trade continued to produce enormous wealth for its investors. (Sieuwert van der Meulen, A Ship Caught in a Storm and Dashed to Pieces on the Rocks, early eighteenth century. Rijksmuseum, Amsterdam.)

The next person to join the venture was Thomas Winchcombe, a master pewterer who had, in the approved manner, worked his way up through the ranks of the pewterer's guild to achieve his place in the world. He had been accorded the freedom to practice the trade independently in 1691 and had recently been elected to its livery. Younger than both Starke and Tournay, Winchcombe was only thirty years old and new to the slave trade at the time that the *Henrietta Marie* was preparing to sail. But as far as he and the other investors knew, pewter was much sought after both in Africa and the Americas. (On past journeys, whatever could not

Pewterware such as this tankard, plate, and bottle from the wreck site of the Henrietta Marie, *was in wide use among the middle and lower classes in England and her colonies from the sixteenth to the eighteenth centuries. Indestructible and versatile, pewter was also recyclable so that those who wished to upgrade their tableware simply took it to a pewterer to be recast.*

be exchanged for slaves in Africa could usually be sold to Caribbean planters.) Winchcombe consigned six hundredweight of pewter plates, bowls, basins, and bottles, a value of £3.4.6, to the *Henrietta Marie*. Winchcombe also contributed pewterware to the ship's second voyage, but as it turned out, much of it would end up in a watery grave on the ocean floor. Other makers' pewter was also discovered in the wrecked hold of the *Henrietta Marie*, indicating that the demand for pewter in Africa and the colonies was on the decline.

Robert Wilson was probably the investor who procured the additional pewter. He also consigned twelve hundred copper bars, numerous cases of alcohol, and four dozen felt hats for the first voyage.[16] A Guinea trader of long standing, he was less interested in slaves than he was in ivory, a much sought after luxury in England. Used to fashion handles for knives and forks, combs, hair clips, buttons, ornately carved cane heads, and the keys of musical instruments, ivory had been one of the original trade items that the Europeans brought back from Africa, and it was still highly prized. Less perishable than slaves, it was a sure profit maker, provided the ship returned safely. During the late seventeenth and early eighteenth centuries, Wilson imported hundreds of ivory tusks, along with other items such as malaguetta pepper and redwood from Barbados, which was used in dying cloth. Robert Wilson would remain connected to the *Henrietta Marie* after its first voyage, for in 1701 he would act as the executor of the estate of John Taylor, captain of the *Henrietta Marie*'s second, doomed voyage.

The Lure of the Sea

The *Henrietta Marie*'s consortium of investors knew just how critical the choice of a ship's captain was to the eventual success of a trade venture. Hoping to minimize their economic exposure, they selected a veteran merchant seaman by the name of William Deacon to captain the ship's maiden voyage to Africa. A young man in his thirties, Deacon had already captained at least two other slaving voyages, both on the *Crown* out of London. He was reputed to be a responsible sailor and had successfully delivered 305 slaves to Jamaica in 1695 and 211 in 1696. But his first voyage aboard the *Henrietta Marie* was his last as a slave-ship captain. His involvement in the slave trade continued, however, for he had husbanded the profits from each of his voyages and would use them to invest in the commerce he knew so well.

As captain, William Deacon quickly took on a few men, including John Scorch, his boatswain, and Edward Humble, one of his able seamen. Like Deacon, they were born in the small village of Stepney on the north bank of the River Thames. Their allegiance to Deacon was not surprising, for a man of rank from one's hometown inspired deep respect, and a berth with him was cherished. And Deacon had, in the past, proven himself a fair man, a captain who did not stint on rations. In a profession where a captain's temperament could range from incompetent to indifferent to murderous, sailors followed a captain's reputation.

Shipping records tell us that Deacon's boatswain, John Scorch, brought an apprentice with him. And there was a gunner with a mate; a cooper and a carpenter, each with assistants; a sailmaker; a cook; and possibly a ship's surgeon commissioned to look after the slaves and, only incidentally, the crew. The names of some of the seamen are traceable from official records; they include Englishmen Christopher Trunifo and James Kedd, as well as Peter Christopherson and Claes Johansson, both Danes. The bleak circumstances of these men's lives are suggested by Christopherson's will, in which he left his meager possessions to his countryman, making no mention of any family or additional friends.

The *Henrietta Marie* sailed from London in November 1697 with a crew of about eighteen in all. Only the captain and nine of his men would survive the dangerous voyage as far as Barbados, a rate of loss much higher than the death rate on nonslaving ships but not unusual for slavers. Such appalling mortality rates beg the question: Why would able-bodied men risk their lives in a trade whose profits were capricious and whose voyages offered only a fifty-fifty chance of survival? For the officers on board, the reasons may have seemed compelling, because the captain, his officers, the surgeon, and sometimes even the carpenter all had something to gain if the voyage went well: At the end of the journey, each would receive a commission on the number of slaves delivered alive to the colonies. In a letter to one Captain Ambrose Lace, dated April 14, 1762, his employers stated the terms very clearly: "You are to have the usual commission of 4 in every 104 on the Gross Sales, and your doctor, Mr. Lawson, 12d. per Head on all the slaves sold." In addition, officers were allowed to buy and make room for a few slaves of their own: "The privilege we allow you is as Follows: yourself ten Slaves, your first mate Two,

H M

*These "touchmarks" are the professional signatures of Joseph Hodges (*TOP*) and John Emes (*BELOW*), two of the pewterers who supplied the Henrietta Marie with her cargo. The initials "HM" scratched into the back of the plate probably indicate that it was reserved for the use of the crew. (Robert Cummings, 1994.)*

and your Doctor Two, which is all we allow except two or three Hundred weight of screvelos [tusks of immature elephants] amongst your Officers, but no Teeth [full-size tusks]."[17]

The rank and file had no such inducements to offset the hazards and hardships of life at sea. For the common sailor, the wages were mean, the labor arduous, the hours long, and the journey far. Family relationships withered in the face of sailors' protracted absences; indeed, the children of seamen were often raised without ever meeting their fathers, for sailors were essentially wandering souls, social misfits out of touch with the mundane realities of landsfolk.

The archetypal sailor of the time was viewed as a drunken spendthrift, more at home with his shipmates than with anyone else, stupid where money or business was concerned, a member of the port city's lowlife. Seamen perceived themselves very differently, of course, regarding their mariners' skills as a true craft. Nevertheless, they recognized that many of their number were outcasts and idlers, dangerous or shiftless men sent to sea as a last resort. Unmanageable children in seventeenth-century London were often dispensed with in this way, perhaps with the justification that if their lives depended on obeying orders, they would do so more readily.

Despite the obvious dangers of the floating world, children were present on most ships of the time, for both the navy and the merchant service accepted boys as young as ten as midshipmen or servants, and some boys went aboard when they were even younger, well before they could possibly have grasped the harsher realities of life at sea. The fictional Robinson Crusoe recalls his father laying out the facts: "He told me [the sea] was for men of desperate fortunes on the one hand, or of aspiring, superior fortunes on the other, who went abroad upon adventures, to risk by enterprise, and make themselves famous in undertakings of a nature out of the common road."[18] It is true that the pay was more than that of a plowman, a porter, or any of the other lowly jobs available to a poor man. Sailors who signed on for a few slaving voyages might return home with enough money to set themselves up in a tavern. Or they might not return home at all, having succumbed to dysentery, tropical diseases, shipboard accidents, squalls on the high seas, or injuries sustained in battles with hostile ships. Or they might be captured by pirates and forced into slavery in the ports of North Africa or Turkey.

Nor was the violence seamen faced from drunken or unstable men within their own ranks to be discounted or ignored. Only the best captains could control their men without physical punishment, for kindness was often exploited by sailors and harsh treatment must have seemed the only way to maintain control. Despite the numerous accounts of casual cruelty, a merchant ship was reputed to offer an easier term before the mast than that of a naval vessel. Few infractions carried the sentence of hanging on a merchant ship; instead, a captain was more likely to offload troublemakers at the nearest port. However, the extreme corporal punishment that made the English Navy such an efficient tyranny was already gaining wider currency in the merchant service in the late seventeenth century. Flogging with a cat-o'-nine-tails was common for both serious mistakes and petty crimes, including the theft of extra rations. And beatings administered with a rope's end or a cudgel-like belaying pin were a common form of "encouragement," meted out to speed up the work at hand or to induce exhausted or frightened sailors to scramble up a ship's rigging in turbulent conditions.

Nevertheless, struck by the glamour of wind, water, and adventures in never-before-seen lands, many young men chose the sea. Others turned to it as a way to escape debtors' prison, unwanted lovers, harsh masters, or simply the grinding poverty of their lives. Thus, by the time of the *Henrietta Marie*, sailors formed one of the largest trade groups in London. But unless one was fortunate enough to rise through the mercantile ranks, the life of a seaman was not one to grow old in. As William Barlow, a merchant mariner involved in the East and West Indies trade, observed: "He that is but a common seaman that goes to sea when he is past forty years of age, that man earns his living with more pain and sorrow than he that endures a hard imprisonment."[19]

The Fate of the Soul

In light of the perils and pains of life at sea, what motivated so many of London's merchants and seamen to persist in the trade in human beings? What habits of mind and body made slavery an acceptable institution to each of them? While it would be tempting to suppose that they were ignorant of the misery they were setting in motion, this was simply not the case. And yet it would be too simple to paint all of these slave merchants as merely greedy, insensitive, callous, or evil. Tournay was typical of many who traded in human cargo. Cultured, wealthy, and charitable, he was considerate of his family and generous with the servants in his employ. When he died in 1726 at age seventy-six, his elaborate will bore all the marks of a man trying to make sure that his family was cared for and that others less fortunate would also benefit. He left £100 to St. Thomas Hospital in Southwark (it still stands today), and smaller gifts were assigned to the local charity school and to the Skinner's School in Tonbridge Wells. Even his servants were well treated in his will, with Tournay arranging to continue their pay for two years after his death. And yet, for all Tournay's efforts to maintain his integrity, he was a blithe participant in the cruelest, most soul-destroying commerce the world has ever seen.

Men of Tournay's kind are found throughout the pages of slavery's complicated history. Guillaume Grou, for example, one of the most successful slave traders of Nantes, France, during the eighteenth century, was by most accounts a pious man. Never blessed with children, he and his wife left their entire fortune to charity, including a large bequest to the local foundling hospital.

Yet neither Grou nor Tournay ever showed any remorse for their role in the slave trade. No doubt they saw nothing morally wrong with what they did. Indeed, few who entered the business of slavery ever emerged from it of their own volition—the financial stakes were too high. Besides, when all else failed to quiet a pious man's doubts, there was always the comfort to be found in the knowledge that at least the African slaves would be baptized in the New World and become Christians. After all, Europe's slave merchants reasoned, of what concern was the earthly fate of an African's body compared to the heavenly fate of his soul?

The Slave Coast

A Culture Plundered

of Africa

Replenished by the wine they had taken aboard in the Portuguese colony of Madeira and freshly supplied with wood and water from the Cape Verde Islands, the crew of the Henrietta Marie *first sighted West Africa, also known as the Coast of Guinea, in about mid-December 1697. It took the merchant slaver another month to reach the region of New Calabar in the area of what is now Nigeria. The Henrietta Marie's investors had chosen that particular spot just east of the Bight of Benin based on intelligence from the crews of other ships recently returned from trading there. Wars between sovereign states were raging all along the West

African coast, the seamen revealed, and each battle waged garnered a new pool of prisoners, ensuring an abundant supply of potential slaves.

New Calabar lay beyond the Niger Delta. The town itself was at peace, but its location on a major river made it ideally situated to receive the bounty of surrounding wars—slaves. The captives arrived by canoe not just from Benin but also from the hinterlands to the north, where skirmishes and raids among Igbo villages had led to yet more prisoners being rounded up. In fact, the majority of the Africans who would eventually be transported to the New World aboard the *Henrietta Marie* were Igbos (or Ibos), a proud agrarian people whose descendants still

This early map presents West Africa upside down, as though viewed from Europe. (West Africa, from the Vallard Atlas, c. 1547.)

inhabit modern Nigeria. Centuries later, words and phrases from the Igbo language would surface in the patois and creole dialects of nations half a world away, used with little thought of their origin by the inhabitants of such West Indian islands as Jamaica, Haiti, and Barbados.

An appreciation of Igbo society is essential to our understanding of the cultural elements that were transported to the New World aboard the *Henrietta Marie* and other ships of trade. Although the crew of the *Henrietta Marie* would have encountered the Igbo in the coastal regions of New Calabar, their geographic roots lay at the confluence of the rivers Niger and Benue, almost a thousand miles north of lands they occupy today in Nigeria. Some two thousand years before, the Igbo had begun moving southward along the banks of the Niger, displacing or absorbing other cultural groups until they eventually fanned out across a roughly circular territory, almost one hundred miles in diameter, reaching from the west bank of the Niger to as far as the Cross River in the east. The Niger Delta formed the southern border of Igbo territory, which was set into the southeast region of modern Nigeria.

The history of Igbo culture is not particularly well documented and must be pieced together from oral accounts, archaeological evidence, surviving art, shifts in linguistic development, colonial records, and other such sources. A. E. Afigbo, a twentieth-century Igbo historian, has labored to create whole cloth from these remnants of the past, and his landmark study of Igbo culture, *Ropes of Sand*, has advanced our knowledge greatly. We know, for example, that the Igbos had evolved from hunter-gatherers into proficient farmers who practiced conservation techniques. Although the local soil was meager, they successfully cultivated such staples as yams, cassava, and maize, avoiding depletion of the land by clearing new crop areas on a regular basis and supplementing their diet through hunting and fishing. The Igbos were an industrious people. Farms might be as much as an hour's walk away from the village, and everything was cultivated by hand—no beasts of burden were utilized.[1] As their settlements prospered, the Igbo established complex social institutions, initiated new trade alliances with their neighbors, and practiced their indigenous arts.

Invoking the Ancestors

Unlike in Benin, the ascendancy of Igbo culture in the regions around New Calabar did not bring with it centralized government; rather, the Igbos organized themselves into small, autonomous political units, each with its own cultural variations and internal influences. If the Igbo were fragmented politically, they were nonetheless united by a dynamic spiritual and philosophical ethos in which the Earth Goddess, La or Annie, was regarded as the supreme natural force.[2] Particularly heinous crimes such as murder, manslaughter, or suicide were counted as crimes against the earth. But as one Igbo proverb states, *"Ike di na awaja na awaja"* ("Power runs through many channels"),[3] and so a panoply of other gods and goddesses also had to be appeased. This hierarchy of spiritual beings populated a belief system among the Igbo that regarded life's changes, paradoxes, and conflicts as inevitable, even desirable, aspects of a ceaseless, universal flow.

In Igbo culture, the ancestors, though not exactly worshiped, could be appealed to, and the living and the dead could assist each other to affect the outcome of earthly experiences. The head of each household—invariably a man since, despite the Igbos' worship of the Earth Goddess, the culture was a deeply patriarchal one—kept a figure of his own personal god along with the figures of his ancestral spirits in a shrine in his compound. Such shrines pos-

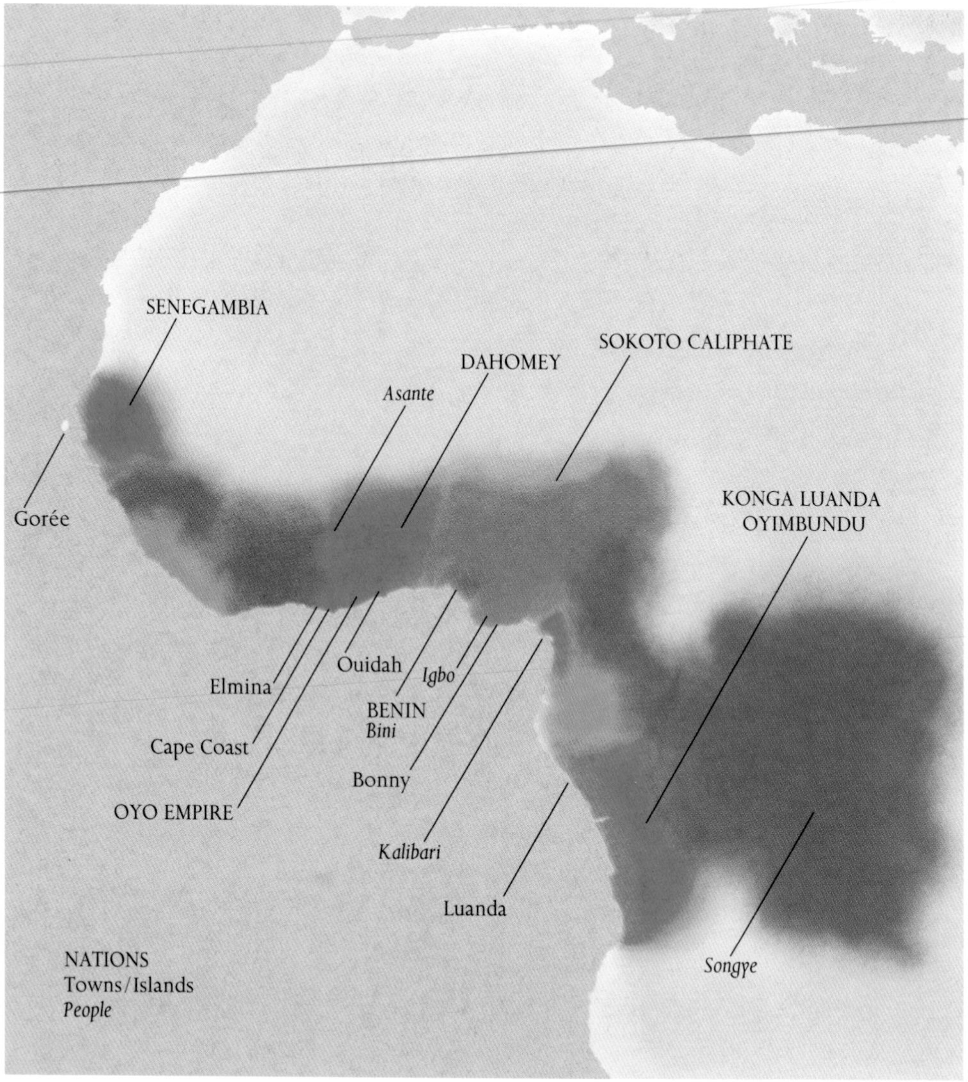
SENEGAMBIA
DAHOMEY
SOKOTO CALIPHATE
Asante
Gorée
KONGA LUANDA
OYIMBUNDU
Ouidah
Igbo
Elmina
BENIN
Bini
Cape Coast
Bonny
OYO EMPIRE
Kalibari
Luanda
NATIONS
Towns/Islands
People
Songye

Although the Europeans established outposts all along the West African littoral, the coast was controlled by those African nations from which the Europeans rented the land for their outposts.

sessed both sacred and historical power, allowing one to call on ancestors from as far back as six or seven generations.

The Igbo dead were often invoked in masquelike ceremonies during which costumed dancers took on elaborate ritualized roles. The ancestors could even be reincarnated if they were sufficiently possessed of *chi*, the animating life force of all things.[4] To this end, Igbo clan leaders would mask themselves during ceremonies and celebrations, assuming the spirit personality of an esteemed ancestor in an enactment similar to that performed during the ancestral rites of the kachinas of the American Southwest. Contemporary Igbo writer Chinua Achebe describes one such spirit ceremony, which takes place at the funeral of an important elder in *Things Fall Apart*, the author's re-creation of life in the Igbo interior before the arrival of whites:

> *Now and again an ancestral spirit or* egwugwu *appeared from the underworld, speaking in a tremulous unearthly voice and completely covered in raffia. Some of them were very violent. . . . But the most dreaded of all was yet to come. He was always alone and was shaped like a coffin. A sickly odor hung in the air wherever he went, and flies*

went with him. Even the greatest medicine men took shelter when he was near. Many years ago another egwugwu *had dared to stand his ground before him and had been transfixed to the spot for two days. This one had only one hand and it carried a basket full of water.*

But some of the egwugwu were quite harmless. One of them was so old and infirm he walked with a stick. He walked unsteadily to the place where the corpse was laid, gazed at it a while and went away again—to the underworld.

The land of the living was not far removed from the domain of the ancestors. There was coming and going between them, especially at festivals and also when an old man died, because an old man was very close to the ancestors. A man's life from birth to death was a series of transition rites which brought him nearer and nearer to his ancestors.[5]

The Igbos' fundamental appreciation of things animate and inanimate, as well as their sacred regard for earthly rhythms and ancient wisdom, allowed the society's decentralized system of power to work. Each subgroup understood that their commonalties were woven together like fine fabric, creating patterns of social interaction that were ever mindful of the cyclical as well as the linear nature of existence. One expression of this dual consciousness could be found in the symbolism attached to the Igbo calendar. While the Igbo week spanned four days, the monthly moon cycle was comprised of seven weeks, and so the numbers four and seven were used in myth and folklore to signify the dynamism between linear time and cyclical layers of repetition. The world was perceived as an intricate evolving reality in which all things were constantly being acted upon by the play of natural forces. This spiritual philosophy informed every aspect of Igbo life.

"The Igbo Make No Kings"

European accounts of African life around the time of the *Henrietta Marie* offer further insights into Igbo culture by detailing its evolution after the arrival of whites. Jean Barbot, who served as an officer aboard at least two English ships between 1699 and 1704, visited many areas of the West African coast and kept extensive journals of his travels. He later published these journals, along with those of his nephew, James Barbot, who also traded for slaves on the West African coast at the turn of the eighteenth century. The Barbots' observations provide vivid descriptions of the environment encountered by the captains and crews of the *Henrietta Marie*, for the interval covered by their journals exactly coincides with the period during which the *Henrietta Marie* made her two journeys to New Calabar.

In his writings, Jean Barbot notes that the rulers of such cities as New Calabar were often referred to by Europeans as "kings," but he doubted that they held such supreme authority. The Frenchman observed that the "king of Bonny" (Ibani), known to the Europeans as William, acted in consensus with other community leaders when decisions had to be made. All these leaders had to be courted for the Europeans to achieve a favorable trade outcome, and presents had to be given generously.[6] Barbot also records that at the end of the trading venture, when a ship was ready to sail, these leaders offered him and his fellow officers parting gifts: "At that time also…the natives as have received from us a present, use to present us each with a boy or girl slave in requittal."[7]

The Igbos, from whom the *Henrietta Marie's* cargo would ultimately be drawn, had a similar social structure. There was no single "king" but many leaders working in concert.[8] The Igbos' loosely knit society, with its associated villages forming political subgroups, supported the existence of not one but many men of high title who wielded authority in communities of varying complexity. Some Igbo villages were quite large with several thousand inhabitants; others were much smaller, formed by a single family in search of arable land or a small group of individuals who might have been exiled from their original community for a crime against the earth.

The Igbos' decentralized system of government represented an effective alternative to the more familiar oligarchies of the time. In Europe and many parts of Africa, a single omnipotent monarch, whose power was the gift of heredity, reigned supreme. By contrast, the Igbos granted temporal power within a village by common consent or widespread acclaim. The proverb "The Igbo make no kings" finds its basis here, in a world where status had to be earned by the individual and endorsed by the community at large.[9] Power was the province of men of title, but such titles were not hereditary. Rather, a man claimed a particular title for himself in a ceremony in which he ritually declared his wealth and gave monetary gifts to members of his village. Every adult male was expected to take at least one title, and not to do so was considered a sign of indolence. Young men who worked hard and seemed destined for a high title were encouraged and praised by their elders, for the taking of titles was the cornerstone of a village's social and economic design. The assumption of rank was an expensive business, requiring as it did a sharing of wealth that both enriched the community and defused individual power. As a man's economic means increased, the culture demanded that he take on additional titles, thereby continuing to redistribute the communal wealth.

While a rich man might buy his son's first title, a poor man's son could make his way in the world through hard work. "A child who washes his hands may eat with kings," an Igbo proverb says, meaning that no one in Igbo society would be spurned as long as the person was doing his or her best.[10]

Skill at farming was one of the chief ways in which Igbos demonstrated their talents and their commitment to the community. Ouladah Equiano, an Igbo captured by African slave merchants as a child, described his kinsmen's agricultural talents in a remarkable account of his life published in the eighteenth century. For Igbos at home, success as a farmer of yams meant communal status and wealth. Not only would one's dependents eat well, but one could afford to distribute seed yams to neighbors at a handsome profit. However, as Equiano also pointed out, the very familiarity of the Igbo people with agricultural techniques, and the long hours they spent toiling over their crops, led to their being much sought after as plantation workers in the New World.

If the attainment of wealth facilitated movement within the social structure, lateral ties to family provided ongoing support. Each village was a microcosm of the larger Igbo division of power. A wealthy man would build his house in the center of a compound around which the dwellings of his dependents, including wives, children, and slaves, would be scattered.[11] His power would be measured not only by the continued success of his farming and trading ventures but also by the number of dependents that he could afford to sustain.

Igbo women, though cast in a subordinate role, also contributed to the overall wealth of the family.[12] A man with many wives could expect them to work for him, donating their efforts to the family's welfare—whether through farming, weaving, childrearing, attending the sick, or performing varied household duties. Although a man's wives were by no means slaves, they were a significant source of labor and were recognized as such. Thus, a suitor who hoped to marry was required to pay a bride price to the woman's family, for the fruits of her labor would henceforth be lost to her father and gained by her husband. Although few Igbo men took more than three wives, some African societies had potentates with a thousand wives or more, all laboring to produce fine cloth or some other commodity for the kingdom.[13]

Among the Igbos there was little difference in the lifestyle of a man of title and his dependents. Both master and dependents dressed in a similar fashion, shared the workload, and ate the same food.[14] Each wife was responsible for cooking for herself and her children as well as preparing a share of her husband's meals. Since all Igbos were expected to produce agriculturally, few men or women could afford full-time occupations outside of farming. In spite of this, artists and artisans were highly skilled and produced accomplished works that were strongly individualized within the culture's stylistic canon. As in other areas of the culture, both men and women contributed to the arts, but there were marked differences in their creative spheres. Men became smiths, builders, and carvers, as well as priests and specialists in the making of ritual objects. Women, in contrast, worked more often in ephemeral media, performing such tasks as decorating the exterior walls of buildings or adorning the human body. Women were also potters, weavers, and painters, and

Jean Barbot's illustrations of his travels reveal his eye for detail. Other captains studied his accounts in order to improve the chances of their voyages' success. ("Meeting with the King of Sestos," from Barbot's Journal, in Awnsham and John Churchill, Collections of Voyages and Travels, Vol. 5, 1732. Mariners' Museum, Newport News, Virginia.)

they served as the culture's "seers"—clairvoyants whose sanctuaries punctuated the Igbo landscape much as they had in ancient Greece.

While men were likely to learn their craft in the course of a formal and lengthy apprenticeship, women came by their knowledge informally, usually taught by the senior women of their households. For both men and women, however, training in the arts did not encourage imitation of the teacher, and creative innovation was valued over subscription to an established formula. An individual artist was expected to reinterpret the ethos of his or her time, in much the same way that Western artists since the Renaissance have been valued for their original interpretation of contemporary themes.

Despite the ephemeral character of the arts practiced by Igbo women, their work was not considered secondary to the more concrete trades that engaged the men. In this regard, the defining Igbo philosophy prevailed. In the arts as elsewhere, all things were perceived to be in a constant state of flux, and so it was more critical that creative output be pertinent, not permanent. Artists were valued as long as they were making relevant art, and artworks retained their significance only as long as they were useful—that is, able to be incorporated into the rituals and masquelike ceremonies of the culture. Thus, the work of Igbo artists, like much of African art, was created in wood, raffia, or other media not designed to survive the damp tropical climate of the West African coast. For the Igbo, this was a desirable state of affairs in that ritual symbols were constantly being re-created and modified as the culture evolved. However, for anthropologists and historians seeking to grasp the essence of Igbo culture, the loss of this potentially instructive art is lamentable indeed.

Not all aspects of the Igbo tradition were lost in this way. The best-known and oldest Igbo cultural site, known as Igbo-Ukwu, dates to the ninth century.[15] Situated at the approximate center of Igbo territory, a dozen miles from the home of the major Igbo subgroup, the Nri, on the eastern banks of the Niger, Igbo-Ukwu is comprised of three extraordinary archaeological sites—a storehouse of ceremonial objects, the tomb of an important man, and a pit holding decorative ornaments and jewelry. The first objects from these sites were accidentally uncovered in 1938 by an Igbo man digging a cistern in his backyard. The importance of his discovery was soon verified by the Nigerian department of antiquities, and in the late 1950s and early 1960s, the area was formally investigated by a team of Nigerian and British archaeologists. An excavation of historical significance comparable to that of the Egyptian tomb of King Tut, the sites are important not only to our understanding of Igbo culture but to the culture of West Africa as a whole.

From the artifacts discovered, archaeologists have determined that the man interred at Igbo-Ukwu possessed great wealth and community stature. Buried seated on a throne, his arms resting on metal supports, Igbo-Ukwu's entombed lord wore a crown, breastplate, and bracelets as he gazed into eternity. Beside him was a staff bearing a leopard skull, and the ten thousand beads found scattered about his body were presumed to have once decorated his clothing. He was attired in full ceremonial regalia and carried a fan and an ornate fly whisk surmounted by the figure of a horseman. This detail alone marks the man as an uncommon

Njinga, the Queen-King

Angola's First Freedom Fighter

BY IONE

Playwright and author Ione wrote and directed the acclaimed *Njinga, the Queen-King: The Return of the Warrior*, a play with music and pageantry. In this essay, she weaves the richly imagined voice of Angolan legend Njinga Mbandi with the narrative of her story:

I was a girl child in a woman's body, leaping and floating and flying inside the rosy dark of the beautiful Kengela Kacombe, and then there was no more room, and the feeling was worse and worse, and I was forced to leave Kengela Kacombe, only to take up air, never to be so completely woman again.

In 1592, in Ndongo, a part of the Central African country now called Angola, a dancing child entered this world to become Njinga Mbandi. Njinga means entwined, as a vine twists, and the name is given to infants born with their umbilical cords wrapped around the neck. "Ai Mama!" the court shamans and astrologers cried in astonishment at the birth of this child, seeing immediately from the cord that she was a force to be reckoned with.

Njinga was the favored child of a marriage between *Ngola* Kiluanji, ruler of Ndongo, and Kengela Kacombe, a former slave to whom the king had given his heart. A powerful old woman who had served the royal family for decades trained the young princess shaman in the ways of spirit.

In my teacher's dwelling place, I learned many things. I told her my dreams until my voice was strong. She taught me that it is through dreaming that a people hold together. She taught me to hear without ears, to see without eyes, to speak with no

Refused a chair by the Portuguese governor, Njinga devised one of her own. (Giovanni Antonio Cavazzi, Istorica descrizione dé tre regni, Congo, Matamba e Angola, Bologna, 1687. British Library, London.)

tongue—so that eventually any animal, any man or woman whose power I needed would come to me.

The powerful *Ngola*, or king, was the descendant of many great leaders before him, and he taught his daughter to hunt and to fish and to be a warrior. It is said that he even took her into battle with him when she was yet a young child.

With my father I hunted crocodiles and hippopotami, birds and snakes. Our palm trees gave life, oil, fruits, and building materials for our houses. Our women tended the crops as our ancestors had through all time, raising millet and beans, yams, radishes, bananas. They reared cattle, pigs, chickens, goats and sheep—and dogs good for eating. Our eggs and honey were greatly valued by all the surrounding peoples.

Njinga had a brother, Mbandi, who was jealous of their father's attention to her, and two beloved sisters, Kifungi and Kambu.

My sisters' breathing was like music in my ears. Music I always wanted to hear. Scent of the oils on my skin, my knees smooth against each other. What I did not know began to come in the night like whispering dreams—and later they became a part of me. I could not separate myself from them. We laughed and sang in the game circle and Mbandi could not keep up. And I danced as the other children stood back, my arms outstretched so that my fingertips touched the outer edges of the world, beyond the circle of the children, beyond the walls of our royal city high on a precipice overlooking the sea. And each time I danced, I hoped he would be watching. He stood tall and black against the blue of our sky, tall as the Palm source, heart of our people. He was my father, the king. I was dancing the world for Ngola Kiluanji.

The tension between Njinga and her brother, Mbandi, mirrored a much fiercer court rivalry. The brothers of the *Ngola's* principal wife had designs on the throne. When Njinga was thirty-five and the mother of a son of her own, her beloved father was murdered in an ambush staged by this faction of the family. Her brother, Mbandi, always unstable, chose this moment to seize the throne, engaging in a killing spree that included his own mother and most of her kin. He executed Njinga's son as well and placed his own son with a powerful Imbangala leader hoping that he would be taught to protect himself against Njinga's vengeance. Mbandi, now the

Ngola, knew that vengeance was sure to come, and it was probably this certainty, along with the pressures of the steady inroads being made by the Portuguese colonizers in Ndongo, that contributed to his mental and physical deterioration.

I waited. I was good at waiting. I knew how to bide my time. I watched as my brother became more and more deranged. I treated him respectfully and showed him not a sign of my pain, my heartbreak. But alone with my dear sisters, we mourned our mother and healed ourselves. And I listened to the messages from the bones of my father in order to know just what to do.

In 1622, probably hoping to appease her and those in court who favored his sister, Mbandi made Njinga his ambassador to Luanda, where Portuguese governor João Correia de Sousa was ensconced. Her task was to negotiate a peace treaty with the Portuguese slave traders and colonizers.

One thousand servants accompanied me to Luanda. I wore my father's royal leopard skin, bound with the belt of a buffalo tail, my bark cloth apron, my palm cloth over my arm, a small bone in each of my nostrils. In my hair there were beautiful beads and shells. In my ears there were magnificent earrings. Everywhere we stopped the people greeted us joyously and there was much celebrating.

The details of Njinga's meeting with the Portuguese have become the stuff of legend. In Luanda, the governor, himself seated on a chair, offered Njinga a mat with a cushion to sit on, their standard seating arrangement for Africans. Haughtily, Njinga refused it and ordered one of her female servants to kneel down. Taking a seat on the woman's back, she continued the interview with the astonished Portuguese. Njinga negotiated a fair treaty with the governor and refused to pay tribute, pointing out that her brother was a head of state and that Ndongo had not been conquered by the Portuguese. According to Father Giovanni Cavazzi, a Capuchin priest who resided many years in Njinga's court and was greatly fascinated by her, she further exclaimed, "He who is born free should maintain himself in freedom, not submit to others and lose freedom, which is so esteemed by all, as there is nothing worse or more abhorrent than slavery." The Portuguese were so impressed by Njinga that they gave her the royal treatment during her stay.

While in Luanda, Njinga was baptized into the Christian faith and was given a new baptismal name: Ana de Sousa. Scholars still debate the sincerity of her conversion to Catholicism, many claiming that it was a political ploy. In any case, Njinga returned triumphantly to Kidongo, Ndongo's capital, carrying many presents for the king. Her prestige in court rose enormously even as her brother Mbandi's health continued to fail. Although he was consuming many medicines for a stomach problem, he grew more and more despondent, and in 1624 he took his own life.

Upon *Ngola* Mbandi's suicide, Njinga capitalized on her strength in court and claimed the throne by becoming regent to her nephew, Mbandi's son. But this was the moment for Njinga to avenge the death of her mother and her own son. She had the boy poisoned, and, adopting an Imbangala custom normally abhorred by the Mbundu, she ate his heart ritually.

In taking the throne, Njinga circumvented a custom that allowed no women to rule, although they had done so in the far distant past. Njinga simply declared herself the *Ngola*, or king. Dressing in her father's ceremonial garments, she gathered her best warriors and chose thirty concubines, as was the custom of the king. But there was a difference: Njinga's concubines were men whom she ordered to dress as women. She even directed these concubines to sleep among her maidens.

"Now," I told them, "see that your garments come as you have come—as we all have come—from women. You will sleep with the women, but if you touch one, you will never be able to sleep with a woman again, and you may choose to give your life!"

Witnesses attest to the queen-king's ferocious battle appearance and to her fierce war cry, reputed to be heard for miles. As ruler, Njinga enticed many slaves from Portuguese-held areas to escape to her territory, upon which she reclaimed them and integrated them into her vast army. This created so many problems for the Portuguese that they declared war on Njinga in 1626. After two failed campaigns against the colonizers and the capture of her sisters by the enemy, Njinga fled Ndongo, taking her army and the seat of government with her.

To bolster her position, she forged an alliance with the ferocious Imbangala, a notorious company of mercenary soldiers. With their support she rebuilt her army and established a base in Matamba, some distance to the north of Ndongo. Striking out from this new territory, she was able to progressively reoccupy areas of Ndongo that the Portuguese could not hold on to. A peace treaty with Portugal in 1639 recognized the legitimacy and stability of her new government.

But the Portuguese encroachment on Ndongo's lands continued. A few years later, in 1641, Njinga's armies joined with the Dutch to attack the Portuguese and nearly succeeded in driving them out of Ndongo. But the Dutch were distracted by other spoils, and in 1648 the Portuguese retook their lost positions. Six years later Njinga negotiated another peace treaty with Portugal. By then, her sister Kifungi had been drowned in the river Kwanza when it was discovered she was sending spy messages to Njinga from Luanda. But the queen-king was finally able to achieve the release of her other sister, Kambu, now a devout Catholic known as Dona Barbara. Once her sister returned home, Njinga moved against her former allies, the Imbangala, and brought Christianity to her country. In this way, she strengthened her position with the Portuguese and ensured her sister's right to succeed to the throne at her death.

Kambu I have seen it. One day you will rule after me. Kambu, never stop fighting. Never give up! One day Ndongo will be free!

The court shamans were correct in their forecast about the baby born with her umbilical cord wrapped around her neck. Njinga ruled for forty years, keeping the Portuguese colonialists at bay through a combination of diplomacy, fierce fighting, and mythology, and holding the Mbundu people together in the face of enormous odds. But her wars with Portugal led to the export of thousands of her people as slaves. Many went to the American colonies, and records in both New York and Virginia show that the slave population in the mid-seventeenth century was largely of Angolan origin.

Brazil, however, received the largest number of Angolan slaves. In modern-day Brazil, descendants of these slaves hold ceremonies to celebrate Njinga, and perform chants and dances to commemorate her. They believe that Njinga sent many warriors "in disguise" to Brazil. These warriors were committed to sowing the seeds of rebellion among the slaves and to maintaining the fighting skills of the mother country. Njinga's fighting spirit was certainly alive when her contemporary, a dedicated African warrior leader named Zumbi, created the Kingdom of Palmares in the north of Brazil in the mid to late seventeenth century. Also known as Angola Janga, or Little Angola, the fortress city became a refuge for thousands of runaway slaves and grew to roughly the size of Rhode Island. Palmares would remain a safe haven for Njinga's people in Brazil for almost a century, until it was finally destroyed by the Portuguese colonizers.

In Ndongo, Njinga was already a living legend at her death, regarded as a powerful shaman by many of her subjects and respected by the Europeans who knew her. Documents attest to the fact that shortly before her death at age eighty-one, Njinga rose from her sickbed and danced for several days, executing the old war dances before an amazed court, as she had in her youth. Revered today in war-torn Angola, Njinga is widely known throughout Africa as a champion of African nationalism, a fierce freedom fighter against the Portuguese, and, by implication, against all European aggression.

individual, for until the arrival of Europeans in the Igbo interior, horses were available only through trade with Arabs, and Igbo horsemen were rare souls indeed.

Above the man's burial chamber, five people, possibly the man's slaves, had been sacrificially entombed. Since the Igbo had no kings, the chief archaeologist at Igbo-Ukwu suggests that the individual buried at the site may have been an *ozo*, or "big man"—one who had taken the highest of titles and whose interment was typically accompanied by grand ceremonies and masquerades.[16] In his autobiography, Ouladah Equiano describes an Igbo burial which echoes that of the man at Igbo-Ukwu, offering insight into the role of the *ozo* in Igbo society:

> Though we had no places of public worship, we had priests and magicians, or wise men…held in great reverence by the people. They calculated time, foretold events…and when they died, they were succeeded by their sons. Most of their implements or things of value were interred along with them. Pipes and tobacco were also put into the grave with the corpse, which was always perfumed and ornamented, and animals were offered in sacrifice to them.[17]

A large number of bronze sculptures made of an alloy of copper and tin were unearthed at Igbo-Ukwu, representing the earliest bronze pieces discovered in West Africa. These bronzes exhibit an extremely sophisticated technique whose artistic precedents have not yet been found. Clearly, Igbo artisans of the period possessed a great facility with the art of lost-wax casting. Their bronzes are notable for their elaborate surface decoration, usually featuring geometric patterns along with highly realistic depictions of insects, frogs, and snakes. Among the numerous bronze objects found at the site are ceremonial bowls, drinking vessels, and staff fittings, many of which imitate the form of natural materials such as the calabash and seashells.

How was all this wealth and luxury obtained? While earlier doubts about the existence of active copper mines in Nigeria have been dispelled, the excavations at Igbo-Ukwu leave no question that long before the arrival of the Europeans, the Igbo traded slaves, ivory, and kola nuts in exchange for metals, beads, perishable goods, and even horses. Beads were especially important; over sixty thousand were found in the ceremonial storehouse at Igbo-Ukwu. The beads appear to have been imported from the Islamic countries to the north, indicating a well-established system of trade that predated the arrival of the Portuguese by centuries.

Masks such as this were not meant to cover the face but were intended as belt ornaments to be worn by the oba. The mask's brooding features are emphasized by the ritual scarification of the brow. The stylized figures around the top represent Portuguese visitors. (Benin, Ivory hip mask, c. 1550. Metropolitan Museum of Art, New York.)

This musician wears a coral necklace and a leopard-skin kilt trimmed with feathers. (Figure, Standing: Horn-Blower, bronze, c.1550–1680. Metropolitan Museum of Art, New York, The Michael C. Rockefeller Memorial Collection, Gift of Nelson A. Rockefeller, 1972.)

At the time the *Henrietta Marie* anchored offshore at New Calabar, many Africans had already converted to Christianity, among them the Owarri, who occupied lands north of Benin called Warri, close to the Niger Delta. Warri had become a Christian state at the end of the sixteenth century when its ruler consented to be baptized by Augustinian friars. Although the form of Christianity practiced by the Owarri was intertwined with local religions, contemporary commentators were nevertheless impressed by the Africans' sincerity in adopting the tenets of the Christian faith.[18]

The fact that Africans were already Christians did not preclude their enslavement by the Europeans, however, and the argument put forth by many advocates of the transatlantic trade—that slavery was an opportunity to convert African heathens by transporting them to Christian lands—was never set against the fact that many Africans had embraced that faith while still in their homelands. But if Christianity did not save the Africans from slavery, it also did not blind them to the true intentions of early European mariners. Aware that the seafarers meant to exploit their wealth, the Africans hastened to secure their coasts and inland waterways. Skilled warriors, expert fishermen, and seasoned navigators of the uncharted waters, the West Africans were virtually invincible—and they would prove it if necessary. They owned large canoes capable of carrying twenty or thirty men, more than the total crew of many European ships that reached their shores. Indeed, those Europeans who survived the arduous sea voyage around the bulge of Senegal did not have the resources to meet such a contest. Arriving in small vessels battered by the high seas, with scant crews and a few guns, they might hope to intimidate the locals but were clearly no match for a contingent of African warriors.

So Europeans sought to establish formal trading relationships instead. But they found the Africans slow to abandon their suspicions toward them, for although the pattern of raids in which the first Africans had been seized did not continue for very long, such raids continued to be staged often enough to make the Africans wary of doing business with the Europeans unarmed or in small numbers. Captain Thomas Phillips, an Englishman whose voyage on the *Hannibal* was commissioned by the Royal African Company in 1693, reported, "At Caba-la-ho the Africans are distrustful and before they will engage in trade they require that the captain come down the side of the ship and drop three drops of salt water in his eye as a pledge of friendship, and of the safety for them to come aboard." Phillips himself performed this ceremony but added, "They came aboard, but seeing so many men on deck, were mistrustful and went into their canoes again."[19]

A number of African slaves, captured during the earlier raids on the coast and brought back to Portugal, now returned as translators to help negotiate trade with their countrymen. Soon the Portuguese, like the other Europeans who followed them, sought to set up trading outposts or "factories" patterned after those they had previously built on Africa's Mediterranean coast. By establishing a permanent presence in West Africa, the Europeans hoped to secure their right to trade in the sub-Sahara and to forge long-lasting relationships with local rulers who could help them fulfill their commercial needs.

When the Portuguese first opened trade with the Africans, both parties were less put off by cultural differences than they were impressed by the possibilities of material exchange. One culture's surfeit, they understood, could become the other's indulgence. Ivory, for example, was so plentiful in Africa that ivory objects were available for what the Europeans considered outrageously cheap prices. The abundance of ivory also meant that African artisans had much experience and therefore great expertise in carving the precious substance, and the elaborately crafted pieces, in particular salt-cellars, were much in demand among the nobility of Europe. But African ivory could be had by more common folk as well, with sailors purchasing spoons and other trinkets for the price of a piece of their clothing. Both the Europeans and the Africans were well satisfied with the exchange: The Africans regarded the beads or items of clothing they purchased as pieces of exotica to be worn, shared, traded, or paraded as a triumph of commerce, while the Europeans knew that their purchase of ivory, ubiquitous in Africa, would be highly prized at home. The trade was a success, and the ivory industry boomed.

As the trade expanded, Portuguese officials, ever vigilant in their attention to monetary bureaucracy, began levying taxes on African imports. By the turn of the sixteenth century their official ledgers recorded a wealth of imported ivory, fabrics, and other goods. European artists such as Albrecht Dürer studied the exquisite workmanship of

Africans carved ivory into delicate horns, bowls, spoons, and other utilitarian objects. (Carved Altar Tusk, ivory, nineteenth century, 1888–1897. Metropolitan Museum of Art, New York, Gift of Mr. and Mrs. Klaus G. Perls, 1991.)

In this engraving, Africans are trading gold for European goods. Not all areas of Africa sold slaves to the Europeans, nor did those involved in the trade sell all the time; instead, they sold whatever surplus wares were available locally. Europeans often referred to areas of Africa by the commodity for which they most frequently traded in that region. The territories of the Akan people that today comprise much of modern Ghana were known as the Gold Coast for their abundant supply of the precious metal. (William Bosman, A New and Accurate Description of the Coast of Guinea, London, 1705. Carl A. Kroch Library, Cornell University, Ithaca, New York.)

imported carvings for inspiration and included them in paintings. Princes and aristocrats developed an appreciation for African art, especially those aspects that appeared to share a European aesthetic. Patrons and collectors began to send drawings to Africa to have custom work executed, and in time ivory saltcellars, hunting horns, cutlery, and the like entered the treasuries of Europe's monarchs.

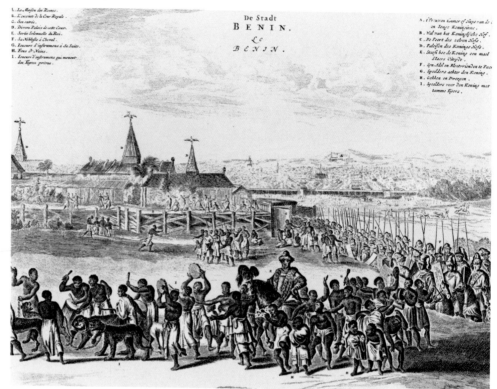

The city of Benin was one of the largest in the world during the sixteenth and seventeenth centuries, with art, culture, and nobility comparable to many European cities and surpassing others. (Olfert Dapper, "De Stadt Benin," from Naukreurige Beschrijvinge van Africa Gewesten, *Amsterdam, 1668. Musée Dapper, Paris.)*

The Europeans started to feel at home in Africa. Olfert Dapper, a Dutch writer who published his *Naukreurige Beschrijvinge van Africa Gewesten* in 1668, compared Benin favorably to his native Haarlem, observing that it was larger and describing it as a well-kept city of remarkable architecture, thriving commerce, and industry. The differences between the two worlds, African and European, might have seemed plain in terms of local customs but were less so in terms of the wider culture. The bronzework created in Benin was considered then, as it is now, to be some of the finest craftsmanship of the period, and Europeans of the Renaissance era could appreciate its brilliance. Europeans also did not find the Africans' architectural hierarchy unfamiliar, accustomed as they were to their lords living in grand houses and their peasants in thatched cottages. And there were other similarities. In both cultures, people ate using their hands, assisted by a knife and sometimes a spoon, and the smoking of tobacco after meals was a shared pleasure. Among the common folk, few in either culture could read and fewer still could write.

Even religious differences were not incomprehensible. They mainly involved the distinction among followers of God and his Son (Christians), God and his Prophet (Moslems), or one God and many Gods (indigenous faiths). Such distinctions could readily be bridged by a shared

A Cultural Exchange

1400–1700

When European voyagers first encountered West Africans in the fifteenth century, they were much taken by their creative achievements. Back in Europe, artists and craftspeople were only beginning to embrace the humanist ideals of the Renaissance, and they were impressed to discover that African artists had already attained many of the aesthetic goals for which they strove.

The Portuguese arrived first in the area of Sierra Leone, where they met the Sapis, craftsmen of extraordinary versatility and sophistication. The light, airy, ivory carvings of the Sapi people dazzled European collectors, who found the artistic virtuosity startling. Sapi carving made as much use of negative space as it did of detail, with arched bases enclosing voids over which a salt container perched. Huge tusks were used to create these effects, ivory of a size and quantity the Europeans had never seen. The amount of the precious substance that was discarded in order to achieve the typically light and graceful Sapi carving must have seemed to Europeans shockingly wasteful for such a fabulous luxury.

As the Renaissance ushered in Mannerism, the interplay between European and African art deepened. While Africans may not have influenced Renaissance art directly, European sculpture of the period began to exploit negative space and displayed a feeling of movement similar to

Ancestral heads played an important part in Benin's spiritual life. At the beginning of the sixteenth century the famous oba, or king, Esiege, commissioned a number of fine, heavily decorated heads made in memory of his deceased mother. (Head of an Oba, brass, sixteenth to seventeenth century, c. 1550–1680, Metropolitan Museum of Art, New York, The Michael C. Rockefeller Memorial Collection, Bequest of Nelson A. Rockefeller, 1979.)

African work. The Sapis' patient carving of links and linked spaces is echoed in the Mannerist ideal of *difficultà*—works that demonstrated technical wizardry and a mastery of spatial as well as iconographic skills.

The aesthetic of the Bini people of Benin differed strongly from that of the Sapi, but it, too, was easy for the Europeans to appreciate. The bronze funerary portraits evoking the mothers of various *obas* (kings) are considered among the world's finest examples of bronze casting during the period. Naturalistic, bold, and full of dramatic character, these sculptures equaled those of Renaissance masters. Indeed, the flowering of Bini art starting in the fifteenth century has been compared to the Italian Renaissance partly because of the overlapping time periods and partly because of similarity in stylistic preoccupations.

Artists of the European Renaissance had turned from the stylized aesthetic of the medieval period toward naturalism and spontaneous observation. Experimenting with new techniques and refining old ones, they were casting about for stimulation and studying every new or exotic element that came their way. African artists already had a long tradition of naturalism, and their technical skills were highly developed. When African and European artists met, not in person but through their works, a cross-fertilization of style and content was inevitable. As a result, from the late fifteenth century to the present, this mingling of artistic intentions has pulsed through the art of both continents, sometimes boldly, sometimes subtly, but always with the power to transform.

In 1520, while traveling in the Netherlands, the German artist Albrecht Dürer bought two African ivory saltcellars. Like so many other European collectors, he had been struck by the virtuosity of African art. Although African ivories could still be purchased inexpensively, they were highly prized in Europe, for Europeans realized that because of the scarcity of the medium in their region, they themselves were unlikely ever to produce works of such technical brilliance in this medium. So they turned to Africans, requesting that they carve ivory pieces for them and commissioning specific decorative motifs. Designs sketched by artists with whom Dürer would have been familiar, and perhaps even by Dürer himself, were among those sent to Africa. Responsive to this new market, Africans quickly learned the elements of European design, incorporating these into their already intricate style and introducing European subjects into sculpture of extraordinary power and beauty.

From this interchange and others it is clear that neither the Europeans nor the Africans regarded the other as a "primitive." Rather, during the early period of trade between the two continents, there was an equal exchange of commodities on both sides: English iron for African gold, ivory and cloth for beads and firearms. Gradually, two different and aesthetically sophisticated cultures came to appreciate each other's art.

Although the names of African artists from this period are not recorded, the wealth of surviving art has allowed scholars to piece together the story of their workshops, or guilds. The ivory carvers of Sierra Leone banded together according to distinct stylistic canons, while Bini artisans—bronze casters, ivory carvers, basket weavers, and fabric makers—organized into guilds accord-

OPPOSITE: *Bas-reliefs depicting important personages and scenes were a standard genre of art in the Benin area. (*Mounted King with Attendants, *brass, sixteenth to seventeenth centuries. Metropolitan Museum of Art, New York, The Michael C. Rockefeller Memorial Collection, Gift of Nelson A. Rockefeller, 1965.)*

ing to their specific crafts. Like their European counterparts, these guilds provided quality control, regulated workers, and dictated the iconography of a particular craft. The Bini guild of bronze casters, known as the *iguneromwon*, also made sure that artisans were trained to create various types of objects. Interestingly, the work-

the finest ivory was reserved for the king. The guild itself probably regulated iconography, specifying the amount of European imagery that could be used, and incorporating it into their traditional designs. Full-length sculptural portraits of Europeans figure prominently on the lower sections of the Bini saltcellars, and detailed renditions of clothing, weaponry, and equestrian gear reflect a precise moment of contact between Europeans and Africans at the turn of the sixteenth century. Interestingly, the Europeans depicted in these ivory pieces are of much greater wealth than those shown in Bini bronzes, suggesting that the bronzes portrayed the Europeans as the Africans most often saw them, while the saltcellars, carved from designs sent from Europe, reflected Europeans' highest notions of themselves, their wealth, and their aristocracy.

Congo craftsmen also fashioned exceptional works of art that included evidence of European contact. Crosses, statues of the Madonna, and various saints were all cast in bronze, many with decidedly African details, indicating a blending of European and African iconography to create a modified version of Christian symbolism.

Of course, Europeans also sought artifacts made in less durable media than ivory and bronze. Woven fabrics in particular appealed to them, with the best of African cloth being traded alongside the finest European weaving. Neither culture needed the other's cloth since both produced exquisite materials of their own, but a mutual desire for the exotic made the trade viable. Duarte Lopez, the Congo ambassador to the Vatican in the late sixteenth century, speaks of "weaving in different cloths such

ABOVE: *Open forms and delicate arches are the hallmarks of Sapi-Portuguese style. (Ivory saltcellar, the Paul and Ruth Tishman Collection of African Art, Walt Disney Company, Los Angeles.)*

ABOVE RIGHT: *Many magnificent saltcellars were commissioned by the European aristocracy. (Benin, Ivory saltcellar, early sixteenth century. Metropolitan Museum of Art, New York.)*

shops of the Bini bronze casters, like those of the ivory carvers (the *igbesamwan*) were all located in a specific district, just as the European guild system was organized in London, Paris, and Rome.

In Benin, ivory production was strictly limited, much as gold was in Ghana. The king had a right to one of every pair of tusks brought in by a hunter and could also exercise the right to buy the second one. Thus,

as velvets with and without pile, brocades, satins, sendals, damasks, and similar cloths." Since the Africans had not established trade with the Far East, they did not use silk but threads from palm leaves with which they achieved "equal Finesse and delicacy."*

This trade of indigenous arts and crafts with Europe would ultimately provide Africa with better access to imported materials such as bronze, coral, and glass beads, all of which were used to great advantage by African artists. The intercontinental trade would also ensure a lasting artistic legacy that might otherwise have been lost. The damp, humid climate of West Africa was not conducive to the conservation of artwork in organic media. Wooden sculpture, for example, was part of a long-standing artistic tradition, with clearly defined regional styles and elaborate craftsmanship. But little of it survived the ravages of climate, war, insect rot, and colonization. What has survived is a large cache of African artifacts imported into Europe, a remarkable trove of African art in private collections and later in museums, all spared by Europe's more temperate conditions. Eventually, the founding of institutions such as the British Museum, established in 1753, provided homes for these extraordinary ethnographic treasures.

Ironically, the preservation of so much of Africa's art would not have been possible but for the presence of European merchants on African soil. But the devastation wrought by the slave trade would finally undermine

This naturalistic figure of a Portuguese musketeer shows one aspect of European contact with which the Africans were familiar: warfare. (Benin, Portuguese Musketeer, bronze, sixteenth century. Museum of Mankind, London.)

Ivory spoons such as this were brought home as mementos by Europeans in large numbers. (Benin, sixteenth century. Metropolitan Museum of Art, New York.)

three centuries of heady and inventive inter-mixing of European and African art.

The drawing apart of the two worlds can easily be traced through each culture's depiction of the other. In the early years of the trade, Africans were represented in European art as magi, kings, or other notables, usually richly attired and adorned with dramatic jewelry. In like manner, Africans represented Europeans as nobles bearing arms, sometimes mounted and often accompanied by servants, just as their own *obas* might be. On both sides, the respect was evident.

As the transatlantic trade ground on, how-

Ivory spoon. (Benin, sixteenth century. Metropolitan Museum of Art, New York.)

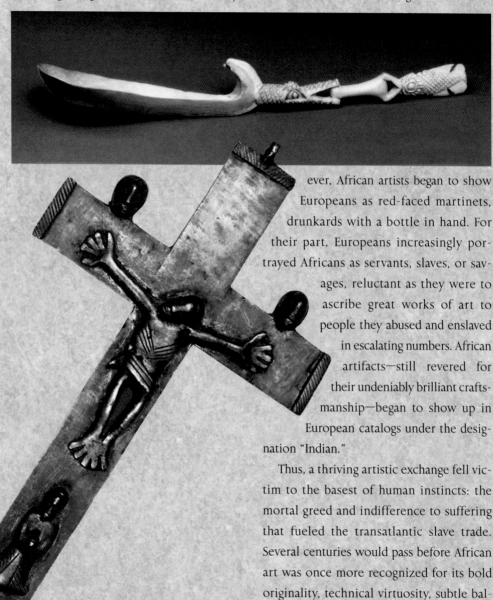

Christian converts in Africa produced religious art that combined European and African themes, or showed Christian religious figures with African features. (Bronze Congo crucifix, seventeenth century. Metropolitan Museum of Art, New York.)

ever, African artists began to show Europeans as red-faced martinets, drunkards with a bottle in hand. For their part, Europeans increasingly portrayed Africans as servants, slaves, or savages, reluctant as they were to ascribe great works of art to people they abused and enslaved in escalating numbers. African artifacts—still revered for their undeniably brilliant craftsmanship—began to show up in European catalogs under the designation "Indian."

Thus, a thriving artistic exchange fell victim to the basest of human instincts: the mortal greed and indifference to suffering that fueled the transatlantic slave trade. Several centuries would pass before African art was once more recognized for its bold originality, technical virtuosity, subtle balance, and dramatic force.

belief in spirits, witches, and saints. Thus, when the Catholic missionaries arrived in the Congo in the late fifteenth century, brought by Portuguese mariners, they did not find the task of converting people to Christianity any more difficult than when the Roman Church had reached out to western Europeans centuries before.

At the turn of the sixteenth century, the *Mwene Congo*, or king of the Congo, was baptized by the Catholic missionaries, taking for himself the name of João and instituting the use of Portuguese names among his people. The Portuguese missionaries became important advisors to João and his descendants on matters of religious orthodoxy and heresy. Congo bronze casters soon added religious icons to their repertoire, including images of Christ on the cross and the Virgin Mary, but they substituted African symbols and figures for European ones. Thus, African and European belief systems mingled, sometimes with confusing results, but the Catholic missionaries found it more productive to compromise on the details of their faith to get the gist of their message across.

The exchange of cultures was more easily facilitated in some African societies than in others. In Benin and the Congo, both major kingdoms with centralized seats of power, the forms of government and cultural organization would have been familiar to the Europeans. The *Mwene Congo* and the *oba* (king) of Benin commanded vast territories with sophisticated monetary systems and social hierarchies. Manuel I of Portugal referred to João's son, the *Mwene Congo* Afonso I, as a "brother monarch," and Afonso's son, Henrique, was educated in Lisbon along with the sons of other Congo nobles. In 1512, Manuel suggested to Afonso that he send a mission to Rome. Afonso heeded his advice and two of the Congo oliphants (ivory trumpets) later found in the collection of Rome's famous Medici family are believed to have been gifts from Afonso's Congo ambassador to Pope Leo X.[20] The Congo tradition of keeping missions in Europe continued throughout the next century, and among the Africans who visited under these terms was the marquis of Funta, ambassador to the Vatican. His importance as a member of Roman society is attested to by the fact that in 1608 a bust of him was placed at the church of Santa Maria Maggiore in the Holy City.[21]

João I of the Congo, who reigned during the fifteenth century, was the first West African ruler to be converted to Christianity. (Awnsham and John Churchill, "Baptism of the King of the Congo," from Collection of Voyages and Travels, *London, 1746. Mariners' Museum, Newport News, Virginia.)*

The Measure of Bondage

Despite the Europeans' early appreciation of African culture, the transatlantic slave trade was never abandoned, nor even lessened. The Europeans had encountered and accepted slavery in North Africa, so they were not surprised to find it in the sub-Sahara. Moreover, southern Europeans, particularly the Portuguese, Italians, and Spanish, were used to the presence of slaves at home. Skilled craftsmanship, intellectual brilliance, political power—none of these attributes would have precluded enslaving the Africans who possessed them. If northern Europeans found the institution of slavery at all strange, they were quickly reassured by the knowledge that slavery was common in warmer climates. Besides, they were eager for the "free" labor that slavery made available to them.

In Africa, the circumstances of slavery differed widely. In many parts of the continent, slaves were treated as family members, accorded privileges and comforts similar to free-born members of a household. Although enslaved, such individuals were often able to work in roles that were familiar to them, and they might even rise to lofty social stations depending on their talents and the benevolence of their masters. Slaves in such settings were not necessarily drudges but could be artisans and administrators, respected members of their communities who could even take

Slavery was a widely used form of labor in Africa before the arrival of the Europeans. But African slavery differed dramatically from New World slavery in that the bondspeople, who were usually prisoners of war, lived out their days within a culture similar to their own. (John Hanning Speke, "Steboko's Slaves Carrying Fuel and Cutting Rice," from Journey of the Discovery of the Source of the Nile, *New York, 1869.)*

slaves of their own. Ouladah Equiano, kidnapped and forced into slavery as a child, began the account of his life with a description of Igbos in his homeland—the very region of West Africa from which the *Henrietta Marie*'s slaves were taken. Equiano expressed clearly the difference between slavery in the European colonies and the enslavement of one African by another.

In Africa, "the spoils [of war] were divided according to the merit of the warriors," he wrote.

Those prisoners which were not sold or redeemed, we kept as slaves; but how different was their condition from that of slaves in the West Indies! With us, they do no more work than other members of the community, even their master; their food, clothing and lodging were nearly the same as theirs (except they were not permitted to eat with the free-born); and there was scarce any other difference between them, than a superior degree of importance which the head of a family possesses in our state, and that authority which, as such, he exercises over every part of his household. Some of the slaves even have slaves under them as their own property and for their own use.[22]

Eventually, the children or grandchildren of those enslaved in such circumstances might be absorbed into their new "family" and granted full rights. Such manumission was more likely in the case of female slaves, whose children by their masters became a second line of descent. This family model made the acquisition of female slaves highly desirable in Africa, where women possessed the requisite farming and craft skills and, having been taught to submit to authority, were therefore less likely to disrupt the communal peace. The preference for female slaves in Africa stood in stark contrast to the situation in the Caribbean, where backbreaking labor conditions increased the European demand for male slaves.

The benevolence of certain African masters toward their slaves notwithstanding, a bondsperson could never afford to lose sight of the cruel reality of the institution of slavery itself, for even in the most generous of African households, a slave could be treated as a son or daughter one day only to be sold to strangers the next.[23] Slavery could never be equated with true freedom. Thus, an important slave official always understood that any power he might wield was dependent on the will of his master, for no one else in the community could offer him any form of patronage or independent support.

An essential difference between the African and European conceptions of wealth is implied by the general beneficence of African masters toward their slaves. In Europe, land, along with whatever wealth it could produce, could be legally owned by an individual. Serfs and later tenant farmers were required to pay part of their earnings to the landowner. Their health and well-being were of little interest to the landlord, and as long as the tenant farmers continued to pay their rent, they could be largely ignored. Peasants who starved to death were easily replaced by others eager to increase their chances of scratching out a living, albeit at the landowner's profit.

The reverse was true in Africa, where land was available to anyone who could marshal the labor to clear it. Here, a man's wealth was judged less by the size of his farm than by the quantity of food it produced. Since a family could cultivate only as much land as it had workers to do so, the wealthy man had a stake in the welfare of his dependents, including his slaves, for they increased his workforce. A key indication of this important difference in the value of land and labor was the fact that in Europe a landowner was taxed on land, whereas in Africa, the tax was on heads.[24] In Africa, private ownership of labor rather then land provided a household with its most secure investment, one that could be expected to pay dividends as the population itself increased.

Even so, the attitude toward slaves, serfs, and peasants—in Africa as in Europe—did not always lend itself to kindly treatment of its bondspeople, and the condition of slaves in Africa differed even among countries in close proximity to one another. In many states, slaves were selected to perform difficult and dangerous tasks such as gold mining—work so arduous that in some parts of Africa slave masters considered it too expensive in terms of slaves' lives to be worth the investment. In time, the bondspeople who worked the gold mines were themselves sold to Europeans, for their African owners found it more economical to sell the slaves for gold than to maintain them as workers.

Malnutrition and dehydration contributed to the sense of hopelessness that overtook many captives even before they were taken aboard European ships. (Thomas W. Knox, "A Slave Offered in the Market," from Boy Travellers on the Congo, New York, 1871.)

Other slaves were traded to the Arabs of North Africa and were forced to march across the unforgiving Sahara to the shores of the Mediterranean at the rate of some ten thousand per year. The volume of the North African trade bears stark witness to the harsher side of the African experience of slavery, confirming that sub-Saharan slaves were not always hailed as lesser members of an extended family but were frequently regarded as mere chattel to be bought and sold.

But there was yet another fate that bondspeople in sub-Saharan Africa might face, a fate that sometimes accorded the slave a degree of personal respect and communal status: Slaves could be pressed into military service to fight a king's wars. Like the Pope with his elite Swiss Guard and the Moors with their crack troops of *janissaries*, African kings knew that troops of foreigners, even slaves, were often more trustworthy than armies comprised of the king's vassals, who, being free, might aspire to seize power from the king and could marshal the support to do so. Indeed, the ascendance of the Songhai Empire during the fifteenth and sixteenth centuries was largely the result of the skillful military deployment of the state's slave population. The *Tarikh al-Fettash*, a contemporary chronicle composed in Arabic, details the allocation of slaves to rice plantations and villages as well as to staff both the armies and the bureaucracy of the Songhai emperors.[25] This clever manipulation of enslaved workers allowed the emperors to consolidate their political power.

The opening of major slave trading ports along West Africa's Guinea coast and the European demand for slaves provided a powerful incentive for Africans to reevaluate their perspectives on the enslavement process and the handling of bondspeople. While enslavement was still the penalty for a few major crimes such as adultery and kidnapping,[26] the judicial system did not produce an abundance of slave labor. However, the enslavement of prisoners of war was easily expanded, particularly when European mercenaries and weapons bolstered the resources of warring parties. The losers were immediately handed over to the Europeans. Thus, wars that might have failed before they started because of minimal support suddenly became profitable ventures. And, increasingly, slaves were obtained not only through war but by kidnapping as well, provoking a desire for revenge that could in turn escalate into wars, providing yet more slaves.

Ouladah Equiano described a pattern of interaction between local rulers and traders, whom he believed pushed his people far beyond their natural limits in the quest to meet the European demand for slaves:

From what I can recollect of these battles, they appear to have been irruptions of one little state or district on the other, to obtain prisoners or booty. Perhaps they were incited to this by those traders who brought European goods. . . . Such a mode of obtaining slaves in Africa is common; and I believe more are procured in this way, and by kidnapping, than by any other. When a trader wants slaves, he applies to a chief for them and tempts him with his wares. It is not extraordinary, if on this occasion he yields to the temptation.... Accordingly he falls upon his neighbors and a desperate battle ensues. If he prevails and takes prisoners, he gratifies his avarice by selling them; but, if his party is vanquished, and he falls into the hands of the enemy, he is put to death; for, as he has been known to foment their quarrels, it is thought dangerous to let him survive, and no ransom can save him, though all the other prisoners may be redeemed.[27]

The concepts of *community* and *personal dignity* can perhaps provide a context for assessing the ultimate psychological and historical toll of slavery. For those who served their masters in a familiar community, and whose human worth was affirmed, the bondage could seem rel-

Prisoners might be held in slave sheds, sometimes for months, awaiting the arrival of European merchants. (Thomas W. Knox, "Slave Shed," from Boy Travellers on the Congo, *New York, 1871.)*

atively light. In contrast, those who were treated harshly and viewed as nothing more than chattel would find slavery psychologically damaging in the extreme. One English trader revealed his instinctive understanding of this truth when he candidly described his commercial concerns: "Our greatest care is to buy none that are pox'd, lest they should infect the rest aboard...and that distemper they call the yaws is very common here, and discovers itself by almost the same symptoms as the *Lues Venerea* or clap does with us; therefor our surgeon is forced to examine the privities of both men and women with the nicest scrutiny, which is the greatest slavery, but which can't be omitted."[28]

The English trader's insight makes plain that one measure of slavery's cruelty was the dignity accorded or denied a bondsperson. The very state of bondage could be rendered all the more grievous by the failure of the slave owner to recognize a captive's humanity. The removal from one's community, from the place where one's history was known and one's customs observed, only increased the burden of slavery a hundredfold.

West Africans traded for European arms, and soon coastal nations that found themselves better armed than inland states began to prey on them for slaves. (L. Degrandpré, "Noir au Bois Mayombé," from Voyage à la Côte Occidentale d'Afrique, *Paris, 1734. Bibliothèque Municipale, Nantes, France.)*

In the broader communal sense, the transatlantic slave trade had a devastating impact not just on individual Africans but on the African continent as a whole. The fact is, even in its most desperate form, slavery in Africa was different from slavery in the Americas in this overwhelming particular: As a result of the Triangle Trade, Africans and their labor, and the labor and talents of their children, would forever be lost to the future inhabitants of the African continent.

A Life of Exile

As the Europeans became familiar with the various West African nations, they began to pick and choose where they would trade. During different periods, natural disasters, civil war, or geography rendered one part of the West African coast more hospitable or more profitable than another. In addition, Europeans might face difficulties if the Africans they sought to do business with had recently been preyed on by less scrupulous white traders. Rivalries and warfare among the Europeans themselves also affected the course of trade, and the establishment of safe harbors and safe routes was essential in seas on which sailed the ships of friend and foe, merchant and privateer.

Tensions between Africans and Europeans simmered and occasionally boiled over as traders on both sides sought to gain the upper hand. Of necessity, however, both sides generally endeavored to maintain a relationship just cordial enough for the trade to prosper, although there is little doubt that each side complained bitterly about the other once out of earshot. Captain Thomas Phillips shares one tale of friendly but wily Africans, which was told to him by a European associate: "Animabo lies in the kingdom of Fantine and is a pretty large town," he wrote. "The Negro inhabitants are accounted very bold and stout fellows, but the most desperate treacherous villains, and the greatest cheats upon the whole coast, for the gold here is accounted the worst, and most mix'd with brass, of any in Guinea."[29] One can only imagine what the "stout fellows" of Animabo had to say about the Englishmen!

Yet there were many examples of real accord between the Europeans and the Africans with whom they lived. Jean Barbot, in his memoirs written at the turn of the eighteenth century, describes several instances in which the Africans not only lived in harmony with the Europeans but provided enlightened mediation among them.[30] The king of Whydah, for example, arranged a formal treaty among the French, Dutch, and English, requiring them to observe the state of Whydah as neutral ground on which their rivalries and wars could not be furthered.[31] And if Africans were able to mediate for peace among the Europeans, they were also capable of generous hospitality toward them. Phillips describes a scene at Winniba, near Accra, where one Nicholas Buckeridge was stationed as the agent of England's Royal African Company at a coastal outpost, also known as a factory or fort:

> We fill'd some water and cut a good store of firewood, with the Queen's permission. The queen is about 50 years old, as black as jet, but very corpulent. We went with Mr. Buckeridge to pay our respects to her under a great tree where she sat. She received us very kindly, and made her attendants dance after their manner before us. She seemed very free of her kisses to Mr. Buckeridge, whom she seemed much to esteem; and truly he deserved it from all who knew him, being an extraordinary good-humoured and ingenious gentleman, and understood this country and language very well. We presented her with an anchor of brandy each, and some hands of tobacco, which she received with abundance of thanks and satisfaction, and so bid her goodnight.[32]

The company agents, or "factors" as they were called, were almost always Europeans. Their investors back home kept them abreast of what ships to expect, enabling factors to negotiate trade terms in advance, purchasing slaves, ivory, and other cargo in preparation for the arrival of the next scheduled ship of trade. Ideal as this arrangement must have seemed to the shareholders of the nationally charted slave trading companies back in Europe, the reality for those men who chose to work as factors in Africa was that the assignment was demanding and dangerous—if not fatal. Indeed, few factors survived beyond two years, which was the average life expectancy for Europeans stationed on the West African coast, and many new factors became mortally ill within just a few days of their arrival. Phillips describes one of the least hospitable outposts that he visited:

> Our factory... stands low in the marshes, which renders it a very unhealthy place to live. The white men the African Company send there, seldom returning to tell the tale; 'tis compassed round with a mud wall, about six foot high, and on the south side is the gate; within is a large yard, a mud thatch'd house, where the factor lives, with

the white men; also a store house, a trunk for slaves, and a place where they bury their dead white men, call'd, very improperly, the hog-yard; there is also a good forge and some other small houses....The factory is about 200 yards in circumference, and a most wretched place to live by reason of the swamps adjacent, whence proceed noisome stinks and vast swarms of little flies, called musketoes, which are so intolerably troublesome.[33]

Yet there were compensations in a factor's life of exile. European laws barely applied, and those that did needed to be observed only when dealing with other Europeans. Slavery and concubinage were local customs that many expatriots were eager to adopt, and most factors took African lovers at will. The children of previous factors were generally added to the pool of available servants and mistresses, with the benefit that they might already speak some English and have some grasp of European customs. Again, Phillips's observations offer a clear picture of European life in Africa:

Mr. Cooper, the factor, who is a very ingenious young gentleman, gave us a cordial reception, having the company of his wife (as he call'd her) to dine with us, as we had of Mrs. Searle's at Animabo, being both mulattos, as was Mr. Ronon's at Cabo Corce. This is a pleasant way of marrying, for they can turn them off and take others at pleasure; which makes [the women] very careful to humor their husbands, in washing their linen, cleaning their chambers and the charge of keeping them is little or nothing.[34]

With such entitlements, new company agents could always be found for assignments on the West African coast. In his journals, Jean Barbot suggests that the majority of these agents were men of dubious character, with "no education or principles, void of foresight, careless, prodigal, [and] addicted to strong liquors."[35] Some factors fared better than

Barbot observed. One legendary Dutchman, William Bosman, who was stationed at the fort of Elmina near Accra toward the end of the seventeenth century, survived for fourteen years on the Guinea coast and was by reputation a well-liked man. But regardless of whether they thrived in Africa or succumbed to sundry distempers, the company agents came, willing to brave the searing heat, frequent famine, tropical fevers, and the very real possibility of being attacked, for the chance to make some quick money and experience the freedoms of exile.

Modern visitors to West Africa who examine the now-ramshackle slave factories expect to find them heavily armed against assault from surrounding areas. They are surprised to discover that, in fact, much of the artillery is pointed out to sea. While Africans who did not have a stake in preserving trade with the Europeans might have been interested in stealing their captives, the forts were more likely to be attacked by European predators than by Africans. The relatives of enslaved Africans were not, as some have supposed, able to organize themselves to redeem their kinsmen by violence. Slaves were almost always brought to the coast from the interior, and it would be many days' journey through hostile territory before rescuers from their homeland could arrive. In almost every case, such a rescue mission would prove hopeless, resulting in yet more people being taken as slaves. Nor could those held prisoner in the barracoons, or slave pens, hope to be freed by local Africans, for any slave thus "rescued" would simply find himself working for an African master.

The captured Africans were a far more precious—and potentially scarce—commodity to the Europeans than they were to the Africans. And the Europeans, who arrived by sea, were perfectly equipped to match fire with the factories for they possessed similar weapons. They could also possibly influence the local inhabitants to stay neutral since the Africans held prisoner in factories did not belong to the community. While a light gun might be all that was necessary to frighten away ambitious locals, serious cannon fire was the only deterrent when European pirates arrived at a slave fort's door. Thus, the larger factories were always strategically built and heavily armed. Jean Barbot described the fortifications at the English outpost at Cabo Corso Castle:

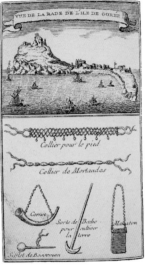

View of the Isle of Gorée, off the coast of Senegal, where Europeans held slaves for export. (Awnsham and John Churchill, Collection of Voyages and Travels, *London, 1746. Mariners' Museum, Newport News, Virginia.)*

Its shape is quadrangular. It is built of locally baked brick and black stone, and is situated on a point which juts out so that it is only connected to the mainland on its northern side. The rocks in the sea surrounding it make it almost inaccessible, because the sea breaks furiously on them. But it is fairly easy to disembark. There is a little bay formed by the rocks on the east side, where longboats enter and are beached on the sand. This however, does not pose any threat to the castle, which commands this landing place with 16 large 18-pounder iron cannon and with the small-arms of the garrison…the walls are high and thick. The lodgings inside the castle are very comfortable and spacious….The most notable item is the slave-house, which lies below ground. It consists of vaulted cellars, divided into several apartments which can easily hold a thousand slaves. This slave house is cut into the rock, beneath the parade ground, which is very large and spacious. There is also a fine cistern in the castle capable of holding a hundred tuns of water. In the castle I counted 38 fine pieces of iron cannon and a garrison of 60 white men, excluding the blacks of the country in the company's pay, whose number is far larger. This garrison is clothed in red and maintained at the expense of the Royal Company in London. The only fault of the place is that from all sides except the sea one can look over the facing battery and see everywhere inside the castle. This battery is totally commanded by the Danish fort at Mafrou, which is on a mountain only an 8-pounder cannon-shot away. This consideration makes the English very circumspect towards that northern nation.[36]

These outposts provided much needed support for the company captains, affording a secure landing for their ships and generally facilitating the trade of cowrie shells, iron bars, guns, basins, mirrors, knives, pewter tankards, linens, silks, or beads for a specified number of African slaves. Two of the largest trading forts of the late seventeenth century were

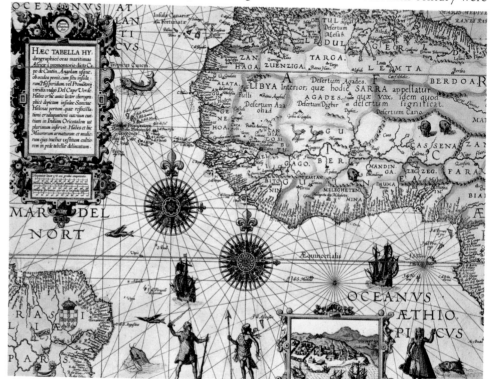

The simple charts that a ship's captain would have used were much less decorated than this elaborate presentation map, yet would probably have had no more detailed information. (Jan van Doetecum, Chart of West Africa, *c. 1595. British Library, London.)*

Elmina, near Accra, which was founded by the Portuguese but was captured by successive European countries until it was finally retained by the English; and the Isle of Gorée, near Dakar, Senegal, which was Dutch at the beginning of the seventeenth century but was captured by the French in 1677. Such thriving European outposts could be established only with the cooperation of the Africans in whose territory they lay. Usually located in or close to a large African town, the trading forts were situated to provide easy access to slave markets and to those who controlled them. Local rulers charged rent on the land that the forts occupied and also levied taxes on the slave trade, sometimes charging whites as much as one hundred slaves per ship in export duties. Such taxes were at the sole discretion of local potentates, and their amount varied widely. Jean Barbot compared the situation at one trading port with another: "Here [at Ardres] as at Juda, it is necessary to arrange the price for the trade with the king. From start to finish, all the duties you pay come to 70, 75, or 80 slaves, whereas at Juda, you pay from only 32 to 35 slaves."[37]

For almost three hundred years this economic affiliation between Europe and Africa constituted the intricate underpinnings of the Triangle Trade. In the interests of commerce, the Africans tolerated, encouraged, used, and sometimes massacred the Europeans but never surrendered their lands to them. In like manner, the Europeans exploited Africa's human resources to the extent that they could within the boundaries set by Africa's rulers. This pattern of material interaction and cross-cultural exchange would continue into the nineteenth century, to be broken only when Africa's true wealth—her population—was profoundly depleted and the period of European expansion into the Americas had reached its plateau. Only then would the nations of a weakened and economically burdened Africa finally fall prey to the colonizing ambitions of European monarchs.

Africa's Loss

By the time the *Henrietta Marie* sailed to New Calabar under the English flag, the population of the Bight of Benin had already seriously declined, and just thirty years later depopulation would be recognized as a problem all along the West African coast.[38] African complaints ranged from a shortage of young men—the favored prey of the slave traders—to a substantial loss of people. From time to time, local leaders decided to drop out of the slave trade, but this caused the Europeans only a momentary setback before they moved on to another area of the coast.

The price of the transatlantic slave trade for Africa was devastatingly high. The future potential of the continent was dissipated as its sons and daughters were shipped in the squalid holds of slave ships to sprawling estates in the New World, only to die in bondage before they could pass on the fullness of their heritage. These children of Africa carried with them skills and knowledge that would henceforth be lost to their homelands, for their tradition was primarily oral and the passages of their history were seldom written down. Thus, the African "brain drain" that was the by-product of the Triangle Trade represents a loss to the world of monumental proportions. Even more tragic, the squandering of the continent's most vital resource—its people—was not a single, terrible occurrence but was perpetrated again and again over the course of four centuries, as Europeans ferried some 15 million Africans to the New World in ships like the *Henrietta Marie*.

If the *Henrietta Marie* had been the last slaving vessel to sail for Africa, the whole subsequent history of that continent might have been different. Although the damage in 1698 was already significant, Africa was not yet so depleted of her people that she could not keep pace economically. But the arrival of the *Henrietta Marie* at New Calabar was really just the beginning, for the transatlantic slave trade would mushroom during the next two centuries as unprecedented numbers of African craftspeople, warriors, politicians, artists, princes, healers, farmers, and musicians were all sent by their enemies—personal, political, or coincidental—to serve white masters on sugar, cotton, and tobacco plantations on the other side of the world.

The Middle Passage

"The Galling of the Chains"

CHAPTER 4

As Captain William Deacon guided his vessel into the mouth of the Rio Real, the river that would lead the Henrietta Marie to the town of New Calabar, he would have surveyed the shore intently. Deacon was an old Guinea hand, familiar with the geography of the coast and keen to the subtleties of trading with the Africans, and he was no doubt aware that each time he ventured into Africa he risked losing his life. To complicate matters, the majority of his crew were raw recruits, inexperienced in the ways of the African continent, and Deacon knew that many of them would certainly die.

The captain was right to be concerned. All ocean voyagers of the time accepted loss of life as a matter of course, but the trip to Africa, particularly to the region known as the Bight of Benin, was more hazardous than most. Diseases to which Europeans bore no immunity were rampant, claiming far more lives than shipboard accidents, hostile encounters, or storms at sea. Aboard the *Henrietta Marie*, each crewman would have made his will, with those who had lost touch with their kinfolk consigning their meager belongings to a shipmate. Indeed, as officers and crew glided toward their appointed destination on the West African coast, each man may have recalled with some uneasiness the lines of an often repeated seafaring doggerel: "Beware and take care of the Bight of Benin,/for one that comes out, there are forty go in."

Yet in the midst of the apprehension, there would also have been a great sense of expectancy. Deacon had been advised that the trade in slaves at New Calabar was particularly active, and if this was true, he could be assured of a handsome profit on which to retire—if he survived the journey. James Barbot, an English ship's officer who arrived at New Calabar aboard another ship not long after Deacon traded there, described the scene the *Henrietta Marie*'s captain would have found:

> The English do their trade more in Calbory or Oudt Calbary than elsewhere, and they do take more there than any other Europeans. They take 500–600 slaves annually, but do so very slowly, for the vessels sometimes stay 8–10 months in the river, lashed to trees. Furthermore, you cannot imagine the inconveniences they suffer from the malignity of the air, something the Dutch have not been able to endure (for they hardly ever go there to trade), not to speak of the long time it takes to reach Cape de Lopo [from Old Calabar], the currents always bearing rapidly towards Camarones, which troubles not only the crews of the ships but also the captives being transported.

James Barbot went on to describe a ship he encountered, a casualty of the conditions faced by Englishmen at New Calabar and one that amply justified any concerns harbored by Captain Deacon. "I met an English flyboat which was making for Prince's Island," he wrote. "It had traded 300 blacks in Calborgh in a 10 months' stay; already it had thrown more than 100 blacks who had died into the sea, and its crew was so weak that it had no more than five men to run the ship. It seemed that this vessel would not deliver to America more than 100 live slaves."[1] This tragic episode was probably quite typical of the experience of English ships at New Calabar, an inference supported by the fact that Barbot's journals, like the journals of so many other European sailors of the time, were intended less as a memoir than as an instructional handbook. Thus Barbot's extensive discourse—which touched on what to expect in every port, the importance of using up-to-date maps and charts, what provisions to bring, and how to trade in Africa—emphasized how critical it was that European slavers be well informed in order to avoid the misfortunes that could befall them on the Guinea coast.

Deacon no doubt had access to similar accounts, although he would also have relied on his own experience gathered on previous voyages. But would what he had learned in the past prove adequate now? Missing ships and washed-up hulks told sundry tales of well-planned undertakings that had ended in disaster. Nonetheless, as the *Henrietta Marie* gingerly made its passage up the estuary of the Rio Real, her captain would have known the landmarks to look for. "As to Bandy point," Barbot had written, "…it is discernible enough…by a tuft of high trees, overtopping the wood which covers all the coast about it."[2] As soon as the ship reached this area, a captain knew, her crew would be assured of help. The local people would paddle out to meet them in long canoes manned by up to twenty rowers. These Africans spoke a smattering of the languages of the European traders—English, French, Dutch, and Portuguese—and, in the interest of facilitating commerce, they would guide European vessels up the river, assisting them in negotiating the small islands that lay at the mouth of the Rio Real.

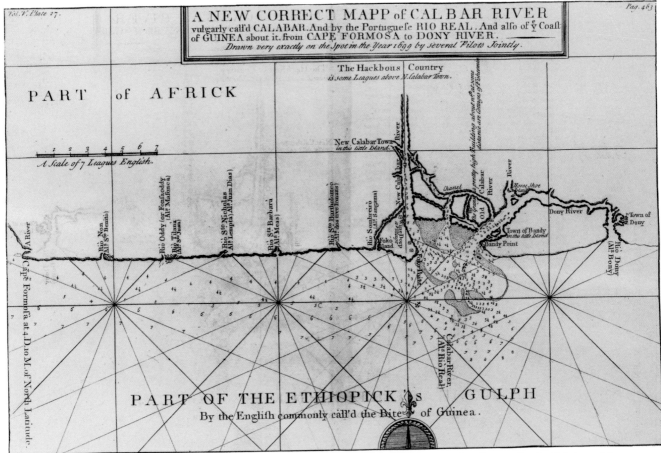

Ships had to navigate the river very carefully, for they could still founder on a sandbank. Barbot described one instance in which a slaver arrived in the Rio Real having already taken on board 350 slaves. The ship struck a bank lightly and found herself stuck. Panicked, her officers and crew abandoned ship and rowed to Bandy in their longboat, leaving their vessel tossing in the tide for three days. At last the king of Bandy, much surprised by the Europeans' behavior, sent canoes to salvage the ship's contents, thereby gaining all the slaves and a large supply of ship parts that he was able to sell to other incoming vessels for a handsome price. The crew struggled home eventually on ships that came in later and whose pilots were more vigilant.

At Bandy proper, a large town comprised of three hundred compounds, the crew of the *Henrietta Marie* may have mounted a three-gun salute to the king, for the dignity of commerce

This detailed chart of the Calabar region is a rarity. It was the responsibility of every mariner to share his knowledge, but accurate charts were often concealed from rivals. (John Churchill, "A New Correct Mapp of Calbar River," 1699, from Collections of Voyages and Travels, *Vol. 5, 1732. Mariners' Museum, Newport News, Virginia.)*

was never sacrificed. Cordial greetings would certainly have been exchanged between Captain Deacon and the king of Bandy before the *Henrietta Marie* continued up the river, probably to Foko on the river's west bank and eventually as far as the town of New Calabar itself. The ship would have passed various hamlets, settlements whose inhabitants relied primarily on trade with the Europeans for their livelihoods, though they also fished the waters of the Rio Real. (The sole exception was a salt-making settlement near New Calabar.)

The crew of the *Henrietta Marie*, many of them in Africa for the first time, were no doubt astonished to discover that the inhabitants of the region were familiar with their customs,

habits, and preferences. The local people knew them and knew all Europeans in a way that the crew did not know Africa. And the Africans were willing to use their insight to good advantage. In each hamlet, the inhabitants rowed out to trade ships in their canoes bearing supplies of all kinds. They called out their wares in a mixture of Portuguese and their native languages, often bargaining with five Europeans at once and never losing track. The Africans were veterans at this game, offering live animals such as goats or calves as well as fresh produce including bananas and yams.

Distracted by so much activity, the *Henrietta Marie*'s crew may have relaxed somewhat. Perhaps they began to feel that their mission might be a success, for the Africans who came to greet, guide, and trade with them seemed knowing, prepared, and confident. They could tell them where they might find a good water supply for the long journey ahead and where they could get enough wood for the building of half-decks to hold slaves. Still, the crewmen could not afford to let down their guard.

By the time the *Henrietta Marie* reached her destination, her crew would already have been suffering from the swarming attacks of mosquitoes, which were known to be bad near Foko and worse in New Calabar. Indeed, insect bites were such a plague to Europeans who visited the region that Captain Phillips even included his recipe for an anti-irritant in his journal.[3] The *Henrietta Marie*'s crew would also have found the air on shore stifling, for here, even the scant breeze that had teased them on their trip up the river would have expired. In this part of Africa, the tropical sun beat down mercilessly, and the atmosphere was intolerably humid. Up on deck, most slave-ship captains wore only a shirt and breeches, and their men wore even less. Crews often ran tarpaulins or spare sails across their decks in tentlike fashion to shelter themselves from the sun.

But the *Henrietta Marie*'s deeper travails were just beginning. In the four months since the crew had left England, a few of their number had died at sea, and now the inevitable distempers of the Tropics seemed to be creeping among their ranks. In an account reflective of the *Henrietta Marie*'s circumstances, Captain Phillips of the *Hannibal* recorded in his journal that his brother had died days before the crew even began to trade for slaves and that several other men were laid low with the same illness.

The West African night brought no relief from the heat. All sleep was permeated by sweat. Journals of the period tell us that some sailors preferred to sleep on the open decks, protecting themselves from the mosquitoes with homemade potions. The night watches sought refuge from the blazing heat of the weather deck, going below and easing themselves into hammocks still damp from the humidity of the day before. Down in his quarters, the *Henrietta Marie*'s Captain Deacon must have felt the full weight of his station. His cabin was no doubt sweltering, but his position required that he maintain the appearance of going there to rest. And this was not a time to set appearances aside. All captains knew how easy it was to lose control of a crew through lax discipline. Unless a captain maintained a strict code of conduct, demanding that each man efficiently perform his appointed tasks, a ship risked having to stay even longer in Africa than planned, each day further endangering the venture. With such concerns a slave ship's captain was inevitably the crew member for whom sleep was most elusive, and as Captain Phillips observed, what rest he got was often a reflection of his investment in "opium, laudanum, or some other soporifick."[4]

The next morning, in spite of the heat, Captain Deacon would have donned his woolen coat, searched out his best wig, and put on his heavy felt hat. His officers would have been instructed to do likewise, and even the rank and file among the crew would have been ordered to put on a clean shirt and brush their hair. The conventions were well established: Both Europeans and Africans were expected to dress in their finery to meet each other, the observation of such niceties connoting a mutual regard for the process of trade upon which they were about to embark.

OPPOSITE: *In this view of Calabar, Africans lament the loss of their countrymen who are being rowed out to a waiting slave ship. Many families and friends were separated in the course of the slave trade, because slavers found that people who knew each other were likely to unite in revolt. (S. Daget,* A View of Calabar, *1725. Bibliothèque Municipale, Nantes, France.)*

Let the Trading Begin

A delegation would have gathered on shore to meet the newly arrived trading vessel. Recognizing the *Henrietta Marie*'s flag, the Africans would have sent their English-speaking translator down to the ship. Gift-giving was an important aspect of this phase, for every local dignitary expected some foretaste of the trade goods: casks of brandy, a few hands of tobacco, barrels of gunpowder, hats. Europeans of the time frequently complained about their stock of valuables dwindling before the real trade occurred, but they also noted that the Africans offered them parting gifts usually of comparable value. Often, a child slave was reserved for just this purpose.[5]

After the initial formalities were observed, the trading would begin in earnest. More canoes now arrived from upriver as African traders from inland towns brought in slaves and ivory. Records indicate that Captain Deacon purchased some of the slaves, a few ivory artifacts, and sundry supplies. He may also have traded for some of the specialty items found in the local markets, including chimpanzees and blue parrots, both highly prized as pets,[6] although their mischief could cause havoc aboard ship were they to escape. The price of all these commodities was determined primarily by the Africans, the Englishmen taking what they could get and striking the best deals possible.

Although the Europeans were often ill-informed about which of their goods were currently in demand in Africa, a captain like Deacon was well aware of the price that African goods would bring him at the end of his voyage. He knew, for example, the going price of ivory in London and the formidable strength of the demand. Indeed, in weight and volume, ivory was a far more valuable cargo than slaves and much less perishable, but the incursions of European traders in Africa since the fifteenth century had made the substance less abundant there. The depletion of this resource had become evident during the *Henrietta Marie*'s first layover in New Calabar in early 1698. Just a year later, on a voyage to the same region, Barbot recorded in his journal that he had been interested in some large ivory tusks but could not afford to buy them. The scarcity of ivory had driven the price of such items so high in Africa that they were no longer worth the cost of transporting them to Europe.

The *Henrietta Marie* did take some ivory items aboard, but they were small pieces, a fact that lends credence to historical reports that, by the turn of the eighteenth century, Europeans traders could find only *scrivellos*—small tusks from immature elephants—for trade on the Guinea coast. This is a sobering comment on the fate of the elephant population in Africa as a result of the transatlantic trade. The enormous tusks, some weighing as much as one hundred pounds,[7] recorded in the journals of early travelers and depicted in illustrations of past centuries, were produced by massive animals, the vast majority of which would eventually be slaughtered for the purpose of providing decorative accouterments. As the animals were progressively hunted and killed, the genetic lines that produced these giant tusk-bearers gradually disappeared, and lesser tusk-bearers became the standard.

The fate of the elephant population in Africa parallels the ultimate fate of the human population and of West African culture as a whole. The civilizations that produced magnificent ivory sculptures and other highly evolved artistic artifacts would finally be decimated by European demand for slaves. The indigenous people, the richest resource of any culture, would eventually go the way of the African ivory. The *Henrietta Marie* herself participated in sealing this ominous fate, sailing as she did at a time when the slave trade was beginning to expand its scope. Twice as many slaves were exported in 1690 as in 1640,[8] and, by the time the *Henrietta Marie* first navigated the waters of the Rio Real in 1698, the decline in population at New Calabar had become critical.[9]

But few individuals on either side of the trade were willing to admit just how serious the situation had become. Thus, when Deacon stepped ashore at New Calabar, he could be confident that the Africans were as eager to trade as he was. Shrewd negotiations called for bluffing and cheating where possible—the Europeans, for example, were notorious for the sale of second-rate guns that could not be aimed accurately, outmoded weapons that ensured the Europeans would have the edge in any armed confrontation with the Africans. On the other hand, since the Europeans frequently supported one African country or faction against another, deploying their superior weaponry, the Africans were anxious to stay up to date in the arms race.

Slaves were often transported long distances downriver to the coast to be sold to Europeans. (Thomas W. Knox, "A Slaver's Canoe," from Boy Travellers on the Congo, *New York, 1871.)*

Their own ruses aside, the Europeans often complained about the tactics of the Africans with whom they did business, and Jean Barbot's grumbling was typical:

> You discover daily that the natives have a splendid mental capacity with much judgment and sharp and ready apprehension, which immediately understands whatever you suggest. They have so good a memory that it is beyond comprehension, and although they cannot read or write, they are admirably well-organized in their trading and never get mixed up. I have seen one of the brokers on board trading four ounces of gold with 15 different persons and making each a different bargain, without making any mistakes or appearing the least harassed.
>
> Yet they do not keep their word with whites, and are very skillful thieves, working together in this business and passing very rapidly from hand to hand what they steal, without arousing the least suspicion. The highest in rank are not exempt from this vice. They never rob each other but consider it a virtue to rob us.[10]

Aboard the *Henrietta Marie* the trade goods were varied. Her English investors had sent as much as possible in the way of British goods, supplementing these commodities with merchandise purchased from other countries, which they hoped would grease the wheel of successful negotiation. French brandy was a must, as was tobacco from the colonies of the New World. The ship also carried a wealth of pewter in the form of basins, tankards, bottles, and spoons, all of which had proven very popular trade items in the past. And glass beads, paltry trinkets to the British, were always in demand in Africa, for such beads had long provided the

Ivory rivaled both slaves and gold in importance as a trade item. On the first voyage of the Henrietta Marie, tusks like this one formed a considerable portion of the cargo. In England they were made into decorative pieces such as cane handles, musical keys, combs, and the like.

medium for some of Africa's most delicate craftsmanship and had been trade items with the Arabs centuries before the arrival of the Europeans. The *Henrietta Marie* also brought basic items such as iron bars, linen, chintz and calico cloth, tallow, red paint, Spanish wine, rum from Barbados, blunderbusses, cutlasses, and knives.

One of the oddities of the African-European trade was that many European ships also carried African goods from other parts of the coast. In his journal, James Barbot mentions "cloths from Cape Verde, Quaqua, Ardres, and Rio Forcado, akory [blue coral from Benin], a few cowries…"[11] as well as North African and Turkish carpets. Prices varied widely. While the Royal African Company set standard prices at least once a year in response to changes in the market, interlopers observed these only as a reference point to try to undercut. At the time of the *Henrietta Marie*, the profit on European trade items averaged about forty-five percent. Thirty years later, the profit margin would rise as high as seventy percent as the demand for European commodities climbed in response to the increasing loss of labor in Africa. With so many of her people gone, many African states found it cheaper to trade slaves for goods rather than marshal the workforce to create them. The economic noose was tightening.

Wood Shelves and Yams

As the trade negotiations continued, a ship's carpenter and some of her sailors were normally dispatched to the interior with axes to cut down trees for wood. In the extreme heat and humidity, this was miserable, even dangerous work, for any injury might be subject to a tropical infection. Funguses, too, could be picked up, and insects and other unfamiliar creatures of the forest also plagued the workers. Eventually, when they had gathered enough wood, they hauled it back to the ship, where they fashioned it into shelves and supports. As the trade cargo was sold and removed from the hold, the ship's carpenters began to install the shelves, or half-decks, on which the slaves they had purchased would lie for the crossing of the Atlantic. The moist, stifling heat and the copious sweat of the carpenters' labor were just a mild foreshadowing of the conditions that would prevail in these quarters for the duration of the Middle Passage.

After leaving New Calabar, ships traveled for several months up and down the river, trading for slaves and other commodities at every hamlet. The captain commonly enlisted the assistance of the local traders, for the Africans could negotiate among their own far more easily than the Europeans. Barbot described how such an arrangement might be made: "We…advanced to the king, by way of loan, the value of 150 bars of iron, in sundry goods; and to his principal men, and others, as much again, each in proportion of his quality and ability," he recorded. "This we did in order [for them] to repair forthwith to the inland markets, to buy yams for greater expedition; they employing usually nine or ten days in each journey up the country, in their long canoos up the river."[12]

Along the Calabar River, with its decentralized governments and lack of European forts, slaves may have been held in large cages built on the outskirts of a village. Many might already have been employed in local households until such time as they could be sold. Abused and dispirited, the captives held in this region would have walked miles from their homes and would perhaps have served many masters before finally arriving on the coast, where fresh horrors awaited them. Here, strange-looking men with long hair and pale skin examined the slaves carefully for signs of poor health, some of the Europeans going as far as tasting the sweat of a captive, an act they believed could tell them if someone was sick or not. One can only imagine the alarm of the captive who, having already suspected that he was to be eaten by these strangers, found himself tasted in this way.[13]

The examination complete, the negotiation of prices would begin. Again, the journals of Jean Barbot are instructive: "Slaves are priced the same way as all other goods, and hence one says 'so much gold's worth of slaves,' 'so much gold's worth of goods,'" the Frenchman explained. "However, slaves are fairly often traded by the 'piece,' for a certain amount of goods, as is appropriate. For instance, three *ancres* of brandy for a young male slave, etc.; one *ancre* of brandy, one piece of Coesvelt linen, and a dozen knives for a woman; and so on."[14]

But these European goods were not always regarded with favor. By the time of the *Henrietta Marie*, Africans had traded for such items for generations and knew what they wanted. Further, African fashions changed, rendering some goods outmoded. The younger Barbot, James, described an occasion on which the local king "objected much against our basins, tankards, yellow beads, and some other merchandise, as of little or no demand there at the time." Later,

This type of pewter spoon, which commonly included a portrait on its handle, was typical of the late seventeenth and early eighteenth centuries. These spoons were found in the wreck of the Henrietta Marie.

"the blacks objected much against our wrought pewter and tankards, green beads and other goods, which they would not accept of."[15] Incidents like these explain why the *Henrietta Marie* carried so much in the way of trade goods to the ocean floor when she sank on her last voyage, which departed England late in 1699, the same year as James Barbot's journey. Indeed, the *Henrietta Marie*'s wreck site yielded a large number of the scorned yellow and green beads as well as a few blue ones. Since the ship transported beads of all colors, it seems a fair assumption that red beads and most of the blue beads sold well. The pewter basins, found on the ocean floor with their straw packing intact, may also bear testimony to the changing needs of the Africans for whom they were originally destined.

This reconstruction of a cross-section of the Henrietta Marie *shows how trade goods were accommodated, later making room for the construction of half decks to provide quarters for the African prisoners during the Middle Passage. Note also the barbed fence that was constructed amidships as a defensive barrier to keep the Africans away from the officers' quarters or the ship's steering mechanism.*

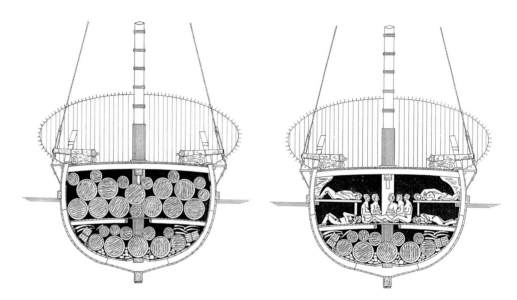

Ironically, African goods were often the fastest selling commodities on the Guinea coast, and the role of European merchants in the trade between African nations is an interesting one. Captain Thomas Phillips observed that in the places that he traded, the goods most in demand were cowries, with brass basins a close second. "The price is about 100 pounds [of cowries] for a good man-slave," Phillips wrote. If an African merchant had five slaves to sell, "he [would] have two of them paid for in cowries, and one in brass, which are dear slaves; for a slave in cowries costs us above 4 pounds in England; whereas a slave in coral, rangoes, or iron, does not cost above 50 shillings; but without cowries and brass they will not take the least goods."[16]

Before the slaves could be taken on board from their onshore holding cages, the construction of the half-decks had to be completed and a supply of food for the captives had to be obtained. The *Henrietta Marie* probably arrived on the coast in January, a good time of year for collecting yams. Yams were vitally important, because it was recognized that the captive Africans were more likely to survive the rigors of the Middle Passage if they could be given food to which they were accustomed. Africans from the Calabar region considered yams a staple, just as they do today. Thus, a captain proposing to transport 500 slaves would have been prudent to lay in a supply in excess of 100,000 yams. Although this requirement was expensive and burdensome, and the storage of so many yams reduced the space available to transport other goods, only the most shortsighted of captains would stint on the slaves' food supply, for as Jean Barbot pointed out, "no other food will keep them; Indian corn, Beans and Mandioca, disagreeing with their stomach; so that they sicken and die apace."[17] Barbot spoke from experience, having witnessed voyages in which the captives began to die as soon as they ran out of yams.[18]

The price of the yams, like all other supplies, had to be negotiated. In solidarity with one another, the African merchants fixed their prices on each item in advance so as to avoid sell-

Europeans sometimes tasted the sweat of African captives in a misguided effort to determine if they suffered from tropical diseases. One sick slave could wreak havoc in the congested hold of a slave ship during the Middle Passage. (S. Daget, An Englishman Tastes the Sweat of an African, *1725. Bibliothèque Municipale, Nantes, France.)*

ing against one another. "The price of provisions and wood was also regulated," Barbot recorded. "Sixty king's yams, one bar; one hundred and sixty slaves yams, one bar; for fifty thousand yams to be delivered to us. A butt of water, two rings. For the length of wood, seven bars, which is dear; but they were to deliver it ready cut to our boat. For a goat, one bar. A cow eight or ten bars, according to its bigness. A hog, two bars. A calf, eight bars. A jar of palm oil one bar and a quarter."[19]

Jean Barbot's nephew, James, further explained that slaves were often priced in copper or iron bars like those the *Henrietta Marie* carried. The king of Bandy drove what was considered a particularly hard bargain, requiring thirteen iron bars for a man and ten for a woman, reasoning that slaves were scarce because so many ships had recently come that way. James Barbot refused this price, declaring it too high. The argument went back and forth, and after a few days "the king sent for a barrel of brandy of thirty-five gallons, at two bars of iron per gallon, possibly to prove he already had bars to spare, but Barbot would not budge."[20] A few days later the king's "brother," more likely a titled elder of lesser rank, came to negotiate, offering thirteen bars for a man but only nine bars and two brass rings for a woman.

The Englishmen also knew how to bargain. When the king sent them thirty slaves, they chose only nineteen and sent the rest back. When a settlement was finally reached and all the slaves were loaded, the captain had to pay duty to the king. Barbot recalled that he had been charged one iron bar per slave but eventually paid only two copper rings.[21]

Of course, such firsthand accounts of human commerce on the African coast during the late seventeenth century are unremittingly one-sided since journals from European seamen have survived, but the oral nature of the African cultural tradition meant that their side of the story was seldom set down. More to the point, all the existing records of commodities and price negotiations obscure the deeper emotional experience of the African slaves themselves, the men, women, and children who were bought and sold as so much chattel and whose futures were decided by the posturing and petty power plays of merchants on both sides of the trade.

Later slave narratives, many of them published through the efforts of abolitionists in Europe and the Americas, do offer some insight into the slave trade from the perspective of its human quarry. One such narrative is particularly enlightening as to the conditions that African captives faced during the latter part of the seventeenth century. Ouladah Equiano's account of his childhood in an Igbo village in West Africa, his kidnapping as a young boy, and his subsequent enslavement specifically informs our inquiry into the life and times of the *Henrietta Marie*. Equiano, who was ultimately traded to whites in the environs of New Calabar, was captured and sold into slavery during roughly the same period that the *Henrietta Marie* voyaged there, securing for her investors a cargo of African slaves, the majority of whom were young, male, and Igbo—as Equiano was.

Made in the famous glassworks of Venice, these glass trade beads were of the type used as currency by Europeans on all their voyages of exploration and colonization. At the time of the Henrietta Marie, Africans used the beads to decorate ceremonial regalia.

A Stolen Child

A boy hides in a tree. Only eleven years old, he feels very grown up, because he knows that the other children are relying on him as their lookout. And this is not a game. The children of the village have been raised to be always on the alert for kidnappers, people who will seize them and carry them off to work as slaves. The adults of the village and their own slaves are elsewhere cultivating a distant farm, for while the threat of abduction is constant, it is sufficiently rare so as not to merit the adults' full-time attention at the expense of feeding the family.

On this day, the boy spots a man prowling outside the compound and gives out the alarm. The older children rush forward with ropes and quickly ensnare the man. All the children feel self-reliant, bold, and pleased with their capture. When the adults return and the story is told, the young boy gets much of the praise. The captured man will remain in the village as a slave.

A few weeks later the same boy is playing in the yard with his beloved sister when two men and a woman scale the compound wall and bind and gag the children before they can call out. The boy and his sister are hustled away. Once at a safe distance, their gags are removed, but they are forced to march for many hours with their hands tied. They see no one else on the road until the second day. Immediately, the boy shouts for help, but his captors quickly gag him again and stuff him into a sack until the travelers are out of sight.

The third day brings a new disaster, the worst yet. The brother and sister are separated, carried off by strangers in different directions so that now they have not even the solace of each other's company.

So begins the tale of Ouladah Equiano, born in 1745, the youngest son of a titled Igbo man, an earnest child who had once thought himself destined to follow in his father's and brother's footsteps, becoming a farmer and a man of high rank. Instead, Equiano would become the boy slave of a series of African masters, all of whom treated him quite considerately although none would grant him his freedom, much less help him return home to his family. Escape was futile, as Equiano discovered on his sole attempt. Too young to have developed much of a

Huddled together for comfort, these young boys represented the slavers' favorite cargo. (Harper's Weekly, 1860.)

sense of direction, the boy spent the day wandering about in the bush and successfully eluding his captors. But at nightfall, he sheepishly returned to his master's house, for it was the only place he knew how to find.

After a fortuitous but very brief reunion with his sister, Equiano was once more separated from her and taken to a land he called Tinmah, a place of rich pastures and abundant harvests, where his masters were mild-mannered and not unkind. Displaying a child's gift for adapting quickly to new circumstances, the boy resolved to live in the present rather than dwell on the painful suspicion that he might never see his family again. In Tinmah, he tasted coconuts for the first time and found them "superior to any nuts I had tasted before."[22] Here, he was also introduced to sugarcane, the sweet harvest that would prove so bitter for millions of Africans transplanted to the Americas. Though he did not yet know it, Equiano, too, was bound for America. But he would make a few more stops along the way.

Not long after he arrived in Tinmah, the boy was sold again, this time to a local widow and her son who paid the sum of 172 cowrie shells—a widely used form of currency in many African cultures. Equiano described this new experience:

Ouladah Equiano's story was published to draw attention to the plight of enslaved Africans everywhere. (British School, Portrait of Ouladah Equiano, late eighteenth century. Royal Albert Memorial Museum, Exeter, England.)

Her house and premises...were the finest I ever saw in Africa: they were very extensive, and she had a number of slaves to attend her. The next day I was washed and perfumed, and when meal time came, I was led into the presence of my mistress, and ate and drank before her with her son. This filled me with astonishment; and I could scarce help expressing surprise that the young gentleman should suffer me, who was bound, to eat with him who was free....Indeed, everything here, and all their treatment of me, made me forget that I was a slave. The language of these people resembled ours so nearly, that we understood each other perfectly. They had also the very same customs as we. There were likewise slaves daily to attend us, while my young master and I, with the other boys, sported with our darts and bows and arrows, as I had been used to do at home....I now began to think I was to be adopted into the family, and was beginning to reconcile to my situation.

But Equiano had sorely miscalculated his circumstances; he had forgotten his true station as a slave, and the reminder, when it came, was all the more painful: "All at once the delusion vanished," he wrote, "for, without my least previous knowledge, one morning early, while my dear master and companion was still asleep, I was awakened out of my reverie to fresh sorrow and hurried away."[23]

Equiano now fell among a new group of people whose customs were unfamiliar to him. The men were circumcised, their facial scarification was different and possibly not associated with rank, and they also filed their teeth. The young boy was shocked to discover that these new masters did not wash their hands before eating and used a large number of utensils of European rather than native origin. In the months that followed, Equiano was passed from trader to trader, sometimes marching alongside a large river, sometimes bundled into a canoe with other bondspeople for the journey downstream. At last he caught sight of the ocean, rippling water that stretched as far as the eye could see, a larger body of water than a child from the interior could ever have imagined. But young Equiano had no time to revel in his wonder: His fascination with the ocean changed abruptly to terror as strange hands carried him roughly aboard a ship.

"I was immediately handled, and tossed up to see if I was sound, by some of the crew," Equiano later recalled, "and I was now convinced that I had gotten into a world of bad spirits, and that they were going to kill me. Their complexions too, differing so much from ours, their long hair, and the language they spoke (which was very different from any I had ever heard), united to confirm me in this belief. Indeed, such were the horrors of my views and fears at that moment, that, if ten thousand worlds had been my own, I would freely have parted with them all to have exchanged my condition for that of the meanest slave in my own country."[24]

On the deck of the ship, Equiano noticed groups of disconsolate Africans from various nations chained together—and a large copper cauldron boiling. Convinced that he was about to be eaten by the evil spirits with their white skin and strange, pale eyes, the boy fainted.

Equiano's experience echoed that of millions of other Africans from the fifteenth through the nineteenth centuries. Though many of these embarked on the Middle Passage as mature adults, young boys like Ouladah Equiano were the most prized quarry of all, for they were considered old enough to do the work of a grown man but young enough to learn a new language quickly and be broken of an excessive attachment to their former lives. Stark evidence of this fact would be found three centuries later in the shackles brought up from the wreckage of the *Henrietta Marie*. Among almost one hundred pairs, some were so small that they seem to have been forged for the wrists and ankles of a child Equiano's age, or younger.

"Last Friend, Death"

Almost 100 pairs of shackles were found at the Henrietta Marie *wreck site. Hand-forged in different sizes and weights, these shackles were commonly used to restrain men, particularly while the ship was in sight of land. People were shackled together in pairs at the ankles.*

Once aboard ship, the prisoners entered a frightening new world. If they thought they had met strangers before, they had never met the likes of these Europeans—pale-skinned, red-faced, long-haired, and violent. Whatever miseries they had experienced in Africa were nothing compared to the ordeal they now faced, and however ignorant they were of the exact course the nightmare would take, they could sense its real horror. Some of the captives, like Equiano, feared they would be eaten or sacrificed. Others realized that every chance of seeing their families and homelands again had vanished.

Branded with a hot iron and shackled in pairs, the prisoners were unable to move about the deck freely. Instead, they were forced to huddle and watch as the Europeans processed each new arrival for the long voyage ahead. Finally, the prisoners were thrust below, where they were packed in between decks with less than five feet of head room in the center and half that on the shelves on which they slept. With brutally misguided logic, the Europeans sought to minimize the economic losses that resulted from high slave mortality rates by cramming as many people into the hold as they could. In one famous and disturbing illustration of the tight pack of human cargo aboard the slave ship *Brookes*, the captives barely had room to turn over, none to walk, and no allowance for latrine buckets. And yet, other ships were said to be much worse, with slaves literally lying on top of one another. Not until the end of the eighteenth century would regulations be adopted governing the number of slaves allowed on a ship, and then the capacity was judged by a ship's tonnage. For English ships the number was five slaves to every three tons[25]—an appalling, claustrophobic vision.

Reeling from the stench and the heat of the half-deck, some of the captives sat where they fell, plunged into abject despair. Many contemplated suicide and some attempted it, conspiring with their shackle mates to jump overboard when they were finally allowed back on deck. Others tried to starve themselves. But few were successful in embracing what Equiano called that "last friend, death,"[26] because the Europeans were quick to recapture those Africans who jumped ship—most were from the interior and were therefore awkward swimmers—and starving was not permitted. A prisoner who would not eat was persuaded with a number of brutal methods: he might be flogged hourly until he agreed to take food; his lips might be burned with a hot coal; molten lead might be poured on his skin; or, more simply, his jaws might be forced open and food shoved down his throat. European-style slavery, the captives soon learned, meant that they had lost all rights to their bodies and, indeed, their lives.

Desperate to be delivered from such bondage, the Africans relentlessly plotted among themselves. When not isolated from one another by language, they attempted to organize an

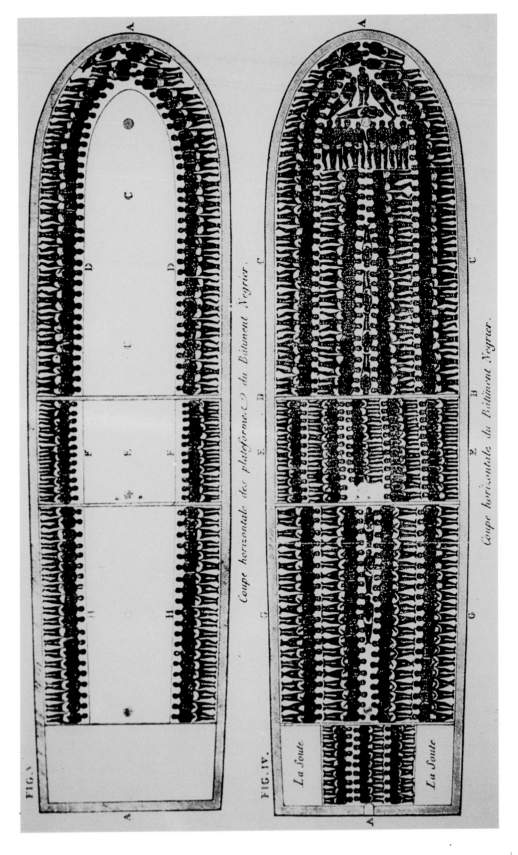

The tightly packed slave holds were unimaginable to many until the publication of drawings such as this famous one of the arrangements aboard the Brookes. In fact, this eighteenth-century ship's plan may have represented an improvement over earlier conditions, when people were packed one on top of another like logwood. (Slave Deck of the Brookes, *Paris, 1802. Library of Congress, Washington, D.C.)*

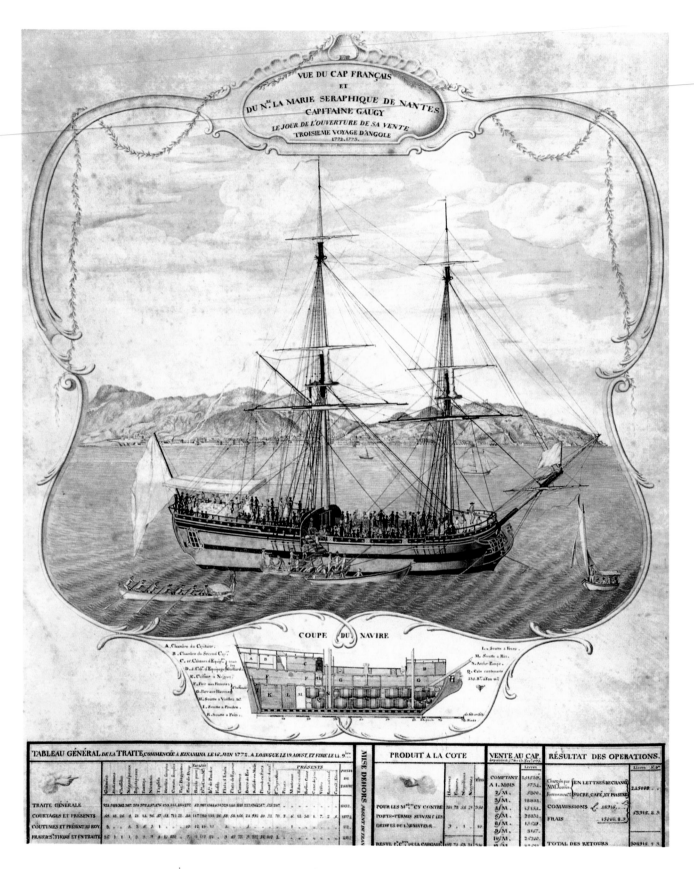

escape, for they had observed that although the crewmen were heavily armed, there were not many of them. A headlong rush had a chance, even though some of their number would almost certainly die in the pursuit of their freedom.

Every European writer of the period remarked on these frequent uprisings, and every crew had to be prepared for such an event. "When our slaves are aboard we shackle the men two and two, while we lie in port, and in sight of their own country," Captain Thomas Phillips reported, "for 'tis then they attempt to make their escape, and mutiny; to prevent which we always keep centinels upon the hatchways, and have a chest of small arms, ready loaden and prim'd, constantly lying at hand upon the quarter-deck, together with some granada shells [grenades]; and two of our quarter deck guns, pointing on the deck thence, and two more out of steerage, the door of which is always kept shut and well-barr'd."[27] The deck itself was divided by a heavily constructed wooden fence topped with spikes, a structure that provided shelter for the crew if they needed to suppress a rebellion.

Despite these odds, the captives were quick to grasp any opportunity for escape. One factor ironically stood in their favor: To the Europeans, the Africans were essentially commodities of trade, acquired for the sole purpose of turning a profit. The prisoners could see that the crew had carefully prepared a defense, but it was also apparent that they were hardly eager to attack since doing so might maim or kill a captive, eating into the profits of the voyage. For the slaves, an uprising must have seemed well worth the risk. If the crew became distracted in any way, if any weapon fell into their hands, if sheer anger at their plight bubbled over, a revolt took place. Usually it was quelled, however, for the crew had the advantage of firearms, which allowed them to triumph over even large numbers of mutineers.

Once the rebellion was put down, the crew would rout out the leaders. Often, the Africans would confess their responsibility, either because they sought death as an alternative to slavery—many Africans, in fact, simply jumped overboard when it became clear that the battle was failing[28]—or because they were tortured until they agreed to bear witness against each other. John Newton, the slave ship captain who later became an ardent abolitionist, recounted how captains would get to the bottom of a mutiny plot by applying thumbscrews to the boys, who were less able than the men to endure the pain. A more humane captain might reason with the captives, pointing out that escape was fruitless since they would simply be recaptured and resold by other Africans wherever they came ashore. But such a reasonable approach in the aftermath of a mutiny was rare. More frequently, the participating slaves were flogged and their leaders killed. Many slave ship captains also believed it prudent to dismember publicly the leaders of a revolt, letting their fate serve as a warning to the others.

Captain William Snelgrave, an English slave ship captain writing in the 1720s, recalled several incidents of mutiny, including one involving a captain who, against better advice, purchased all his slaves from one location. Snelgrave warned the captain that when a large number of captives speak the same language or, worse, have been acquainted with one another in their homelands, they are more likely to mount a damaging mutiny. He further cautioned the captain that if the slaves were denied the food to which they were accustomed—

OPPOSITE: La Marie-Séraphique, a merchant slaver based in Nantes, France, was equipped with an iron fence that isolated slaves from the quarter-deck. (Anonymous watercolor from Capitaine Gaugy, "Vue du Cap Français et du Navire 'La Marie-Séraphique,'" from Troisième Voyage d'Angole, 1772–1773, Paris, 1778. Nantes Musée du Château, Nantes, France.)

in this case rice—the situation would be much aggravated. The captain failed to heed Snelgrave's advice and compounded his recklessness by freely moving among the slaves while they were eating on deck. About ten days after leaving Africa, the prisoners beat the captain to death with their food tubs.[29]

Snelgrave himself had a prisoner shot to death for killing a white man, much to the dismay of other would-be mutineers who were counting on his not wanting to take the monetary loss of a dead slave. However, Snelgrave seemed satisfied that his response to the slaying of his crewman constituted a sort of rough justice. After all, he had prevented the African from being torn apart by enraged crew members, had allowed him to confess publicly, and had then engaged in a fact-finding procedure before executing the murderer.

In fact, the primal violence of Snelgrave's crew was more in line with what Africans might expect on most ships, particularly in response to any attempt by the captives to reclaim their freedom. Tales of horror abound. James Arnold, a ship's surgeon on the brig *Ruby*, which completed a slaving voyage in 1788, endured the captaincy of a sadist who enjoyed goading his crew into gross maltreatment of the captives on board. The ship had not left Africa before the slaves mutinied, grabbing a sailor who had constantly flogged and tortured them. The sailor escaped, and the crew fired through the gratings into the hold until the rebellion was quelled. The next day most of the captives were dragged on deck, their arms pinioned. But three men at first refused to come up. Two were eventually lured by promises of leniency from the crew and the entreaties of African traders who had been brought on board to help put down the insurgency. The third man shouted a vow that he would never give up, and so the torture began. Boiling water and fat were poured on him through the grating. When he at last climbed up a rope, having been assured that he would be mistreated no more (and probably realizing that he had no chance of actual escape), he was stabbed and clubbed senseless. Still unconscious, he was then chained to the mast, with orders from the captain that he was not to be helped or fed. For three days the West African sun beat down on him, his skin peeling from his body where he had been burned. On the third day, he died.

His two companions met a swifter fate. According to the ship's surgeon, they were decapitated, and all the captive Africans were forced to hold the bloody heads and kiss their lips. Those who refused were flogged.[30]

In the midst of such horrors, the Africans imprisoned in slave ships would sometimes turn against one another—hardly surprising given the brutal circumstances. Old rivalries between nations flared up, and the Europeans exploited these antagonisms, selecting members of one nation to be in charge of the captives while their rivals were consigned to the bottom of the temporary hierarchy. Captain Phillips knew just how to employ such divisive tactics to maintain order on his ship. He explained:

> We have some 30 or 40 Gold Coast negroes which we buy…to make guardians and overseers of the Whidaw negroes, and sleep among them to keep them from quarrelling, and in order, as well to give us notice, if they can discover any caballing or plotting among them, which trust they will discharge with great diligence; they also take

The Planter's Son

"Negroes Passing To and Fro"

In the year 1819, the twelve-year-old son of a French planter with lands in Guadeloupe was sent as a passenger on the slave ship *La Rodeur*, which was traveling from France to Africa and then to the West Indies. On this infamous voyage, many of the slaves and crew were temporarily struck blind by ophthalmia. The captain, assuming that the Africans were permanently blind and could not now be sold, threw thirty-nine of them overboard in the hope of recouping his losses from the ship's insurance underwriters. The young boy, J. B. Romaigne, watched this and many other violent proceedings of the voyage with an innocent's horror, recording all that he witnessed in letters home to his mother. In the following two excerpts, he relates events deeply familiar to all slave traders. In the first, he describes the trading scene on the African coast, and in the second, he recounts a slave revolt at sea.

Since we have been at this place, Bonny Town on the Bonny river, on the coast of Africa, I have become more accustomed to the howling of these negroes. At first, it alarmed me, and I could not sleep. The Captain says if they behave well they will be much *better off at Guadeloupe; and I am sure, I wish the ignorant creatures would come quietly and have it over. Today, one of the blacks whom they were forcing into the hold, suddenly knocked down a sailor and attempted to leap overboard. He was caught, however, by the leg by*

Slaves being thrown overboard.
(Harper's Weekly, 1860.)

another of the crew, and the sailor, rising up in a passion, hamstrung him with a cutlass. The Captain, seeing this, knocked the butcher flat upon the deck with a handspike. 'I will teach you to keep your temper,' said he with an oath. 'He was the best slave in the lot.' I ran to the main chains and looked over; for they had dropped the black into the sea when they saw that he was useless. He continued to swim, even after he had sunk under water, for I saw the red track extending shoreward; but by and by, it stopped, widened, faded, and I saw it no more.

We are no fairly at sea again. . . . Today, word was brought to the Captain, while we were at breakfast, that two of the slaves were dead, suffocated, as was supposed, by the closeness of the hold; and he immediately ordered the rest should be brought up, gang by gang, to the forecastle, to give them air. I ran up on deck to see them. They did not appear to me to be very unwell, but these blacks, who are not distinguished from one another by dress, are so much alike one can hardly tell.

However, no sooner had they reached the ship's side, than first one, then another, then a third, sprang up on the gunwale, and darted into the sea, before the astonished sailors could tell what they were about. Many more made the attempt, but without success; they were all knocked flat to the deck, and the crew kept watch over them with handspikes and cutlasses till the Captain's pleasure should be known with regard to the revolt.

The negroes, in the meantime, who had got off, continued dancing about among the waves, yelling with all their might, what seemed to me a song of triumph, in the burden of which they were joined by some of their companions on deck. Our ship speedily left the ignorant creatures behind; their voices became fainter and fainter upon the wind; the black head, first of one, then of another, disappeared; and then the sea was without a spot, and the air without sound.

When the Captain came on deck, having finished his breakfast, and was told of the revolt, his face grew pale, and he gnashed his teeth. 'We must make an example,' said he, 'or our labor will be lost.' He then ordered the whole of the slaves in the ship to be tied together in gangs and placed upon the forecastle, and having selected six, who were known to have joined in the chorus of the revolters and might thus be considered as the ringleaders, he caused three of them to be shot, and the other three hanged, before the eyes of their comrades.

Last night, I could not sleep; cold sweats broke out over my body. I thought the six negroes were passing to and fro through the cabin, and looking in at the door of the Captain's stateroom. The Captain, I could hear, was sound asleep, and this made me more afraid. At last I began to pray so loud, that I awoke him, and he asked me, what was the matter. 'I am saying my prayers,' said I. 'That is a good boy,' replied he, and, in an instant he was as sound asleep as before.

care the negroes scrape the deck where they lodge every morning very clean, to eschew any distempers that may engender from filth and nastiness. When we constitute a guardian, we give him a cat of ninetails as a badge of his office, which he is not a little proud of, and will exercise with great authority. [31]

A Floating Hell

Once a ship was out of sight of land, the threat of rebellion all but ceased. The Africans knew they could not run the ship by themselves, and so they were forced to endure until land was spotted again. In all respects, life aboard ship now became a floating hell. Unfamiliar food brought on digestive disorders among the Africans, and almost all the captives were seasick, especially during such difficult passages as that from New Calabar to Cameronnes (now Cameroon). And no matter how careful and invasive the European health checks had been, there were always captives on board who developed dysentery, also known as the "bloody flux." The bane of every slaver, dysentery was caused by the consumption of food contaminated by feces. In the notoriously unsanitary conditions aboard slave ships, the illness spread rapidly.

In addition, many captives exhibited symptoms of smallpox, malaria, and yellow fever. Indeed, the spread of yellow fever to the Americas may be blamed entirely on the slave trade, for the disease is borne by a highly specialized mosquito, *Aedes aegypti*, which can only reproduce in small, stagnant bodies of water, notably cisterns, calabashes, and water barrels such as those that were carried aboard European ships of trade. Not surprisingly, the first cases of yellow fever were reported in the Americas as early as 1648. [32]

At sea, both slaves and crew were also susceptible to an eye disease called ophthalmia, and sometimes the entire crew was blinded at once, causing numerous shipwrecks. Though this disease was usually temporary and the victim recovered his or her sight, there was no question of its danger. Such diseases also provided an excuse for less humane captains to indulge their sadism, as in the case of the captain of the French ship *La Rodeur*, who in 1819 ordered that thirty-nine slaves be thrown overboard, ostensibly to prevent the spread of infection but actually to facilitate a fraudulent insurance claim.

Still another common shipboard illness resulted in hearing damage. Captain Thomas Phillips was so affected with deafness that he had to retire from the sea after one slaving voyage and died in poverty. Scurvy also affected the captives and crew of slave ships. A problem that showed up frequently among seamen of the time, scurvy is the result of continuous deprivation of vitamin C over a five- or six-month period. Since few slaves were on board ship for that length of time, the presence of the disease among Africans testifies as much to the poor diet fed to the captives while on land as it does to the fare served during the Middle Passage. Diarists of the period observed that many a ship's surgeon gave slaves a mouthful of lime juice for scurvy prevention. In fact, food aboard ship may have represented a dietary improvement for some Africans, particularly those who had been stricken with famine in their homelands.

By virtue of their smaller numbers, crew deaths may have been proportionately higher than that of slaves,[33] but the slaves' suffering was far more acute. Not only were they ill, but they had to endure their fevers in the stifling heat below deck. Portholes and windsails brought some relief in fair weather, but all ventilation was closed off when it rained or blew hard. "The closeness of the place, and the heat of the climate, added to the number in the ship, which was so crowded that each had scarcely room to turn himself, almost suffocated us," Ouladah Equiano recalled. "This produced copious perspirations, so that the air soon became unfit for respiration, from a variety of loathsome smells, and brought on a sickness among the

This contemporary watercolor of the slave deck of the Albanez *shows Africans among barrels, sacks, and supplies. The painting was made by an English crew member of the antislavery vessel* Albatross. *(Francis Meynell, The Slave Deck of the* Albanez, *c. 1860. National Maritime Museum, England.)*

slaves, of which many died....This wretched situation was again aggravated by the galling of the chains, now become insupportable, and the filth of the necessary tubs, into which the children often fell, and were almost suffocated. The shrieks of the women, and the groans of the dying, rendered the whole scene of horror almost inconceivable."[34]

The dying lay shackled to the living, the living to the dead. Even when the chains were removed, as they often were at sea, the slaves were little better off. They could reach the latrine buckets only by crawling over other human beings in a tossing ship, an endeavor that must have presented enormous difficulties and produced complaints and misery among the captives. The result of this inhuman state of affairs is suggested by the fact that at the end of the journey, those Africans who survived were often so ill that they were unable to stand without excrement running down their legs or to walk from the ship without having to pause every minute to relieve themselves.[35] In the face of such humiliation, survival must have seemed a worthless objective, one that only the strongest and most determined would be able to achieve.

European crews tried to stave off disease by forcing the prisoners to move their cramped limbs. The Africans were brought up on deck and ordered to sing. Sing they did—mournful songs in their many languages. For exercise they were compelled to dance, sometimes to the melody of a fiddler or bagpiper, sometimes to the beat of a drum struck by one of their own. And sometimes the slaves were simply flogged until they moved around.[36]

Violence continued to be the norm. "I had never seen among any people such instances of brutal cruelty," Equiano wrote, "and this not only shown towards us blacks, but also to some of the whites themselves. One white man in particular I saw, when we were permitted on deck, flogged so unmercifully with a large rope near the foremast that he died in consequence of it; and they tossed him over the side as they would have done a brute."[37]

Sexual predation was also to be expected. Although far fewer enslaved women were taken to the Americas than men, those aboard ship inevitably became the prey of the officers and crew. In some cases, a young woman agreed to become the lover of a particular sailor, and a relationship, however temporary, evolved. In most cases, however—such as in the particularly brutal rape of a pregnant woman aboard a ship that John Newton captained[38]—the sexual act was one of violence.

James Barbot attempted to paint a more benevolent picture of the intercourse between captives and crew in his journal, referring to the Africans' behavior during what he disingenuously called "free time on deck." The slaves "often made us pastime, especially the females, who, being apart from the males and on the quarter-deck [with the crew] and many of them young sprightly maidens, full of jollity and good humor, afforded us an abundance of recreation,"[39] he wrote. To give the benefit of the doubt, perhaps Barbot's experiences were always aboard the more judiciously run ships, for he also described punishing crew members in front of the Africans if they had harmed them in any way.[40] But Equiano, who eventually became a shipping agent for one of his owners, tells a different story. In the course of his job as a shipping clerk in the Caribbean, he witnessed a crueler and possibly more realistic picture of life at sea. Referring to the officers and crew of his master's vessels, he wrote, "I have even known them to gratify their brutal passion with females not ten years old; and these abominations [are] sometimes practised to scandalous excess, that one of our captains discharged the mate and others on that account."[41] In another account of the same period, the surgeon of the *Ruby* described his captain's habitual rape of female prisoners:

> It was his general practice on the receipt of a woman slave—especially a young one—to send for her to come to his cabin so that he might lie with her. Sometimes they would refuse to comply with his desires and would be severely beaten by him and sent below. There was one young girl that he retained for some time as his favorite and kept her in his cabin, until one day when she was playing with his son, she accidentally tore his shirt. When the captain learned of it he whipped her unmercifully and beat her up with his fists until she threw herself from him against the pumps and in doing so injured her head so severely that she died three days after.[42]

Female slaves had a fair idea of their fate and spent miserable hours in anticipation of it. The surgeon of the *Ruby* recalled hearing them sing sad songs about their former lives and lost countries. Another ship's doctor, Alexander Falconbridge, who traveled to Africa on a slaving voyage in the mid-eighteenth century, described a deep melancholy that descended over the women before the ship left port. As an example, he cited one particular case: "A young female negro, falling into a desponding way, it was judged necessary in order to attempt her recovery to send her on shore to the hut of black traders. Elated at the prospect of regaining her liberty she soon recovered her usual cheerfulness, but hearing, by accident, that it was intended to take her aboard the ship again, the young woman hung herself." Falconbridge further observed that total breakdowns were not uncommon. "It frequently happens that the Negroes on being purchased by Europeans, become raving mad and many of them die in that state, particularly women," he wrote. "One day at Bonny, I saw a middle-aged, stout woman, who had been brought down from a fair the preceding day, chained to the post of a black trader's door, in a state of furious insanity. In a former voyage we were obliged to confine a female negro of about twenty-three years of age, on [account of] her become a lunatic."[43]

The "Good" Captains

Confronted by such despair, could the white slavers really have remained the unfeeling participants that so many historical records suggest? Was there no demonstration of humanity on their part, no concern for the Africans even as a valuable cargo that must survive if a profit was to be made? In more than a few instances, the answer was yes. Many European writers of the period expressed a view of African slaves as unfortunate souls in a dire predicament, and for whatever reasons—simple or complicated, economic or political—they advocated a more humane approach to caring for these captives. "Mutinies," wrote Captain Snelgrave, "are generally occasioned by Sailors ill usage of these poor People, when on board the Ships wherein they are transported to our Plantations. Wherever, therefore, I have commanded, it has been my principal Care, to have the Negroes on board my Ship kindly used; and I have always charged my white People to treat them with humanity and Tenderness; In which I have usually found to my account, both in keeping them from mutinying and preserving them in health."[44] Snelgrave even employed a translator on board, a free African who could speak the languages of the slaves as well as English and other European languages. It often fell to the translator to calm the prisoners by explaining what they could expect; if necessary, he also acted as an arbiter in disputes among Africans or between captives and crew. Yet it never seemed to occur to Snelgrave and other advocates of mercy that the institution of slavery was the real crime, one that could not be expiated by softening its sharpest edges.

Even so, while many slavers saw their quarry as barely human savages, others did recognize Africans as people of enlightened character and complex emotions, caught up in devastating circumstances. Even seasoned slavers were sometimes overcome by the sheer tragedy of the enterprise in which they were engaged. "It even happened that I bought, at different times and places, a whole family of five persons," wrote James Barbot in his journal. "I have never seen as much joy as these poor people displayed when they found themselves reunited. They could not look at each other without weeping, but despite their tears one could see that they reckoned themselves extremely fortunate that in their wretchedness they were sharing the hardship and sorrow. I did not care to separate them when I reached the islands. I sold them to a single master."[45]

Equiano, too, experienced a measure of concern from some of his white masters, but even the most benevolent, Mr. King, the Quaker, was reluctant to release him despite the fact that Equiano had saved enough to buy his own freedom. In the matter of slavery, humanity was compromised by greed. Traders and owners were quick to justify their actions by asserting that slavery allowed Africans to be given the benefit of Christian baptism or by claiming that they were already enslaved at the time the Europeans purchased them.

John Newton, the slave ship captain whose later remorse at his participation in the trade would lead him to fight for its abolition, remarked in his letters that no one had ever suggested to him that what he was doing was wrong, nor had he been able to perceive this for himself. Having made the choice to play the role of the slave trader, it was merely a matter of doing what was necessary to run an efficient ship. Marine charts, the right provisions, judgments about how tightly the slaves could be packed and still survive—these were the issues at hand.

"You ought to take care during the passage to caulk the vessel regularly, in good weather on the outside, and in bad weather on the deck and on the inside," Jean Barbot advised in the prosaic tone of a business manual.

After that, have it scraped and tarred all over, to preserve it and give an appearance that pleases the eye. This is very good for all, especially for the slaves, for whom you must also take particular care that the in-between deck is always clean and in good order. . . . Thrice a week you should heat cannon-balls and put them when red hot into buckets full of vinegar standing between the two decks, with the hatches shut, so as to improve the bad air that engenders there. . . . The men and women are usually separated, the men placed in the forepart beyond the main mast, and the women towards the stern, with a stout barrier between them, otherwise there would be dreadful confusion.[46]

The stifling conditions in slave quarters threatened the lives of those who endured the Middle Passage. Europeans knew that to preserve their human cargo they had to allow the Africans at least minimal exercise, and so they would bring them on deck and force them to dance or move around, encouraging them sometimes with music and sometimes with a whip. (Amédée Gréhan, "Slaves Dance on the Deck During the Middle Passage," from France Maritime, Paris, 1855. Nantes Musée du Château, Nantes, France.)

The Price of a Dead Slave

All this talk of clean decks and good sanitation had less to do with treating the slaves humanely than with ensuring the eventual profit of the venture. In every regard, profit was the single most important consideration of the Middle Passage. All actions on the part of slaving captains, humane or vile, had to take a trade venture's potential profit into account. Since intestinal disorders were recognized as the leading form of death among Africans during the Middle Passage, great attention was paid to what the captives were fed, and where possible, differences in African diet had to be accommodated. Just as yams were essential to Africans from the Calabar region, beans and rice were appreciated by those from the Gold Coast. Meals were prepared as a simple stew or mush flavored with lard, palm oil, pepper, and sometimes molasses. At mealtimes, the captives were organized into "messes" of roughly ten people who always ate together. Each group was fed twice a day—on Barbot's ship, meals were taken at ten in the morning and five in the evening. The food was served in one large container, and the slaves were supplied with wooden spoons to eat from it.[47]

The Africans complained of dehydration throughout the voyage, and even the crew spoke of their own constant thirst, for it was seldom possible to carry enough water. Much of what there was became foul during the course of the voyage, growing thick with algae and acting as breeding sites for mosquito larvae. Only recently has dehydration been understood as the underlying medical cause of the depression so often noted in the African captives. Certainly many went into shock at being torn from their homelands, and many more were terrorized by violent crews. Other Africans became intensely seasick or fell prey to a host of illnesses. But on top of all this, progressive and widespread dehydration aggravated the slaves' condition both psychologically and physically.

James Barbot, who by his own account captained what appeared to be a relatively efficient operation, noted that the captives were given a coconut shell of water with every meal—less than two pints a day. James Arnold, the ship's surgeon of the brig *Ruby*, recalled that aboard his ship, the slaves got only one pint per day.[48] Alexander Falconbridge suggests that such rations were the norm, and although the captives may have received additional liquid in soupy meals, the water they took in was barely enough to sustain them. A more appropriate allotment would have been two and a half quarts per day,[49] with additional rations needed to replace water lost through vomiting, diarrhea, and even excessive perspiration from the sweltering hold. Underscoring the pernicious effects of dehydration, historians have noted that shipboard mortality rates rose during the rainy season when ventilation to the lower decks was cut off, and it was highest during the first part of the Middle Passage when ships were still in the hottest weather.[50]

As dehydration crept among the captives, each afflicted slave experienced rapid weight loss, fatigue, and listlessness. Soon, the tongue grew swollen, making swallowing impossible, and the eyes sank into the head. Sodium and potassium levels fell as the body became

State of Grace

John Newton

Amazing grace, how sweet the sound
That saved a wretch like me.
I once was lost, but now am found,
Was blind, but now I see.

The author of these haunting lyrics spent ten years as a slave ship captain, a self-described "infidel and libertine" who in his later years became a clergyman and joined the fight for the abolition of the slave trade. When John Newton wrote of sin and grace, he knew intimately whereof he spoke, and for some, his story embodies the redemptive power of conscience.

The early years of Newton's life were as bleak and cruel as any that can be imagined. Born in London in 1725, he lost his mother at the age of seven and was just ten years old when he first went to sea with his father, a merchant sea captain. The rigors of his life before the mast are far from unique: press-ganged aboard a British naval vessel that he later deserted, he was recaptured and flogged. Released from the Navy, he then fell into a life as a slave trader on the transatlantic route. His involvement with the slave trade may have stemmed from his desire to become a man of means so that he might marry a young woman he loved, Mary Catlett, the eldest daughter in a fine London family.

Newton's soul-searching memoirs and obsessively detailed letters between 1745, when he first traveled to Africa, and 1755,

Ex-slaver John Newton wrote that he had once been one of "Satan's undertempters," a thoroughly evil man. But his love for his wife and eventual conversion to Christianity prompted a change in him—from slave ship captain to pastor. Newton is best known for his composition of the words to the hymn "Amazing Grace." (S. Leney after Russell Pinx, Portrait of John Newton, c. 1780. Library of Congress, Washington, D.C.)

when he last took leave of it, describe the trade in ghastly detail. He captained three grueling trips in all to trade for slaves and was once reduced almost to death by sickness on the Guinea coast. He survived when slaves waiting to be sold shared their meager provisions with him. On another occasion he was overcome by a heartsickness so great that only his love for Mary Catlett stopped him from taking his life. Then, on his final transatlantic voyage, in the midst of a violent storm at sea, Newton, a man famous for his terrible oaths, shocked himself and his crew by calling to the winds: "Lord have mercy on us!" He later expressed the belief that God had spoken to him in that storm.

By this time married to his longtime sweetheart, Mary, he found himself drawn to the Church, and he determined to study for the ministry. Over the next few years, he gradually became aware of slavery's inhumanity, and labored to reconcile the abhorrent acts he had committed in his youth with his own inexplicable call to grace. "Custom, example, and interest had blinded my eyes," he wrote of his years as a slave trader. "I should have been overwhelmed with distress and terror if I had known or even suspected that I was acting wrongly." *

As a priest in England's Onley parish around 1770, Newton wrote the words of the timeless hymn "Amazing Grace." (The current melody was composed closer to 1900.) Today, in a curious twist, many African Americans claim this hymn, written by an agent of their enslavement, as their particular anthem. The words have been raised in praise by Africa's children every-

where, in churches, at family reunions, on civil rights marches in the Deep South. Perhaps the slave trade bound its participants more closely than they understood, and each man and each woman—captor or captive, black or white, slave or crew—was marked both by the tragedy as well as the need for redemptive light.

Newton's own path to redemption was offered by a young abolitionist in London named William Wilberforce, who showed the erstwhile slaver how he might become a positive instrument in the fight to end slavery. Newton's prolific writings provided Wilberforce with compelling evidence of the atrocities that were condoned in the name of commerce. For the remaining years of his life, Newton fought staunchly within the English abolitionist movement, and just before his death in London in 1807, the former slave-ship captain turned clergyman was gratified to see England's centuries-long participation in the slave trade officially brought to a close.

progressively depleted of water, and at last the slave's desperate thirst diminished and the sufferer entered a dreamy state, the precursor to heart failure. This "fixed melancholy" was assumed by many writers of the period to be a manifestation of the Africans' mysterious power to will themselves to death, but the melancholy is now recognized as the result of increasing dehydration.

The lack of water on the long passage to the Americas provided many opportunities for less scrupulous captains to bolster their profits. The most notorious case of this kind occurred in 1783 aboard the slave ship *Zong*, on which Captain Luke Collingwood's prisoners were dying

The story of living Africans being thrown from slave ships into the sea became a rallying point for many who opposed slavery. In response to this and other tragic details, paintings, tokens, and tracts were produced to draw attention to the plight of slaves. (J. M. Turner, Slave Ship, *1840. Museum of Fine Arts, Boston, Henry Lillie Pierce Fund.)*

of the usual Middle Passage afflictions. Collingwood decided he could improve his insurance claim by throwing 132 Africans overboard. He asserted that the water supplies were so low that the slaves would no doubt perish, and the loss would have to be borne by the ship's owners. If the captives were thrown into the sea, however, the owners' insurance company would have to cover the cost. When the *Zong* returned to England, its owners did indeed make an insurance claim for the full value of each murdered slave, but the underwriters protested and the case went to court. The first jury supported the owners, stating that it was permissible for animals to be killed or otherwise disposed of should such an act prove necessary for the preservation of ship, cargo, and crew. The *Zong* incident was, they agreed, simply a case of the disposition of "chattels and goods." The underwriters appealed the case with the help of some of England's most ardent abolitionists, and a second jury rendered a landmark decision determining that the murdered Africans were people, not animals. The case was finally lost for the owners when it emerged that lack of water had been used as an excuse for the massacre, for in fact there had been a reasonable supply.[51]

At its worst, the slave ship became a floating sarcophagus. The crews of other ships claimed they could smell slavers from miles away, and sharks were said to trail them across the Atlantic, devouring the increasing numbers of dead and dying who were tossed to them. Captain Phillips discovered this chilling feature of the voyage to the Americas: "We have likewise seen…sharks, of which a prodigious number kept about the ships…and I have been told will follow her hence to Barbadoes, for the dead negroes that are thrown overboard in the passage."[52] On Phillips's voyage, he purchased 480 men and 220 women for a total of 700 slaves, 320 of whom died on the voyage, along with fourteen of his crew.[53] Aboard the *Daniel and Henry*, which sailed at the turn of the eighteenth century, 116 out of the 452 bondspeople taken aboard in Africa died during the passage.[54] All these men, women, and children were set down in an accountant's ledger, not by their own names but as mere numbers, so much profit or loss. In John Newton's log, he reported: "Thursday, 23rd of May, buried a man slave (No. 34)….Wednesday, 29th of May…buried a boy slave (No. 85) of a flux….Thursday, 13th of June…this morning buried a woman slave (No. 47). Know not what to say she has died of, for she has not been properly alive since she came aboard."[55] And yet Newton's ship was among the more fortunate—only 24 died on that particular crossing.

No records survive to indicate the number of slaves William Deacon of the *Henrietta Marie* purchased in Africa, but he delivered 250 of them in Barbados on the ship's first voyage and was considered to have made a profitable trip. On her second and final voyage, the *Henrietta Marie* brought only 190 slaves to Jamaica, but it is unlikely that more than 206 were purchased,[56] which means that the loss of life would have been relatively small and well below the average mortality rate for that period: twenty percent.

To the degree that each dead slave represented a corresponding loss of income, slavers took the dying personally. The frustration that Captain Phillips expressed at the death of Africans during the Middle Passage would be ludicrous if it were not so horrific:

> *What the smallpox spar'd the flux swept off, to our great regret, after all our pains and care to give them their messes in due order and season, keeping their lodgings as clean and sweet as possible, and enduring so much misery and stench so long among a parcel of creatures nastier than swine; and after all our expectations to be defeated by their mortality. No gold-finders can endure so much noisome slavery as they do who carry negroes; for those have some respite and satisfaction, but we endure twice the misery; and yet by their mortality our voyages are ruin'd, and we pine and fret ourselves to death, to think we should undergo so much misery, and take so much pains to so little purpose.*[57]

The blurring of identities between victim and torturer is an old paradigm, one that Phillips exemplified in his penchant for blaming the slaves for his plight: if only the slaves would not despair; if only they would respond to his efforts with gratitude and willpower; if only they would live so that the ship owners would know how hard he worked for them. Ironically, Phillips perceived his labor on behalf of the captives as a form of slavery, too. It was as though the masters and the mastered had become one floating entity of desolation and fear, all of them struggling to survive for the greater profit of their London investors and absentee plantation owners.

Barbot, Snelgrave, and many others must also have felt the blurring of roles that Phillips sensed, albeit incompletely. Snelgrave, whose palpable self-delusion and belief in his own sense of fairness was never threatened by a deeper understanding of the implications of the slave trade, once confronted a slave mutiny by asking the captives why they were rebelling. He was astonished to learn that the prisoners considered him "a great rogue" for snatching them from their homelands and families. Ever the eighteenth-century rationalist, Snelgrave pointed out that they were already enslaved when he purchased them, and that the decision to ship them away had been made by the sellers, not himself. Other than that, he asked them, did they have anything to complain of? Was their food sufficient, their lodging as comfortable as could be expected, their treatment fair? Uneasy with the logic but unable to fault it, the slaves agreed that Snelgrave could not be blamed. Caught up firmly in the captain's view of their situation, they abandoned their mutiny.

Few slave traders would have considered themselves hardened by their choice of a career. John Newton, for example, often paced the deck over the heads of the shackled, praying for the health and safety of his beloved wife. No doubt he believed he was risking his life to support her, and not until many years later did he see the monstrosity of his actions as a slaver.

As Newton had, those slave ship captains who took pains to record their experiences saw the trade simply as a job to be performed to the best of their abilities. Among earlier diarists, the motive for record-keeping was the desire to give others much-needed information on how to proceed. Later, however, as the abolitionist movement in England and the Americas was gaining support, Alexander Falconbridge, James Auburn, and others who testified in favor of ending the trade wrote down their recollections with a different mission: to educate others to the horrors they had witnessed. One cannot discount the possibility that both groups of observers may have exaggerated; the one their successes, kindness, and good management; the other the evils they had seen. But even those writers who sought to put the best face on their own participation pointed to atrocities they had personally witnessed through their involvement in the trade.

Ultimately, the question of who exaggerated and to what degree is a vain and useless inquiry. The point itself is moot, since the sadists who lost half their crew and cargo were not ultimately responsible for maintaining the slave trade over the space of four centuries. No, it was the so-called decent men, those who treated their captives with a degree of humanity, who became the backbone of the industry, for their ships delivered the greatest profits to their London merchants, encouraging them to send new ships to the Americas laden with slaves. Without these "good" captains—men such as Snelgrave, Barbot, and the Henrietta Marie's William Deacon himself—the fickle, often financially disastrous business of slavery might have crumbled sooner through lack of sufficient returns. Even given the relative humanity of some captains, however, one should recognize that, among slavers, there could be no real compassion or empathy for the plight of the slaves—only a chimera of these sentiments born of the base desire for profit, a cold shadow of charity that might later be transmuted into regret or shame. To paraphrase an age-old aphorism, the "good" captains, too, were on a voyage to hell, only freighted with good intentions.

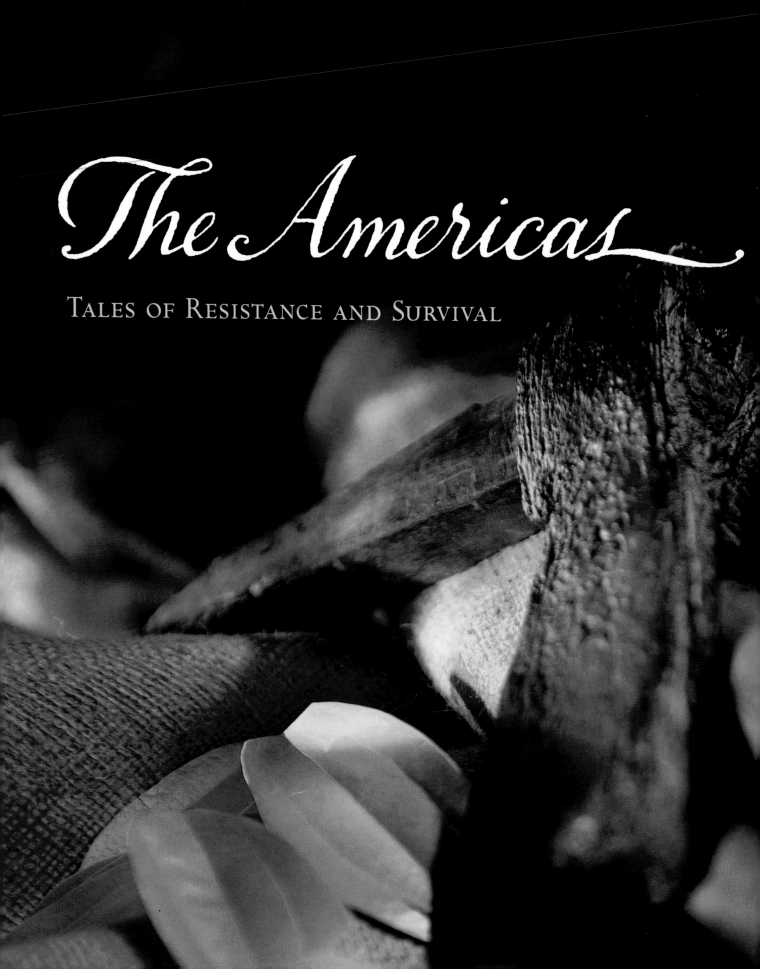

The Americas

TALES OF RESISTANCE AND SURVIVAL

The Henrietta Marie arrived in Barbados on July 9, 1698, with 250 Africans aboard. The ship had followed the Atlantic currents, surviving violent storms, enervating calms, and the horrors of the Middle Passage to anchor at last in the clear turquoise waters of the Caribbean. Barbados was the first stop for most slavers of the seventeenth century, and on this, her first slaving voyage, the Henrietta Marie was no exception. Covered in lush green vegetation, the island must have appeared an exotic earthly paradise. The crew would have welcomed the sight of it, and even the Africans arriving in chains would have found the landscape reassuringly familiar.

But the tranquil beauty of the Caribbean belied its reality. Diseases, insects, and the intense heat of the tropics made the conditions barely tolerable to most Europeans, and their survival rate here was almost as low as it was in Africa. Nor did the Africans have much to look forward to, for in this place they would be sold at humiliating auctions, only to die of overwork and heartbreak in a few months or a few years. With death such a predictable result of the African's tenure in the colonies, slaves were in constant demand, with new blacks being purchased to replace the dead in an ongoing cycle of abused and wasted lives.

As the *Henrietta Marie* sailed into Barbados's Carlisle Bay, however, these were probably not Captain William Deacon's preoccupations. He would have been relieved to see the island's gently rolling landscape, for it meant that the most dangerous part of the trip was finally over and the culmination of his voyage was near. The Africans would be sold, and the price he received for each slave would determine his profit and that of the other investors associated with this deadly concern.

In most respects, the voyage had been a success. The majority of the Africans had weathered the passage, the food had held out, the water supply had proved adequate, and disease had not overtaken the ship. Still, there had been many deaths, both among black cargo and white crew, but that was to be expected. As captain, Deacon had to look at the overall percentages, not the individual losses, even of his crew. No captain on this route could afford to be sentimental.

Now, in anticipation of going ashore, Deacon would have inspected the slaves and ordered that they be allowed extra food, shaved, washed, and given palm oil with which to coat their bodies. The captain was not doing the Africans any favors; rather, he was fattening and grooming them for the market. A few days of this treatment would improve the Africans' appearance considerably and lessen the visibility of their misery. Certainly, Deacon's experience had shown him that a gleaming slave with a glimmer of hope in his eye fetched a better price than a despairing one.

As a further hedge against the Africans' deep despondency, captains often arranged for slaves from local plantations to be brought to the ship to counsel the frightened captives. The African captives feared cannibalism, a terror that only increased when new white men began coming on board to inspect them. As they had been charged, the plantation slaves dutifully assured the newcomers that, no, they would not be eaten, they would merely be given work to do. They would even meet others of their own nations who had arrived long before, and everything would turn out all right. No doubt the plantation slaves also peppered their speeches with quick warnings about the nature of the white masters and advice on how to survive the realities of life in the New World.

For slaves aboard the *Henrietta Marie*, arrangements had already been made. The majority of the Africans, 188 in total, were consigned to a slave merchant by the name of William Shuller. A broker rather than a plantation owner, Shuller was a man of considerable importance in Barbados, where he served as justice of the peace. He paid an average of £19 for each slave, buying only those who had survived the journey in relatively good health. Deacon had done well. At the time, the price paid in Africa for a male slave was roughly £3, no more than an English peasant's annual wage. But the sale price in the colonies fluctuated according to the availability of slaves, and since recent conflicts between European nations had interrupted the trade, many slaves who had died had not been replaced. Even with all the expenses of the voyage factored in, it was a good time to trade.

Of the remaining seventy-two Africans whom Shuller did not take, perhaps thirty were the property of Deacon and his officers, to be sold privately. These were probably the strongest slaves, since during the voyage, the ship's officers would have replaced any of their

personal captives who died or became violently ill with those who had a better chance of survival. The rest of the Africans were those who had arrived in the worst condition, visibly ravaged by dysentery or other diseases of the passage. Considered "refuse slaves," they were unlikely to survive many days in the New World. They had clung to life throughout the passage, but now the realization that landfall would not ease their plight only increased their despair. Too weak to rebel, these Africans sought another way out, letting their lives slip from them in the belief that when they died they would return to their homelands.

Unscrupulous captains sometimes tried to pass off the sick Africans who could still walk as healthy, using such cruel subterfuges as packing the anuses of those afflicted with dysentery with oakum, a type of caulk used to keep ships watertight. White newcomers to the islands might be fooled by the ruse, but in the long run it only meant that buyers felt required to subject their purchases to the most demeaning of examinations.

There is no evidence that Deacon tried such means, but he may well have been able to get at least his purchase price back for the refuse slaves, for even in such miserable beings there was a trade. Some merchants specialized in trying to revive these cheaply bought slaves, and occasionally a local doctor might also buy them, hoping to bring enough of them back to life so that a profit could be realized.

Meanwhile, the 188 "healthy" Africans whom Shuller had purchased were being taken to a nearby warehouse. No longer beset by the rolling of the ship, the slaves now stumbled over the land, their march through town revealing to them how foreign their new environment really was. Despite the familiar vegetation and welcome climate, despite the Africans they met and the languages from home they heard spoken, it was immediately clear to the new-

Pages from the Barbados Shipping Returns, which record the first voyage of the Henrietta Marie, reveal that on July 28, 1699, 188 Africans were consigned to William Shuller for sale. (Public Records Office, London.)

comers that this was the white man's place. Buildings were made of brick and rose two or more stories, and Europeans rode through town on horses. To the few Africans who had seen such an animal, a horse was an indication of exalted status; to the others, the animals and their riders were unnatural magical beings, omens of evil.

Roughly herded down the street, the Africans were pushed and poked and even beaten as they went. Shuller's warehouse was probably no more than an open corral with no amenities. There, the slaves would spend the next few days, the men, women, and children all huddled together. After that, again fed and cleaned, they would be taken to the auction block individually or roped in lots. Richard Drake, one of the last of the English slave traders, described the shock of his first slave auction, which he witnessed at the turn of the nineteenth century. A man with a complicated past, Drake had been orphaned as a toddler and raised in an English workhouse. He went to sea at the age of twelve to serve under his uncle, a slave-ship captain. Captured in Africa at the age of fifteen, he spent the next two years as the prisoner and later the son-in-law of the king of Dahomey. He accompanied the Dahomians on several slave raids, only to be captured again and enslaved. He was finally sold to Europeans, who returned him to his uncle.

Drake's memoirs indicate that he saw nothing wrong with the institution of slavery. To his mind it was merely the way of the world. And yet, as his reaction to his first slave auction suggests, he viewed violence against those who were helpless with distaste and loathing:

Africans were sold individually or in lots soon after they landed in the Americas. This sale notice claims that a number of Africans were immune to smallpox—an important consideration for plantation owners. ("To Be Sold" broadside, Charlestown, Virginia, eighteenth century. Library of Congress, Washington, D.C.)

On July 14th the *Coralline* anchored at Berbice, Dutch Guinea. The blacks were landed at once and two days later were placed on sale in the market. There was a scarcity of hands on the sugar plantations and good prices were paid for slaves. The Dutch maids, in short green jackets and scarlet petticoats, walked around inspecting the naked Africans as if it was a common thing. The auctioneer sat on a high chair at one end of the large room and the slaves stood on a stool in front of him. He made them turn round about, as they stood in their breech-cloths before the people, and the purchasers walked up and felt of them to try their flesh and soundness. The darkies were obliged to go through every sort of motion. It seemed at times as if their arms would be pulled out of joint or their jaws cracked by some of the Dutch boors. One dame was not satisfied until she forced a wench to screech by squeezing her breast cruelly. In two days the venue was over.[1]

Among those Africans who lived to tell of being sold was Ouladah Equiano, who was subjected to the most frightening type of sale, the "scramble." Buyers at a scramble were allowed to purchase whichever slaves they could grab. A signal was given, as at the start of a race, and the buyers rushed forward, seizing Africans with their bare hands or encircling a number of them with a rope. The frenzy to corral the best and healthiest slaves provoked a deep alarm among the Africans. Recalled Equiano, "The noise and clamor with which this is attended, and the eagerness visible in the countenance of the buyers, serve not a little to increase the apprehension of the terrified Africans."[2] If men and boys were petrified, women were even more so, having already endured sexual attacks at sea. Alexander Falconbridge, surgeon aboard the *Brookes* and witness to at least one scramble, was struck by how the women "clung to each other in agonies scarcely to be conceived, shrieking through excess of terror at the savage manner in which their brutal purchasers rushed upon and seized them."[3] For the enslaved Africans it was only the next stage of the continuing journey through hell.

Once their ship arrived at its destination in the Americas, slaves were quickly herded to the auction stand. Those who were too ill to walk were sold as "refuse slaves." (William Blake, "Group of Negroes Imported to Be Sold as Slaves," from John Stedman, Narrative of a Five-Year Expedition Against the Revolted Negroes of Surinam, 1772–77, *London, 1796.)*

Equiano's Burden

The Africans transported on the first voyage of the *Henrietta Marie* were comparatively lucky: Barbados was well known for its relatively humane treatment of slaves. But as Equiano pointed out, Barbados was "a place where the slaves meet with the best treatment and need the fewest recruits of any in the West Indies, yet this island requires 1,000 Negroes annually to keep up the original stock, which is only 80,000. So the whole term of a Negro's life may be said to be there but sixteen years!"[4] On some of the other islands, only the hardiest slaves survived the first three years, and the average life expectancy of Africans in the colonies was nine years.

Not all the slaves of the *Henrietta Marie* were destined to remain in Barbados, however. There was a brisk interisland trade in goods and people, and for those enslaved Africans unfortunate enough to be shipped elsewhere, the reality of slavery in the rest of the Caribbean became immediately and terrifyingly apparent. "It was very common in several of the islands, particularly in St. Kitts, for the slaves to be branded with the initial letters of their master's name," Equiano reported, "and a load of heavy iron hooks hung about their necks. Indeed, on the most trifling occasions, they were loaded with chains; and often instruments of torture were added. The iron muzzle, thumbscrews, &c., are so well known as not to need

The young man with the buckets of water looks pityingly on the slaves who are being brought to auction, an image that illustrates the difference between slaves who had worked in the colonies for a while and those who were new arrivals. Although many African nations were mixed together in the Americas, slaves were often able to find fellow-countrymen who would help them face the violent onslaught of new experiences. ("La Vente des Nègres," from Amédée Gréhan, France Maritime, Paris, 1855. Nantes Musée du Château, Nantes, France.)

description and were sometimes applied for the slightest faults. I have seen a Negro beaten until some of his bones were broken, for only letting a pot boil over."[5]

Equiano himself was transported around 1757 to a plantation in Virginia, where, because of his youth, he was set to weeding and picking up stones. But soon after his arrival, the plantation owner fell ill, and Equiano was summoned to the house to help fan his master while he slept. There, he witnessed for the first time the tortures to which slaves in the Americas were routinely subjected. "I had seen a black woman slave as I came through the house, who was cooking the dinner, and the poor creature was loaded with various kinds of iron machines," he later recalled. "She had one particularly on her head, which locked her mouth so fast that she could scarcely speak; and could not eat nor drink. I was astonished and shocked at this contrivance which I learned afterwards was called the iron muzzle."[6]

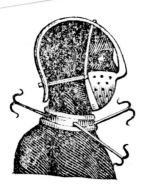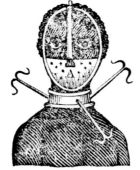

To Equiano's good fortune, he was soon resold to a naval lieutenant, who took him to England and later on a number of maritime adventures. He and his master grew fond of each other, almost in the manner of father and son. The parameter of master and slave was always present, of course, but the affection and loyalty were mutual, and Equiano was treated more like a free servant than a bondsperson. He became fluent in English, learned to read and write, studied mathematics and music, and became a favorite of his master's mistress and her friends. Just as he was beginning to think of himself as part of the family—a critical mistake he had made once before in Africa—changes in the household affected him dramatically. His master acquired a new mistress who was jealous of everything Equiano's old patroness had enjoyed, including Equiano himself. The woman managed to prevail upon her lover to get rid of the boy. Sold to a ship's captain, Equiano once more found himself bound for Barbados.

Mechanical torture, a long-standing form of punishment among Europeans, was inflicted upon slaves for any number of reasons. Many devices were invented to prevent slaves from running away, including shackles and heavy collars, while others addressed specific infringements of the master's requirements. Slaves who ate more than their allotted ration, for example, could expect to be fitted with a device that covered their mouths. (Branigan, "Head of a Negro in an Iron Collar," from The Penitential Tyrant, *1807. Library of Congress, Washington, D.C.)*

Although profoundly distressed by his master's betrayal, Equiano was by nature friendly and resourceful, and he was soon well liked aboard his new ship. The captain, like Equiano's former master, developed a fondness for the boy and resolved to do what he could to ensure that he would have a relatively good life. On arrival in Barbados, the captain arranged to sell Equiano, then about fifteen years old, to a "very good master," a Quaker named Mr. King.

The role of Quakers in the abolition of slavery is an important one. Members of the Society of Friends were among the earliest and most dedicated abolitionists, believing as they did that every person, even the most wretched slave, was a divine vessel for the word and light of God. In Barbados during the seventeenth century, the Quakers had been fined thousands of pounds for encouraging Africans to become Christians and for accepting them into their church. The Quakers were not yet actively protesting the broader institution of slavery in the Caribbean, but they were well known for treating their slaves more kindly than most, dealing with them as people rather than as beasts of burden. On the American

Joseph Cinque and the Case of the *Amistad* Mutiny

Perhaps the most famous successful slave mutiny occurred in the Caribbean in 1839. The uprising began when a number of captives, shipped from Africa and sold in Cuba, were sent to the northern part of the island in a small Spanish vessel, the *Amistad*. The group, all from Sierra Leone, was led by a Mende prince, Singbe, who would later became known by his Spanish name, Joseph Cinque. Cinque planned the rebellion very carefully, and he and about fifty Mende followers, which included a young girl, were able to seize control of the ship, killing the captain and his mate in the process.

The mutineers demanded that the ship head for Africa and forced the crew to sail eastward. But the Africans had no knowledge of celestial navigation, and by night the crew was able to redirect the ship west and north in an attempt to reach land. This zigzag course continued for many days until at last the ship reached the shore of Long Island, New York. There, the mutiny was discovered, and an American naval captain tried to claim the *Amistad* as his prize. News of the rebel slaves spread, however, and abolitionist forces mobilized to make the case a rallying point. In the American courts, Cinque

The Amistad *mutiny is one of the very few examples of Africans successfully taking over a European ship. (La Amistad, mid-nineteenth century. New Haven Colony Historical Society, New Haven, Connecticut.)*

Joseph Cinque's bold rebellion aboard the Amistad *inspired abolitionists, who helped him bring his successful case before the U.S. Supreme Court. (Nathaniel Jocelyn,* Portrait of Joseph Cinque, *mid-nineteenth century. New Haven Colony Historical Society, New Haven, Connecticut.)*

argued that he and his countrymen had been illegally enslaved and should therefore be allowed to return to Africa. Through a Mende seaman who served as his translator, Cinque pleaded his case eloquently. The appeal went all the way to the Supreme Court, where Cinque and his friends were represented by no less a power than former United States president John Quincy Adams.

Adams was seventy-three at the time and almost blind. But he delivered an impassioned eight-and-a-half-hour speech on Cinque's behalf. Despite Spanish pressure to return both captives and ship to Cuban authorities, Cinque and his fellow Mendes won the case and were allowed to return to Sierra Leone in 1842. But few slave rebellions at sea had such fortunate outcomes.

mainland, the Quakers adopted a more radical stance earlier on, and by 1696, any Quaker in Pennsylvania who imported slaves could be expelled from the Society of Friends. It would be another sixty years, however, before the Quakers seriously began to discourage not just the importation but the ownership of slaves, and to challenge the very legitimacy of the institution itself.

King, for the most part, lived up to his reputation as a Quaker. He did not flog those slaves who disobeyed him but simply sold them. "This made them afraid of disobliging him," Equiano observed, "and as he treated his slaves better than any other man on the island, so he was better and more faithfully served by them in return."[7] King recognized that Equiano was a special case in that he was more educated in the Western tradition than other slaves. He started out by asking the boy what he could do, and Equiano was able to recite a range of skills: "[I] could shave and dress hair pretty well; and I could refine wines, which I had learned on shipboard, where I had often done it; and that I could write, and understood arithmetic tolerably well, as far as the Rule of Three. He then asked me if I knew anything of gauging; and, upon my answering that I did not, he said one of his clerks should teach me to gauge."[8] Equiano became King's trusted employee, working alongside free white clerks in his shipping office, where he was given a great deal of responsibility. King often admitted that Equiano was his best clerk and that he saved him over £100 a year, the price of a free man's wage. Despite this, Equiano recalled, "I often went hungry, and an Englishman might think my fare very indifferent."[9]

In the early years, Equiano not only worked for King directly but was sometimes hired out, a typical arrangement. "It is common practice in the West Indies for men to purchase slaves, though they have not plantations themselves, in order to let them out to planters and merchants at so much a piece by the day, and they give what allowance they choose out of this product for their daily work to their slaves, for subsistence; this allowance is often very scanty." Some of these slave owners did not give their slaves any allotment at all, but left them to forage for food and shelter. If slaves had the gall to ask for their due or failed to turn over the full portion of their earnings to their masters, they would be severely flogged. "In particular, I knew a countryman of mine who once did not bring the weekly money directly that it was earned," Equiano wrote, "and, though he brought it on the same day to his master, yet he was staked to the ground for his pretended negligence, and was just going to receive a hundred lashes, but for a gentleman who begged him off with fifty."[10]

As Equiano grew up and learned more of his master's business, his responsibilities increased. He was now often involved in the transportation of slaves between the islands and was forced to watch horrible abuses of his countrymen and particularly his countrywomen. "I used frequently to have different cargoes of new Negroes in my care for sale," he wrote, "and it was almost constant practice with our clerks, and other whites, to commit violent depredations on the chastity of female slaves; and to these I was, though with reluctance, obliged to submit at all times, being unable to help them."[11] The burden of Equiano's position of favor was heavy indeed.

King Sugar

Like Equiano, some Africans who traveled to Barbados on the first voyage of the *Henrietta Marie* may have been transported to other British colonies, but the majority remained in Barbados. At the time of the *Henrietta Marie*'s arrival, there were forty-two thousand African slaves in Barbados,[12] most of them laboring on the island's vast sugarcane plantations. Sugar was more profitable than all the other exports from the British colonies, even tobacco and

Located at the center of the plantation, the sugar mill was active only at harvest time when many Africans were literally worked to death. (Deroy after Lugendas, "Sugar Mill," from Illustrated London News, *March 1845.)*

Slaves feeding the furnaces with crushed sugarcane. Long hours, sweltering heat, and poor food contributed to the overall state of exhaustion as men, women, and children labored to process the sugar crop. ("In the Boiler Room: Feeding the Fires with Crushed Sugar Cane," from The Graphic, *London, 1886.)*

cotton, and it was also less subject to market fluctuations. Thus, during the seventeenth century, European planters raising sugar amassed huge profits very quickly. As their plantations grew, so did the need for laborers. Sugar was so lucrative and demanding a crop that European planters were willing to pay a higher price for Africans who were experienced farmers, and the agrarian Igbo from the regions north of New Calabar were in particular demand.

Sugarcane was first brought to the Caribbean by Christopher Columbus on his second voyage in 1494. Sugar was already being cultivated in Hispaniola in 1507, and by 1535 some thirty animal-driven sugar mills were in operation on the island. In time, sugar became a widespread crop in the tropical and subtropical regions of the Americas. The cultivation of sugarcane was strenuous work. All year long new furrows had to be dug, cuttings set in place, manure and fertilizers spread, and old cane stands removed. Time-consuming and backbreaking as these preparations were, they were nothing compared to the harvesting of the cane. Cutting cane is possibly the single most arduous task of farming, even today. It is best done by hand, and in many parts of the world, including in the United States, much of it is still gathered this way. Each mature cane stalk is over an inch thick and requires a well-placed blow from a machete, applied with skill and force. During the seventeenth century, hundreds of cane stalks had to be cut in a single day, and workers who collapsed from exhaustion were beaten to keep them working.

The hybridization of sugarcane between the sixteenth and nineteenth centuries made increasingly large harvests possible. (M.E. Descourtilz, "Canamelle Sucre," from Flore pittoresque et médicale des Antilles, *Vol. 4, Paris, 1883. Botany Libraries, Harvard University, Cambridge, Massachusetts.)*

Come harvest time, the processing of the cane into sugar crystals was a round-the-clock effort, with slaves allowed only four hours of sleep and no extra food. The furnaces had to be kept stoked, for as one load of cane was being ground into juice, a cart was delivering more stalks to the mill. In the service of King Sugar, men and women worked alongside one another, their bodies naked, sweating and bleeding from the lash of the overseer as they processed cane stalks into the brown *muscovado* sugar that was the mainstay of the industry. Sometimes laborers died where they worked, and their bodies were pushed aside. Others stepped over these stinking, fly-encrusted corpses to continue the grueling routine, uncertain they themselves would survive.

In addition to sugar, each plantation prided itself on its production of rum, which soon became an integral part of the sugar industry. The still house, built next to the sugar factory, contained copper pot stills similar to those used for making cognac. Here, another crew of slaves labored to refine and flavor the alcohol for the pleasure of their master and his friends. Distilled to 140 proof, this by-product of the sugar harvest quickly became an addiction of the planters and of those Africans who could get enough of the rum to deaden the reality of their lives. This habitual recourse to alcohol was common all over the world in the seventeenth and eighteenth centuries, but the consumption of liquor reached new heights on the sugar plantations of the West Indies where, at every opportunity and in the name of faithful service, household slaves offered rum to subdue their masters' daily demands and nightly debaucheries—providing, of course, that liquor did not render these masters more violent.

Historians have observed that the cruelties of plantation life—harsh labor, violence, drunkenness, and the routine raping of female slaves—were exacerbated by the absenteeism of landlords, most of whom resided in Europe and whose estates were run by white factors and overseers. Had they been present, these plantation owners might have been more likely to take a long-term view and, understanding the importance of properly feeding their slaves and allowing them rest, might have kept them in relatively good health. But the overseers and factors left in charge were more interested in a quick profit and thought nothing of sacrificing a few slaves in order to line their own pockets.

In his memoirs, Equiano makes note of this unfortunate state of affairs. "Many humane gentlemen, but not residing on their estates, are obliged to leave the management of them in the hands of these human butchers who cut off and mangle the slaves in a shocking manner," Equiano wrote, "and altogether treat them like brutes." But when owners lived on their estates and not in England, Equiano noted, "the scene is quite changed; the Negroes are treated with lenity and proper care, by which their lives are prolonged, and their masters profited."[13]

Indentured Lives

The pattern of rich colonial landowners living abroad and leaving the running of their plantations to overseers had not always been the case. But the insatiable demand for sugar during the seventeenth century irrevocably altered the lives and attitudes of English colonists in the New World. The cultivation of sugarcane brought the colonial planters wealth beyond their wildest imaginings, making possible a life of greater luxury than they could have in the colonies. In addition, thanks to huge profits from sugar, many members of the colonial plantocracy could now gain acceptance at a level of European society to which they had not previously had access. And since their investments in the New World brought them the means to pay overseers and factors, the more unpleasant tasks of the plantation could now be pushed off on hired hands.

Even so, by the time sugarcane cultivation became widespread, the tenor of the interaction between master and servant on the plantations of the New World had already been set. Before sugar, the main crop in the colonies had been tobacco, and the original means of farming had replicated the peasant societies of medieval Europe. Early workers included white indentured servants as well as slaves. Indentured service in the Americas was part voluntary and part forced, for as it turned out, many who offered themselves under bond of service for a contracted period of years were deliberately deceived about what they were getting into. Indeed, in a scheme that mimicked one common method of acquiring slaves in West Africa, many indentured workers were simply kidnapped from the streets of Europe and forcibly, or through elaborate duplicity, shipped to the colonies of the New World. Between 1660 and 1669, almost two thousand servants were shipped from Bristol, England, to the Caribbean, and twenty-six hundred more went to Virginia and the other mainland colonies.[14]

Many Europeans, used to the terms of apprenticeship and struggling to find work, fell into this fate one way or another. Most of those who went to the West Indies were English and Irish youths who had been abducted, London prostitutes and petty criminals rounded up and transported, or Scottish and Irish soldiers captured by the English and sent as white slaves. Few of those forced into indenture were content in their new circumstances, and many of them banded together in rebellion against their masters. In 1647, eighteen such rebels were executed,[15] highlighting the difficulties of keeping these "contracted" servants in line.

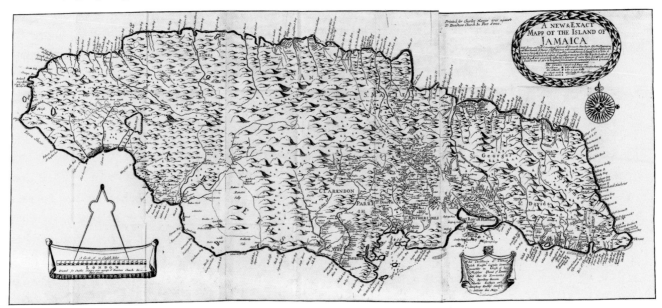

In the English colonies, the violence and physical abuse meted out to indentured laborers became the blueprint for master-slave relationships. In the New World as in England, it was fully accepted that masters might beat their servants for any misbehavior. But although corporal punishment was widespread in England at the time, it did not include such New World innovations as stringing up a servant by his hands and setting lit matches between his fingers. This burgeoning use of torture in the colonies would find its full expression in the context of New World slavery.

Few indentured servants were prepared for the grueling toil and sweltering climate to which they would be subjected in the Caribbean. Still, their status was not that of slaves, for while they were bound for their period of service, usually four to seven years, they automatically became free when the time was up. But in the Caribbean, conditions were harsh and yellow fever raged, and many did not outlast their terms of indenture. Among those who did survive, some stayed on in the colonies to become shopkeepers, tavern owners, artisans, and prostitutes.

All were brutalized by what transpired. Servants raged against their masters, who seemed to have set aside the mores of their mother country. Port Royal, Jamaica, for example, was known as "the wickedest city in the world," peopled as it was by pirates, buccaneers, thieves, gamblers, and whores. Formal justice was nonexistent in this bawdy, freewheeling culture,

The Henrietta Marie *stopped in Jamaica on its second, ill-fated voyage, its cargo of slaves assigned to a plantation owner who was an associate of one of her English investors. By the end of the seventeenth century, Jamaica had become one of the centers of the sugar industry, but it was also the roost of many pirates and buccaneers. Its atmosphere of lawlessness provided the backdrop against which savagery toward slaves would continue unchecked for more than a century. (John Slaney,* Tabula Jamaica, *1678, London. John Carter Brown Library, Brown University, Providence, Rhode Island.)*

where only the craftiest or most ruthless survived. Lost in the clamorous mix was the reverence for reason and quest for personal liberty that was beginning to flower in many seventeenth- and early-eighteenth-century European societies. Indeed, Europe's so-called Age of Enlightenment would shed little light on the colonies.

In 1655, an Englishman named Henry Whistler visited Barbados and was shocked by what he saw. "They have that liberty of conscience which we so long in England have fought for, but they do abuse it," he wrote of the society that he observed. "Our English here doth think a Negro child the first day it is born to be worth £5; they cost them nothing the bringing up, they go always naked. Some planters will have thirty more or less about four or five years old. They sell them from one to the other as we do sheep. This island is a dunghill whereon England doth cast forth her rubbish. Rogues and whores and such like people are those which are generally brought here. A rogue in England will hardly make a cheater here. A bawd brought over puts on a demure comportment, a whore if handsome makes a wife for some rich planter."[16]

In the seventeenth century, the mores of this rowdy frontier society sometimes led to a consensual mingling of the races. African men had few women of their own to choose from, and so they sometimes consorted with the women of the white indentured class. But these liaisons were dangerous, as Equiano related: "In Monserrat I have seen a Negro man staked to the ground, and cut most shockingly, and then his ears cut off bit by bit, because he had connected with a white woman who was a common prostitute. As if it were no crime to rob an innocent African girl of her virtue, but most heinous in a black man only to gratify a passion of nature, where temptation was offered by one of a different color, though the most abandoned woman of her species."[17]

Such incidents notwithstanding, there are indications that during this early period of slavery, African and European servants were treated quite similarly. The first Africans to arrive in England's mainland colonies were regarded by law as indentured servants and, like their European counterparts, were freed after several years. Anthony Johnson, for example, was an African brought to Virginia as an indentured servant in 1621. At the end of his period of service, he had earned enough money to buy himself a plot of land. Soon he was importing African servants himself to help develop the property. Johnson received 250 acres from the Virginia colony in 1651 as reward for importing five such servants, and his sons received an additional 650 acres for similar efforts.[18] The Johnson family's plantation was one of several thriving African estates in the colony. And Virginia was not unique. In 1652, Rhode Island passed a law limiting bound service to a period of ten years for both blacks and whites.

In the Caribbean, however, African slavery rather than indentured service quickly become a way of life. Europeans realized early on that most indentured Africans had no means to protest that their term was up, whereas Europeans had the force of their legal systems behind them. Those Africans who tried to position themselves to benefit under the same laws as white indentured servants usually found themselves shut out. In Barbados, for example, a law of 1636 decreed, "Negroes and Indians that came here to be sold, should serve for Life, unless a contract was before made to the contrary."[19] But, of course, there was no record of any Africans holding such contracts.

Unlike slaves, indentured servants were permitted to sue their masters for mistreatment, and in most colonies, masters were required to care for servants who fell ill. An indentured servant's misdemeanors, if grievous, might result in a court hearing, whereas slaves were punished on the spot for actual or suspected wrongs, and most of their crimes were considered capital offenses. Europeans, even indentured servants, were seldom punished for any misconduct with slaves, and such laws as existed were intended to protect slaves as property

rather than as people. Thus, the punishment or fine for killing one's own slave was considerably lighter than that for killing someone else's.

Being an indentured servant with a set term of service and the protection of English law did not necessarily guarantee an individual better treatment than a slave, however. Indentured servants were of only temporary value, after all, and so they were often abused and underfed to a greater degree than the Africans in whom the planters had a longer term investment.[20] Still, despite the fact that indentured whites could exercise rights that African laborers could not, English planters did not begin to import African slaves on a large scale until the cultivation of sugarcane became widespread. Educated as they were in the production of the crop by

Africans were required to build their own houses on the plantations, but a single room, furnished with mats and simple cooking utensils, was all most people were allowed. (Deroy after Lugendas, "Slave Quarters Inland," from Illustrated London News, March 1845.)

visiting Brazilian sugar barons, English planters in the West Indies observed that South American sugar harvests were reaped by Africans. The first English planters to try the substitution noted that the Africans were better workers, complained less about the tropical foods, insects, and climate, and were cheaper to clothe and feed than indentured workers from Europe. The increasing preference for African labor was soon reflected in the dwindling number of indentured servants arriving from England: Between 1680 and 1686, only 444 white servants left Bristol for the West Indies, and only 157 were shipped to the mainland,[21] a decrease of more than eight hundred percent from just twenty years earlier.

Migrations of the Planter Class

The evolution of Barbados's plantation economy was a critical factor in the development and settlement of the southern colonies of the American mainland. By the latter half of the seventeenth century, there was already a well-established plantocracy in Barbados comprised of English families that had lived on the island for two or three generations. As the island became increasingly populated, opportunities for younger sons, ex-indentured servants, and others diminished, and by the 1680s, the accumulation of land and the growth of real wealth had reached their natural limits in Barbados. Although some members of the plantocracy emigrated to Jamaica and other parts of the Caribbean, the more ambitious colonists looked toward the American mainland, particularly South Carolina. The colonies of the mainland seemed blessed with endless tracts of fertile land, ideal for the development of new plantations. There, the immigrants would be able to reproduce their former lifestyles on an even grander scale, carving out new estates and employing the labor of seasoned slaves whom they brought with them.

If slavery as an economic system was inevitable in the mainland's southern colonies, the immigration of these Barbadian planters hastened its coming and consolidated its uses.[22] Among those who moved to the mainland were scions of Barbados's richest families, who arrived with the means to set up successful new business concerns. These businesses blossomed, creating opportunities for immigrants who were equally ambitious but of lesser means. Through migration to the American mainland, Englishmen who would have remained small planters or struggling businessmen on the island found themselves elected to the state assembly and establishing dynasties of their own. They brought their families, their social habits, and their prejudices with them, and their stamp on the new colonial frontier was unmistakable.

Slavery, of course, was fundamental to the development of this new frontier. Slaves were an expensive proposition—expensive to import, expensive to maintain—yet slaves on the plantations were viewed much as the sugarcane itself: good for a few years before having to be replaced. Numerous examples proved that this was not the most prudent or profitable course, and yet the abuse of slave labor followed the same pattern on the mainland as it had in the Caribbean. Inevitably, despite the fact that farming techniques had advanced considerably, crop returns sank to thirteenth-century levels.[23] But when the land would no longer provide a good yield, when the soil became worn out as it had in Barbados, the planters simply moved on.

Was slavery in Europe and Africa different from that in the New World? Even the most cursory analysis provides a compelling argument that it was: Old World slaves had opportunities both to attain high rank and to achieve freedom; New World slaves lived mostly in squalor and were often worked, starved, or beaten to death. Nor was slavery in the Old World identified with a particular race. Africans toiled alongside Englishmen and Russians, and racial prejudice was not as clear-cut as it was in the Americas, where European colonists considered only Africans and Indians the proper victims of slavery.

The Forbearance of Women

At the time of the *Henrietta Marie*, Barbados was the one place in the Caribbean, perhaps in the Americas, where African women were present in abundance, for the white planters there believed that male slaves would be more contented and therefore better workers if they were allowed wives and families. By 1715, African women in Barbados outnumbered the men, since their survival rate was higher—perhaps because they were assigned less exhausting tasks, or because their average age on arrival was older than that of men, and they had therefore survived many of the tropical diseases to which the younger men fell prey. As the women gradually became acclimatized to life on the plantation, some took their place in the fields with slave gangs, even being promoted to leadership positions such as that of gang driver. Once condemned to fieldwork, women could not escape it until they were too old to perform the tasks. Then they might be assigned the position of gang cook or required to take care of the plantation's young children.

Whereas African men and boys might be encouraged to become artisans and were trained as carpenters, coopers, smiths, drivers, tailors, or for some of the other plantation tasks requiring technical skill, for women, domestic service and sewing were the main alternatives to the drudgery of the fields. African women, like their male counterparts, were often viewed as mere cogs in the plantation machinery, and women's health matters such as menstruation and pregnancy were generally ignored. As Equiano reported, "They pay no regard to the situation of pregnant women, nor the least attention to the lodging of the field Negroes. Their huts, which ought to be well-covered, and the place dry where they take their little repose, are often open sheds, built in damp places; so that when the poor creatures return tired from the toils of the

Flogging was the most common punishment for any infraction, and savage beatings often resulted in death or maiming. This woman's wrapper has been cut to pieces by the blows of a whip. (William Blake, "Flagellation of a Female Lomboc Slave," from John Stedman, Narrative of a Five-Year Expedition Against the Revolted Negroes of Surinam, *1772–77, London, 1796.)*

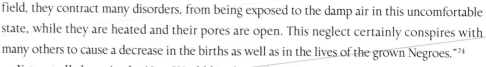

People of mixed race such as this woman were often able to achieve higher status than their counterparts of full African blood. This had to do with the fact that they were often children of a plantation owner who might acknowledge some responsibility for their well-being. (William Blake, "Female Quadroon Slave of Surinam," from John Stedman, Narrative of a Five-Year Expedition Against the Revolted Negroes of Surinam, 1772–77, London, 1796.)

field, they contract many disorders, from being exposed to the damp air in this uncomfortable state, while they are heated and their pores are open. This neglect certainly conspires with many others to cause a decrease in the births as well as in the lives of the grown Negroes."[24]

Yet not all slaves in the New World lived out their days in such meager circumstances. Domestic servants, clerks, and the like were expected to be well dressed and might even own a little jewelry. And during the earlier centuries of the trade, favorite servants could even anticipate gifts from their owners, and sometimes manumission was granted them when the owner died.

Market vendors, too, were generally better off than field-workers, for they had the chance to earn some money on the side—a situation that was often ignored and thus tacitly encouraged by their owners. For the slave vendor, however, this was an opportunity fraught with dangers. "Slaves sometimes brought a few pennyworths of [their own] produce to sell in the market, but because they had no recourse, whites often simply grabbed their offerings and stole them," Equiano explained. He went on to note another peril of the marketplace: "Many others, at the same time have committed acts of violence on the poor, wretched, and helpless females; whom I have seen crying for hours to no purpose, and get no redress or pay of any kind."[25]

As a rule, the slaves' living conditions were as mean and poor as their masters' were grand. As the planters' sugar fortunes increased, they built stately English mansions in the Tropics and filled them with fine art, china, silver, and other appurtenances of the European aristocracy. These thriving plantations were short only one desired resource: European women. The reality was that few European women cared to brave the tropical climate or the cultural isolation of plantation life, a fact that contributed to the owners' making their main domiciles in Europe. Nor were women particularly encouraged to visit the New World when their husbands were in residence there, for in the colonies the legal restraints on sexual violence seldom applied.

Inevitably, black women were forced to fill the void. A pattern had already been established in Africa, where European factors lived with African "wives" whom they set aside at will. But in Africa, women at least had a choice in the matter and could usually return home to their families if they wished. Further, these African "wives" were not considered the servants or slaves of the factors.

Rather than attempt to understand Africa's cultural, ceremonial, and sexual mores, European men interpreted African women's relationships with them as proof of the women's unbridled sexuality. In the West Indies, African women were forced to live up to this reputation by giving sexual favors to their masters—the plantation owners or, in their absence, the white overseers—at a moment's notice, regardless of whether the women had established relationships of their own with African men.

These women soon found that they had escaped the predations of the sailors during the Middle Passage only to be subject to the forceful promiscuity of the white men who were now their legal masters.

Planters and overseers needed no excuse and would brook no argument against what they saw as their right to satisfy their sexual appetites with the women who worked for them—women who were, after all, the very property of the plantations. Secure in their prerogative, planters even shared African women among themselves, offering their female slaves to visitors from other plantations with no thought for the women's personal preferences or other commitments. Not surprisingly, venereal disease was rampant, traveling back and forth between the planters and the women, and wreaking devastation in the lives of the families on both sides.

Perhaps most disturbing of all was the fact that many slave women felt they had no choice but to submit to a master's sexual demands. They were keenly aware that their families could be sold away from them at a moment's notice and that the punishment for resistance to a planter's sexual advances was rape, flogging, or even death. If slave women had few choices, some could at least gain a small amount of control over their own destinies by becoming the mistress or occasional lover of the most powerful men on the plantation. Many slave women took this route, some rationalizing that their master's favor brought them a few comforts, extra rations, or small amounts of money with which to help their families and friends. For such women the Creole proverb, *"Fem tombé na jamè désespéré"*[26] ("A woman who falls always picks herself up") had sustaining relevance.

But other women found themselves unable to bear their owners' unwanted and often violent sexual advances. These women might plot to murder their masters in untraceable ways, most commonly by poisoning them or staging "accidents." More tragic were the women who acquiesced meekly, enduring for as long as they could and privately aborting pregnancies rather than bearing the children of such unhappy couplings. Some of these women eventually took their own lives when their imaginations failed to provide them with any other means of escape from the lasting nightmare of rape.

Color Matters

In this atmosphere of rampant sexual violence, there were, surprisingly, a few long-standing common law marriages between people of different races in which real affection blossomed. Of course, in most of the colonies, it was against the law for Africans and Europeans to marry, but in defiance of the intent of these laws, liaisons between free men and enslaved women or free women and enslaved men were more common than one might suppose.

One of the most extreme examples of a sexual predator was Thomas Thistlewood, who owned a plantation in Jamaica. In his journal, he recorded not only his frequent couplings with female domestics but a passionate affair with one of them, a woman named Phibbah. Was their passion mutual? The answer is obscured by the realities of their relationship as master and slave, yet after they parted, Phibbah sent Thomas presents of food and a gold ring to remember her by, and in his diary, Thomas entreated God to bless her.[27] The fact is, twentieth-century experiences do not prepare us to evaluate the fine points of such unions.

Remarkable in another way was the life of Anna Elisabeth Heergaard, a free person of color who wielded a high degree of influence and power in her native St. Croix. Born to a freed woman in the late 1700s, she was independently wealthy, having inherited a large amount of property in Christiansted from her mother. Indeed, she once owned as many as fifteen slaves but eventually granted them all their freedom.

Anna Heergaard had several white lovers before she met Peter Von Scholten, the man whose life she was to change forever. Von Scholten first arrived in the Danish colonies as a young ensign of twenty. He went home to Denmark but returned a few years later as a captain and "royal weigher," charged with the task of ensuring the fairness of trade. He was soon appointed acting governor of St. Croix and St. Thomas, in which capacity he was first introduced to Heergaard. Their attraction was immediate and mutual. Although forbidden by Danish law to marry, Anna became Peter's mistress and the acknowledged hostess of all his private and official functions for the next twenty years.

The influence of Anna Heergaard on Peter Von Scholten's personal and public life was enormous. Through his lover, the governor came to know the Africans on the island and considered many of them friends. In his tenure as governor, Von Scholten frequently petitioned the Danish government to grant freedom to all slaves, but as might be expected, local planters fought this idea vigorously. Then, during the famous slave revolt of 1848, which the governor is suspected of helping to foment, Von Scholten emerged from his mansion to confront a mob of angry slaves. Ostensibly to quell the potentially bloody revolt, he declared that all slaves in the Danish colonies would henceforth be freed. By the time the Danish home government received the news of what he had done, they were powerless to reverse Von Scholten's historic decision.

Sexual liaisons both forced and consensual between Europeans and Africans soon spawned a population of people of mixed descent in the New World. Since most of the colonies had laws against miscegenation, their societies were at first unresolved about what to do with people of mixed race. The solutions that applied in the early years were gradually harshened as New World slavery became more entrenched. In Antigua, for example, a law of 1644 decreed that people of mixed race should be enslaved until they were eighteen and then freed. But by 1672 this was changed to slavery for life.[28] In Maryland, a law of 1681 declared that children born to white mothers of black fathers were free, but ten years later the level of tolerance for interracial unions had declined to the point that a white man who married a black woman was required to spend seven years as an indentured servant.[29]

White planters in the Caribbean sometimes exercised the option of freeing both their African mistresses and their joint progeny upon their own deaths, as William Bonner, a Jamaican planter, did in 1714. Bonner also bequeathed to his four mulatto children a hundred acres of his best land and a number of slaves. White masters who were less wealthy might secure their offsprings' freedom and apprentice them in a trade. However, despite being free, these mulatto children were subject to the laws governing slaves rather than the laws governing whites.[30]

A Spanish colonist with his African mistress and mixed-race child. Among the Spanish, racial distinctions were clearly defined based on the percentages of white and nonwhite blood a person possessed, and social levels varied accordingly. Under these rules it was possible for someone with a fully African great-grandparent to be considered white. (Miguel Cabrera, Plate I: Depiction of the Mixing of the Races, 1763. Private collection.)

The fact was that most children of mixed descent on the North American mainland inherited their black mother's bonded status, often serving as the slaves of their father's legitimate offspring, but some mixed race progeny were treated with affection by their white fathers and raised in the plantation's main house. A few of these children were even sent to England to receive a formal education. But these more "fortunate" mulattos inevitably faced the misery of returning home after ten or fifteen years' absence only to discover that their mothers had been relegated to menial drudgery as they aged and lost their beauty. As a result of their mothers' fallen status, the children themselves now held a dubious position in the society they thought of as home.

People of mixed descent balanced their lives on the precarious edge of two worlds. If free, they had to be careful not to get sucked back into slavery, and so they refused to perform manual labor for others as much as possible. Instead, they embraced economic self-sufficiency, becoming artisans, farmers, boatmen, and clerks, and making their way in whatever professions and trades they could. In much of the Caribbean and South America, these mixed race people formed a distinct class, slightly more favored by the white man's law than those of full African descent. Depending on the amount of African blood in their veins—and the lightness of their skin—it was even possible for someone with an African great-grandparent to be considered white. This was never the case in the mainland colonies of North America, where any African heritage at all rendered the individual black. Not surprisingly, in North America it has become a point of racial honor among persons of African descent, no matter how light their skin or how mixed their lineage, never to consider themselves actually "white."

Kinship Rituals

In the roiling racial and cultural mix of the New World, the Igbos of the New Calabar region—the *Henrietta Marie's* cargo—were quickly hailed by fellow Africans once they landed in the English colonies. The sheer numbers of Africans brought to the Americas ensured that every newcomer would meet a countryman there. Indeed, all or part of the cargo in which a slave arrived might be sent to the same plantation.

Interestingly, the persistence of African languages in the New World was fostered by European colonists who did not bother to engage in any but the most cursory interaction with those

Many Africans were able to flee plantations and create new lives for themselves in difficult and uninhabited terrain. These maroons had to maintain ceaseless vigilance since their liberty was constantly threatened. (William Blake, "A Rebel Negro Armed and on His Guard," from John Stedman, Narrative of a Five-Year Expedition Against the Revolted Negroes of Surinam, *1772–77, London, 1796.)*

who worked for them, requiring them to learn only enough of the masters' language to understand orders, construct their own lodging, and otherwise perform their assigned tasks. Inevitably, African languages and dialects became secret languages with which the oppressed could communicate unbeknownst to their oppressors. In this secret code, some African words, names, beliefs, and rituals were preserved intact while others were disguised so as not to raise the suspicions of Europeans.

In many of the colonies, Africans greatly outnumbered Europeans and their culture clearly prevailed. By dint of the huge numbers of slaves, white planters and overseers were forced to modify their own languages in order to be understood, and this contributed to the formation of a creole that married elements of the various African languages with elements of the European ones. European visitors were frequently dismayed to find that second- and third-generation colonists talked more like Africans than Europeans, drawling their words and shifting their syntax. Africans even taught Europeans their farming techniques, which, unlike traditional European methods, did not depend on the draft animals that fared so poorly in the tropical climate. Africans also recommended crops that would thrive in the heat of the Tropics, and the planting of rice in the Carolinas is directly attributable to suggestions made by slaves.

The Africans employed whatever means were available to make their bondage more tolerable. Relieved to find that many of the foodstuffs to which they were accustomed grew tolerably well in the New World, the slaves supplemented the meager diet supplied by their masters by cultivating small patches of ground with familiar foods such as cassava and corn, and located medicinal herbs with which to treat their ailments. Europeans, not always oblivious to the slaves' need for some of the satisfactions and comforts of home, imported African foods from time to time and even created "plantain walks" or allowed small gardens and livestock to be maintained for the slaves' use. They purchased more women when male slaves began to demand wives, and they imported cloth, such as the blue-and-white Kwakwa cloth that was typical of African dress. Free Africans, too, could request African imports, and they exercised their prerogative on a regular basis. The existence of varieties of African trees in the Caribbean that were either decorative or used in African rituals is strong evidence of this.

Thus, the Africans were able to maintain their cultural heritage and adapt it to their new surroundings. New experiences were integrated with familiar social structures and concepts to become truly African-American cultural forms. Among these was the adaptation of kinship rituals. In Africa, kinship rituals had served to unify an age group or secret society through initiation rites that might include painful or frightening elements such as facial scarification. These sacred rituals bound the initiated together through a shared memory of courage and endurance.

In the New World, Africa's indigenous religions, with their traditional kinship rituals, were repressed by the Europeans, but the repression itself furnished the means for a new solidarity that transcended Africans' varied ethnic and tribal roots. The descendants of those who had survived the Middle Passage, who had made the crossing huddled in the hold of the same ship, or who had supported one another through the hardships of life on the same plantation, often considered themselves formally bound in kinship groups, connected by new categories of shared experiences that were both horrific and formative. This type of interfamilial link provided a support system that was invisible to the Europeans but that sustained the Africans through even the most dire circumstances.

Europeans led forays into the wild to battle the maroons, escaped slaves who had successfully created new communities. (R.C. Dallas, "March Through a Swamp," from The History of the Maroons, *London, 1803. Division of Rare and Manuscript Collections, Carl A. Kroch Library, Cornell University, Ithaca, New York.)*

Equiano was delighted while he was in Jamaica to find harmony among Africans as well as the preservation of cultural individuality. "When I went to Kingston I was surprised to see the number of Africans who were assembled together on Sundays, particularly at a large commodious place called Spring Path. Here each different nation of Africa meet and dance after the manner of their own country. They still retain most of their native customs; they bury their dead, and put victuals, pipes, and tobacco, and other things, in the grave with the corpse, in the same manner as in Africa."[31]

Africans in the New World quickly understood that it was necessary to put aside old rivalries and band together to survive. Often, there was no possibility of escape, nowhere to run to, and no one to help them if they did not help one another. Used to hard work, many of the Africans labored with little complaint in order to husband their emotional resources, expending their energy on their children, their kinship groups, celebrations of African community, and the business of survival. Faced with the enormous and impersonal machinery of the plantation system, they sustained themselves with the knowledge that together they were strong enough to endure.

Maroon Culture

Any Europeans who were deceived into thinking that outward cooperation and apparent docility meant that the African people went easily into slavery were quickly disabused of that notion. While many Africans sought to improve their conditions in more conventional ways, whether by learning a European-style trade or buying their way out of slavery, still others shook off the yoke of bondage by the simpler method of escape. Such survival strategies were more effective during the seventeenth century than they were later on, for in the 1600s, the New World territories were still going through birthing pains; poorly organized and undermanned, many of these early European colonies could barely control their slaves.

Runaways, or maroons, as they are known, became powerful forces within every slaveholding nation. The word "maroon" comes from *cimarrón*, a Spanish word first applied to stray cattle that became undomesticated in the wild. The meaning was soon modified to describe escaped Indian slaves, and later it was applied to Africans who escaped the plantations and formed their own communities. Organized slave rebellions might take a while to foment, but throughout the history of slavery, the simple expedient of running away was a persistent form of revolt. As early as 1546, more than seven thousand maroons were living in the island of Santo Domingo's heavily wooded mountains.[32]

Punishment for escape was swift and terrible. Early colonial laws dictated that recaptured slaves be hamstrung for a first attempt and have their right leg cut off for the second. The third escape was a capital offense, punishable by death. As repugnant as these laws seem, they had been drafted to codify and restrict even harsher punishments, which included lethal beatings, roasting alive, and the castration of males.[33] Small wonder that, like the Indians before them, the Africans were willing to suffer any fate rather than risk recapture, going as far as committing suicide when cornered with no possibility of escape.

Among the longest standing free communities founded by African rebels and runaways were the maroons in Jamaica, an island where the natural geography provided a host of secure sanctuaries. Here, the history of the maroons followed an unusual path. When the English seized Jamaica from Spain in 1655, the retreating Spanish colonists left behind some fifteen hundred African slaves. These people divided themselves under three leaders and took to the hills. At first they lived in relative isolation, consolidating their forces and cultivating food on the hillsides. The few remaining Spaniards, meanwhile, lived the life of guerillas, preying on the British settlements in a losing effort to survive. In time, the maroons came to the aid of their former masters and supplied much of their food. Together the maroons and the Spaniards raided and harassed the British until a series of peace treaties was adopted.

Revolts were common among Africans, particularly when they knew they could escape the plantation for good and make a new life for themselves in previously uninhabited areas. (German engraving, Slave Revolt in Santo Domingo, 1791. Nantes Musée du Château, Nantes, France.)

By the 1720s the maroons had enlarged their sphere of influence, and two main groups, the Windward Maroons and the Leeward Maroons, emerged under separate leadership. A man of Akan ancestry named Cudjoe was elected leader of the Leeward group. Short and stocky, with a humped back, he was a brilliant strategist who won numerous engagements against the British but was canny enough to forge a treaty just before his supplies ran out. The Windward group made it clear that they lived by Cudjoe's treaty reluctantly; they had little choice since they, too, were short of supplies, particularly weapons. As much as they could, they contrived to avoid contact with the Europeans. The most flamboyant character among the Windward rebels was a former slave named Nanny, a warrior and sorceress who was able to inspire a fierce devotion among her followers. Little is known of Nanny's early life, but tales of her fighting days abound. Her contempt for her enemies is best expressed by the legend that she was able to catch the bullets of the English soldiers in her buttocks and hurl them back at them.

The European colonists' inability to penetrate the dense forests and hilly terrain of the island worked in favor of Cudjoe's and Nanny's freedom fighters, contributing to the survival of these proud maroon communities in Jamaica to the present day. But even in less difficult

Healing Africa's Children

An Atonement in Ghana

BY RENEE KEMP

Renée Kemp, an international reporter for KPIX-TV in San Francisco, frequently covers stories in Africa. In this essay,* she describes an extraordinary and unprecedented ceremonial apology, addressed to Africans of the disapora by Ghana's tribal chiefs.

As an African-American journalist, I traveled to Ghana in 1994 to attend Panafest, a biennial conference held in the hope of bringing the diaspora back to Africa. The event attracted some two thousand people, African Americans and West Indians, many of them visiting the continent for the first time. Dressed in African-inspired robes and head wraps (geles), dozens of us came late one night to see the historic slave dungeons in the oceanside city of Cape Coast.

As we crowded into the dungeons, we shivered in the cold, dark, damp tombs where millions of slaves were crammed, sometimes for months, waiting to be taken to the Americas on a journey of no return. We stood on the floor of the dungeons, now eight inches higher than when they were built due to the tons of compacted excrement and exfoliated skin cells from the bodies of slaves. In the women's chambers, we saw staircases leading to the Dutch and English sailors' quarters, where young African girls were taken. And afterward, as we crossed the courtyard that led to the male dungeons, we glimpsed the shores that were the last sight of home for Africans who might have been our foreparents.

On entering the male dungeons, a middle-aged woman suddenly collapsed, overcome by emotion. Others, holding torches, sat quietly beside her on the floor of the dungeon. Several of us inclined our heads as if listening for voices. Everyone cried.

The time spent in the dungeons gave new meaning to a ceremony many of us had witnessed the night before. Tribal leaders from chiefdoms across Ghana had gathered at midnight in a clearing just outside the capital city of Accra to perform a ritual "washing of stools and skins"† —the Ghanaian ceremony of apology.

The priests and priestesses wore red and black robes—the colors of mourning—and began by asking forgiveness on behalf of their ancestors, those chiefs who reigned centuries ago, who accepted gunpowder, weapons, beads, and promises in exchange for men, women, and children from rival villages. The tribal leaders explained to us that the practice of slavery dated back thousands of years on the African continent. But in Africa, it had been a condition of servitude, and not, by tradition, one of cruelty. The chiefs suggested that their ancestors had not understood the barbarity of slavery as it was practiced in America. Now, with full knowledge of the inhuman nature of American slavery, they wanted to be forgiven.

There was chanting, ceremonial dancing, and the rhythmic beating of drums. There was a mixing of herbs, a letting of blood, and a pouring of libations. Then the Ghanaian chiefs marched in procession through the streets of Accra, spreading the mixture of herbs and libations on themselves and on those of us who joined the procession. Soon, the chiefs shed their red and black robes of mourning to reveal white robes underneath. The white robes represented a new beginning.

As far as we knew, this was the first time in recorded history that the ceremony of atonement had been performed as an apology to African-American and Caribbean people. For all of us who had touched the walls of the slave dungeons and sat holding torches on the impacted floor, it was clear why this ceremony had been necessary. We have always found it difficult to accept that the slave trade could not have flourished without the participation of Africans, but now, the issue of African complicity in the slave trade had been addressed in the only way still possible: by the descendants of those who had helped send their neighbors in chains to the New World, and by the exiled children of Africa who had returned to its soil.

The reality is, Africans of the diaspora may never know exactly how we came by the surnames we carry, and we will probably never know from what part of Africa our ancestors came. But we can take pride in the fact that we are descended from strong stock—strong enough to survive a Middle Passage that claimed the lives of millions; strong enough to withstand beatings, separations, and servitude upon arrival in the Americas; strong enough to parent a generation that, hundreds of years later, would return to Africa to heal its ancestral wounds.

As a people, we must take inspiration from the fact that we have already come through the worst. Africa's children can no longer afford to do harm to one another—that is the message given to us by the Ghanaian chiefs. And though their ceremony of atonement was four hundred years in coming, it was as joyous as a wedding, as solemn as a funeral, and as poignant as a long-awaited family reunion.

terrain, maroon communities existed, albeit with varied success and longevity. In the mainland of North America, escaped slaves often formed alliances with Indians, who perceived a common enemy in the Europeans. In 1526, for example, Lucas Vásquez de Ayllón, a Spanish explorer, attempted to set up a colony in South Carolina comprised of five hundred Spanish settlers and one hundred African slaves. Disease and dissension soon took their toll, and hostility from local Indians was encouraged and fomented by the slaves. Eventually, the Spaniards abandoned the colony, leaving the Africans to join the Indians.[34]

The Jamaican maroons were powerful groups of African descent who preyed on the island's English colony. The last and most famous maroon was Cudjoe, a brilliant general and wily guerilla fighter who only agreed to a treaty with the English in 1738 when he saw that his resources were dangerously low. He was able to forge a lasting compact that maintained freedom for the maroons under his command and gave them a portion of the island to settle. (R. C. Dallas, "Old Cudjoe Making Peace," from The History of the Maroons, London, 1803. Carl A. Kroch Library, Cornell University, Ithaca, New York.)

As in the Caribbean, the mountains, forests, swamps, and those areas of the mainland reckoned inhospitable were chosen by maroons as their strongholds. Indeed, the descendants of many of these maroon communities still live near the original settlements, in places such as the Florida Everglades and the Dismal Swamp on the Virginia and North Carolina border.[35] While some maroon communities were able to farm and raise livestock, for many the hostile terrain afforded them shelter but no livelihood. The rebel members of such communities were reduced to preying on plantations and settlements, and their bid for freedom often ended in violent death as the Europeans, fiercely motivated by the guerilla attacks, organized militias to hunt them down.

Not surprisingly, the American Civil War of 1861–65 encouraged maroon activity, with people of African descent breaking free of their masters to take part in guerilla warfare on their own behalf. And they were not always alone. Several examples are recorded of white Union soldiers, separated from their regiments deep in Confederate territory, joining forces with blacks to fight the plantation system. John K. Jackson, an officer in the Confederate Army, noted, "Many deserters…have organized, with runaway negroes, bands for the purpose of committing depredations upon plantations and crops of loyal citizens and running off their slaves."[36] Harassed by such actions and faced with intense military pressure from the Union troops, the Confederate Army was finally defeated in 1865. By then, the Emancipation Proclamation had already been issued, in 1863. All slaves were officially free.

The Long Voyage Home

Around the time that maroons were consolidating their forces in the hills of Jamaica, the *Henrietta Marie* was preparing to depart the Caribbean for the long voyage home. On September 23, 1698, she sailed from Barbados's Carlisle Bay bound for London. Captain William Deacon had reason to be pleased. His cargo had sold well, and despite the planters' protests that the sugar crop had been poor that year, he had been able to purchase 118 hogsheads of *muscovado* sugar and one hogshead of the more valuable white sugar. He also had in his cargo hold sixty-seven bags of ginger and one hundred elephant tusks that he had secured while trading in Africa.[37]

While no Guinea voyage was pleasant, this one had at least been profitable—so profitable, in fact, that on his arrival in England two months later, Deacon found that he had amassed enough of a personal fortune to allow him to retire from the sea and become an investor. Among the former sea captain's first investments was his contribution of sixteen hundredweight of Venetian beads, rolls of coarse Indian muslin and other imported cloth, and bundles of English linens to the *Henrietta Marie*'s second voyage in 1699.

The *Henrietta Marie*'s next voyage would be commanded by Captain John Taylor, a man somewhat less experienced than Deacon had been. Throughout the summer of 1699, Taylor presided over the repair and refitting of the ship by gangs of carpenters, sailmakers, and riggers, and supervised the purchase and laying in of its cargo. The voyage did not start well. Held up by red tape, the ship missed the convoy with which Taylor had hoped to sail. Perhaps sensing the trials ahead, the captain took advantage of the customs delay to write his will, naming one of the investors, Robert Wilson, as his executor. At last, the customs officers completed their inspection, and the *Henrietta Marie* was allowed to leave London. The vessel would have to make her way alone to Africa, and Taylor himself would have to locate New Calabar, an area with which he was unfamiliar.

The ship arrived at its destination in about mid-December. But when Captain Taylor tried to bargain for ivory and slaves, he found the Africans indifferent to the cargo of pewter tankards, spoons, and bowls he had brought. Complaining that they had enough pewter already, they picked casually through his barrels of beads, choosing only the red and blue ones, and tossing the green and yellow aside. Taylor, feeling unwell, must have cursed as the days of trading dragged on. It soon became apparent

An image of the legendary and much-revered guerrilla fighter Nanny appears on the Jamaican $500 note. Descendants of the maroon leader's fierce band of runaways still inhabit the hilly interior of the island. (Bank of Jamaica.)

that the information which had served Deacon well during the preceding year was already out of date. The slaves trickled on board and lay moaning in the hold as Taylor tried to bargain for a complete cargo. At 206 captives, the captain decided that neither he nor his men would survive another week in Africa. It was late January when Taylor, who by now may have been seriously ill, finally gave the order to load all the slaves they had purchased and weigh anchor.

Taylor himself would die during the Middle Passage, one of many fatalities. A seaman by the name of Thomas Chamberlain succeeded him as captain. But Chamberlain's command was hardly the same sleek vessel that had left London six months before. Rather, the ship had become what one historian described as "a dogged survivor whose sun-parched decks, scorched canvas, peeling paintwork, and faded pennants bore witness to the trials and tribulations of trading along the Guinea Coast."[38] Led by their new captain, the crew of the beleaguered ship first sighted Barbados on May 6, 1700. By then, only nine sailors remained alive. Cheered momentarily by the sight of land, they sailed on, for their destination was Jamaica, where some of the ship's investors had plantations to which the cargo of slaves had been consigned.

The ship reached Port Royal, Jamaica, on May 17, 1700. The Africans, revived somewhat by extra rations, were brought on deck. They had managed the Middle Passage better than the white crew, with only sixteen deaths. Perhaps the Africans had fared so well because of Taylor's decision to travel with a cargo hold at less than capacity—a situation that allowed the captives less cramped quarters and better air circulation than was the case on most voyages.

In Jamaica, the slaves fetched good prices, more so perhaps because no slaver had stopped at the island in several weeks. Purchased for approximately £4 in Africa, the Africans now sold for between £24 and £30, a profit of more than six hundred percent. Perhaps, as he reinvested his profits in new cargo, Thomas Chamberlain was inspired by the thought of William Deacon, who had survived the first voyage and achieved wealth in the process. Chamberlain

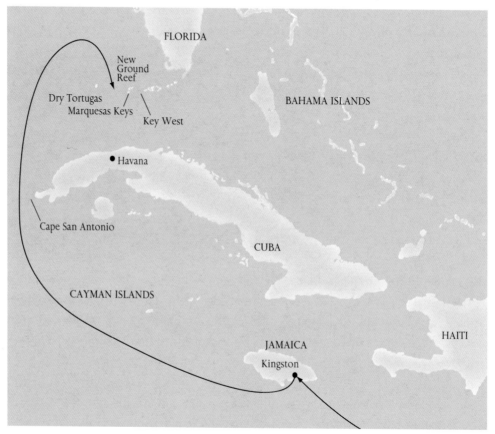

The Henrietta Marie *was on the final leg of her journey, heading home from Jamaica through the Straits of Florida, when she hit New Ground Reef, sinking with all hands.*

was able to load eighty-one hogsheads of *muscovado* sugar, fourteen bags of cotton, eleven barrels of indigo, and twenty-one tons of logwood.

At the end of June, Chamberlain gave the order to set sail for home. The *Henrietta Marie* traveled west and north, past the Cayman Islands, Cuba, and through the Yucatan Channel. Off the coast of Florida, a storm whipped up, part of a powerful hurricane system to which a number of English vessels would fall victim that year. By the time her crew realized the strength of the storm, the *Henrietta Marie* was badly placed to survive it, for the gale force winds caught her in the treacherous Florida Straits, sandwiched between the Dry Tortugas and the Marquesas Keys.

Sudden and deadly, hurricanes afforded a sailing ship no shelter. Wind and rain lashed the decks, flogging the crew. The terror of such storms is captured in the story of Charles May, mate on the West Indies trader *Terra Nova*. May was working to secure his ship during the lull of a storm "when a prodigious wave broke to windward and left us all a-swimming, scarce knowing whether we were within or without the ship, but that on me [rolled] the men, chests, handspikes, shot, and whatever lay windward.... All our masts were gone, and we lay like a wreck. Hereupon we run to clap our helm a-weather; and coming to lay hold of the whipstaff, I found it was fallen into the gun room.... I found the tiller lying in the gun room on the deck...whilst groveling in the dark. I felt my body all covered with rats, as thick as they could stand upon me, on my coat, arms, neck and my very head, so that I was forced to make my escape into the light to get free of those vermin."[39]

Such were the conditions faced by Chamberlain and his men. Frightened and disoriented by the hurricane, the ship's crew pushed onward through the Florida Straits as best they could, but the captain could barely see where they were going, much less chart a course. Certainly, he did not detect the perilous crest of New Ground Reef lurking beneath his bow— not until the ship struck the reef heavily, with a blow that dislodged her stern. The sailors, grabbing at broken spars and fragments of wood, tried to stay afloat as water rushed over the decks. But at last the storm defeated them, and the *Henrietta Marie* perished as she had started out this journey—a lonely traveler on unforgiving seas.

Spirits in the Water

Centuries later, the pain of four hundred years of chattel slavery still marks Americans of African descent, as indeed it still marks Americans of European ancestry, though in a different way. Africans of the diaspora still suffer the everyday indignities of institutionalized racism as both blacks and whites in the New World grapple with the lasting effects of the human trade. The healing has been a long time coming, for even now, the stubborn legacy of slavery continues to hold hostage the descendants of all those who traveled to the Americas in the stench and horror of the slave ships.

The story of the *Henrietta Marie* can serve to remind us that both black and white ancestors made that crossing to the New World. Both races breathed the stink of death; both races felt the heat of desperation in the blood, felt the will to die *and* the will to live that permeated the air of that ship. Two races of people were locked in the nightmare of that experience and were irrevocably scarred by it. Now, through the story of this one ship, two races bound by a painful history can begin to search for the hearts and minds of their ancestors, to piece together their stories, fathom their motives, and perhaps heal the sorrow and anguish and recrimination over what transpired during the deadly passage of American slavery. Perhaps, through this one ship, we can look back at history and claim it in all its untidy complexity, and acknowledge the horror that occurred. Only then might we finally embrace its lessons—as we listen for the voices that whisper through the sunken hold of a slave ship named the *Henrietta Marie*.

The Wreck of the *Henrietta Marie*

By Madeleine Burnside

The renowned treasure hunter Mel Fisher spent part of 1972 searching for the *Nuestra Señora de Atocha*, a Spanish treasure galleon that had been lost at sea in the year 1622. His research had led him to believe that he would find it somewhere near Key West, and so he was concentrating on locating shipwrecks surrounding the island. Day after day his divers would come up with something—debris from a modern pleasure boat, part of a nineteenth-century vessel, even dummy bombs from when the area was used as a practice range by the U.S. Navy. Occasionally, they discovered parts of other Spanish vessels, a cannon perhaps, or some pottery shards.

In the fall of that year, Fisher's divers came up with something else. A magnetometer search, designed to locate metals, locked in on a cannon and two anchors. One diver jumped over the side to take a look. The cannon appeared to be of the right age for the *Atocha*. Had they found the fabulous golden galleon with which their employer had long been obsessed?

Fisher came to the site the next day. On the first dive it became clear that they had the major portion of a shipwreck beneath the water, and so Fisher decided to send a formal team to investigate. Demosthenes "Mo" Molinar received the assignment. Captain of the *Virgilona*, he was also Fisher's only captain of African descent. But the significance of this coincidence would not be understood until later, for there was no hint yet of what the wreck might hold. Molinar and his crew spent about two weeks on the site before the weather got too rough for them to continue. By then they had brought up pewter tankards, some bowls, and a few pairs of shackles. A cursory analysis of the artifacts told them that the ship was not Spanish but English, and of a later vintage than the *Atocha*, closer to the year 1700. Molinar's crew logged the wreck site in Mel Fisher's extensive charts as simply "the English wreck." The ship would lie undisturbed for another ten years.

In 1983, a young graduate student in marine archaeology named David Moore decided that, to get hands-on experience in his field, he would take a job with Mel Fisher. Then as now, the role of the private sector in the excavation of underwater sites was the subject of heated debate. While universities lacked the funds to excavate wreck sites themselves, many academics felt that those in the private sector were ruining valuable archaeological information while looting a wreck's artifacts. But shipwrecks were constantly being discovered by untrained people, who, even with the best of intentions, had no clue as to how to proceed. Moore hoped that as a marine archaeologist, he could help to redress the situation by combining his technical know-how with well-meaning private sector money.

Known as a graybeard, bellarmine, or d'Alva bottle, this salt-glazed stoneware vessel is typical of English ceramic bottles from about 1500–1700 and is linked to Protestant potters who fled to England along with thousands of other people to escape Catholic oppression on the European continent. It is decorated with a bearded face, a classical motif that represented the much-hated Cardinal Bellarmine in the Rhineland and the Duke of Alva, the brutal Spanish governor of the Low Countries.

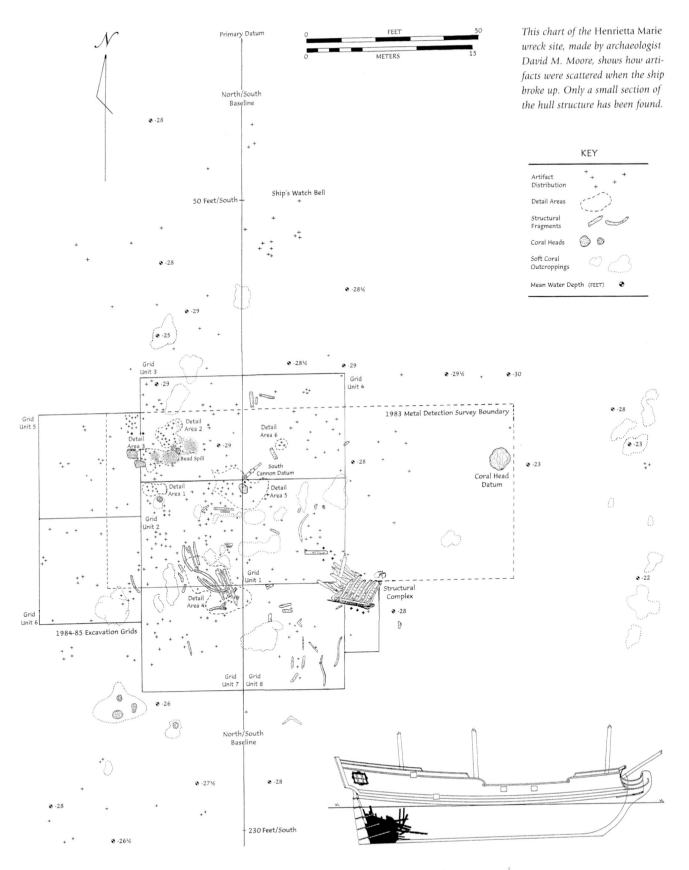

This chart of the Henrietta Marie *wreck site, made by archaeologist David M. Moore, shows how artifacts were scattered when the ship broke up. Only a small section of the hull structure has been found.*

N

Primary Datum

North/South
Baseline

50 Feet/South

Ship's Watch Bell

0   FEET   50
0   METERS   15

KEY

Artifact
Distribution

Detail Areas

Structural
Fragments

Coral Heads

Soft Coral
Outcroppings

Mean Water Depth (FEET)

Grid
Unit 3

Grid
Unit 4

1983 Metal Detection Survey Boundary

Grid
Unit 5

Detail
Area 2

Detail
Area 3

Detail
Area 6

Bead Spill

South
Cannon Datum

Coral Head
Datum

Detail
Area 1

Detail
Area 5

Grid
Unit 2

Grid
Unit 1

Structural
Complex

Detail
Area 4

Grid
Unit 6

1984-85 Excavation Grids

Grid
Unit 7

Grid
Unit 8

North/South
Baseline

230 Feet/South

Moore began his work with Mel Fisher by focusing his efforts on the English wreck. Speculation that the vessel might have been a pirate ship melted as more of its contents were brought to the surface: There were some guns, various personal items, and more pewter objects, including a curious ewer full of spoons but none of the gold, silver, or precious jewels that might have hinted at piracy. The wreck did contain, however, an abundance of one particular artifact: shackles.

Every ship of this period carried a few sets of shackles with which to restrain unruly or drunken sailors, or punish crew members who caused trouble. But only one kind of ship

During the 1991 excavation archaeologist Corey Malcom located several sets of shackles covered with encrustation and shells.

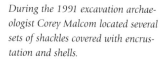

Several lead draft markers were attached to the Henrietta Marie's hull. The number of them visible above the waterline told sailors how low the ship was riding in the water—allowing a simple visual check for problems caused by leaking or the overburdening of cargo holds.

would have carried as many as the ninety-odd pairs of shackles found at the wreck site. The English vessel was a slave ship.

Before long, divers brought up the ship's bell, and Moore set to cleaning the surface. Just a date would have been very helpful or perhaps the place the bell was cast. As the archaeologist chipped away at the sea crust, a date appeared: "1699." Moore sat back, barely able to contain himself. After a few moments, he resumed the cleaning, and letters appeared: "*Henrietta Marie*." Moore shouted with joy. It was a marine archaeologists dream—he had the ship's name and the date of her commission; he knew her nationality and her purpose. Moore could now piece together the rest of her story from archives and shipping records in London and the Caribbean.

By 1991, when I joined the staff of the Mel Fisher Maritime Heritage Society as executive director, most of the *Henrietta Marie*'s artifacts had already been excavated and donated by Mel Fisher to the Society, a nonprofit educational organization that he himself had founded. Located in Key West, the Society was best known for the extraordinary artifacts recovered by Fisher from two Spanish galleons, the *Nuestra Señora de Atocha* and the *Santa Margarita*. Working with such well-known artifacts presented an attractive opportunity, and as I toured the museum during the interview process, I examined the collection intently. Suddenly, in the midst of all the Spanish material, I came upon a very different group of objects in their own case—shackles, beads, tusks, and a large bell.

As encrustation was chipped away from the surface of the bell, the ship's name and date appeared.

What was this? I asked. My guide explained that these were artifacts from an English slaving vessel. I looked more closely. One pair of shackles was extremely small, suitable for a child or perhaps a young woman. I breathed deeply, feeling the sudden flash of connection. *Who had worn these shackles?*

A few people knew about these artifacts, although the collection had not yet received much national publicity. But after a small expedition to the slave ship's wreck site in 1991, the story was picked up by the *Miami Herald*. Ric Powell, then the president of the National Association of Black Scuba Divers (NABS), read about the slave ship with great interest. A young organization dedicated to providing culturally relevant information to its members, as well as dive opportunities, NABS was about to hold its annual summit in Fort Lauderdale. Powell contacted Corey Malcom, director of archaeology and conservation at the Society, and David Moore and asked them to give a talk on the wreck and show some of the artifacts to the group's members.

For the divers, the appalling story came to life. Tangible objects had at last been found to document the Middle Passage experience: heavy shackles; the bell that tolled; remaindered goods of the very sort used to trade in human lives. The black scuba divers decided they had been granted a remarkable opportunity. As far as they knew, no one in the Western world had ever placed a memorial to those who had suffered and died during the Middle Passage. Here was the chance to do so.

Members of the National Association of Black Scuba Divers Dr. José Jones, Ric Powell, Howard Moss, and Oswald Sykes perform a ceremonial handshake during the placement of the memorial plaque.

HENRIETTA MARIE
IN MEMORY AND
RECOGNITION OF THE COURAGE,
PAIN AND SUFFERING OF
ENSLAVED AFRICAN PEOPLE.

"SPEAK HER NAME AND GENTLY TOUCH
THE SOULS OF OUR ANCESTORS."

Dedicated November 15, 1992

As a memorial to those who suffered the agonies of the Middle Passage, this plaque was set in place at the wreck site of the Henrietta Marie by members of the National Association of Black Scuba Divers on May 15, 1993.

Two years later, on May 15, 1993, through calm water and under brilliant sunshine, the divers lowered the memorial—a bronze plaque embedded in a concrete marker—into the ocean. After the plaque was anchored to the seabed at New Ground Reef next to the wreck, a simple ceremony with drumming and reading underlined the stark significance of the event.

Plans for an exhibition also went forward, and I immersed myself in reading about the slave trade. As I studied, I found myself drawn in by the harrowing story. The more I read, the more I felt that the artifacts had their own tale, one that had lain buried in the ocean for so many years, and buried under the desire of too many people, both white and black, to wish slavery away. As I got still deeper into the research, I found myself more and more despondent. How could this have happened?, I wondered. How could people on three continents reach consensus about an enterprise so terrible? And who had worn the smallest shackles?

I realized that until I came to grips with these questions, I would never feel that the exhibition could offer its visitors reasons for hope. I kept returning to those shackles. Partially worn away by the sea, they were still strong enough to hold a pair of small wrists or even ankles. Yet all the literature I had read, including the account of Ouladah Equiano, stated that enslaved children were not shackled aboard ship but were kept with the women or allowed to roam free. Then why had these smaller shackles been forged? As I handled them over and over again, I began to envision my own answer to the questions they raised, to infer my own story about the shackles.

For me, whatever the shackles implied—helplessness, rape, terror—they also implied someone who fought tooth and nail, a young person who could not be restrained in any other way. I tried to picture such a person: a girl, I thought. I could not shake the impression of a girl, as slender as she was young, but intelligent and determined to be a problem. Perhaps in Africa she was a spoiled brat, throwing tantrums and lashing out at those around her; perhaps she had always had to fight to get her own way, struggling against older, more favored siblings; or perhaps she had witnessed or endured trials that filled her with rage. Perhaps she had been forced to defend herself against rapists, murderers, slave merchants. Whatever her story, she was not going to die of despair. She was going to be one of the survivors, and she was going to do her best to make life difficult for her oppressors.

The shackles could restrain but never hold her. Perhaps in the colonies she would be killed for her grit and determination. Or perhaps she would win her freedom, buying it, as Equiano had done, or escaping to the maroons. Suddenly, I understood that whatever her fate, this spirited child would forever maintain her independence. Slavery would not succeed in crushing her will, for she would never relinquish the freedom within.

I have since fathomed that the *Henrietta Marie* is not an ordinary shipwreck. Many of us who have become involved with her story have confessed that we felt driven, guided, cajoled, commanded to take on the work we have done. Each one of us has entered the story at a different place, as though each spirit of the passage had sought a person with whom to communicate. I sometimes think it was the spirit of that rebellious young girl, the one who may have worn the smallest shackles, who called to me.

Accounts of the desperate Middle Passage and slavery as a whole too often characterize the Africans as victims without sufficiently honoring them as survivors, heroes, and role models, as people of great pride and stubborn endurance. For the sake of humanity in general, and African Americans in particular, it is the indomitable spirit of these enslaved ancestors that must be summoned. The pathos of their situation must be understood, the tortures accounted for, the numbers of the dead reckoned with. But their anger and self-will, their defiant laughter and song, their respect for freedom and deep love of life must bear the final witness to the strength and survival of extraordinary people; to the mutual support of individuals, families, and kinship groups; and to the generosity of strangers toward their fellow sufferers.

This is the true legacy of the *Henrietta Marie*.

Like the exhibition and the plaque, this book is intended as a memorial, a testament, not just to the anguish of those who endured the Middle Passage but to their courage and heroism in the face of great odds. In the words of diver Oswald Sykes, which are inscribed on the plaque:

Speak her name
and gently touch
the souls of our ancestors.

Endnotes

Chapter 1
Chattel Slavery

1. The kingdom of ancient Ghana was located between the Senegal and Niger Rivers in the region of modern Mali and Mauretania. In medieval times, its gold was much sought after by North Africa and Europe. Ancient Ghana should not be confused with the Gold Coast, also a gold-producing region, which took the name Ghana on achieving independence in 1957.

2. Stephen Clissold, *The Barbary Slaves* (New York: Marlboro Books, 1977), p. 131.

3. Clissold, *The Barbary Slaves*, p. 32.

4. Clissold, *The Barbary Slaves*, p. 37.

5. Clissold, *The Barbary Slaves*, p. 44.

6. Edward William Bovill, *The Golden Trade of the Moors, West African Kingdoms in the Fourteenth Century* (Princeton, N.J.: Markus Wiener Publishers, 1995), p. 151.

7. The numbers of Africans enslaved in Europe would remain modest, particularly when compared to the millions of African captives who were soon to be transported to the American colonies. By the time the transatlantic slave traffic was outlawed throughout the world in 1824, the use of African bondspeople in Europe had already petered out.

8. T. Bentley Duncan, *Atlantic Islands: Madeira, The Azores and The Cape Verdes in Seventeenth-Century Commerce and Navigation* (Chicago: University of Chicago Press, 1972), p. 10.

9. Kirkpatrick Sale, *The Conquest of Paradise* (New York: Plume Books, 1991), p. 138.

10. Sale, *The Conquest*, p. 161.

Chapter 2
London in the 1690s

1. The ship's bell was the single most important diagnostic artifact recovered from the wreck site. Its inscription of the ship's name and date took researchers into archives in London, Jamaica, and France, and to the logs of such vessels as the *Speedwell*, whose captain mentioned sighting the *Henrietta Marie*. As a result of this inquiry, archaeologists and scholars were able to determine the origin and subsequent fate of the vessel, and the names and contributions of the people involved in her two voyages.

2. Peter Earle, *A City Full of People: Men and Women of London, 1650–1750* (London: Methuen, 1994). p. 7.

3. Robert Latham, ed., *The Shorter Pepys* (Berkeley: University of California Press, 1985), p. 553.

4. Latham, *Pepys*, p. 521.

5. Latham, *Pepys*, p. 494.

6. Latham, *Pepys*, p. 583.

7. Latham, *Pepys*, p. 662.

8. London Guildhall, Archives, MS 12017.

9. Latham, *Pepys*, p. 663.

10. The importance of these high-ranking merchants is suggested by the fact that to this day the liverymen are the only residents of the city empowered to vote in elections for the lord mayor of London and his sheriffs, the administrative core of the city's government.

11. Daniel Defoe, *Robinson Crusoe* (Cutchogue, N.Y.: Buccaneer Books, 1986), p. 38.

12. Nigel Tattersfield, *An Account of the Slave Ship* Henrietta Marie *of London: 1697–1700* (unpublished manuscript, 1994), p. 9.

13. Tattersfield, *An Account*, p. 10.

14. Tattersfield, *An Account*, p. 10.

15. Tattersfield, *An Account*, p. 10.

16. See P. E. H. Hair, Adam Jones, and Robin Law, eds., *Barbot on Guinea* (London: Hakluyt Society, 1992). Jean Barbot mentions trading in hats and giving hats to Africans as presents, p. 691.

17. Letter to Ambrose Lace, in George Francis Dow, *Slave Ships and Slaving* (Brattleboro, Vt.: The Marine Research Society, 1927), p. 103.

18. Defoe, *Robinson Crusoe*, p. 9.

19. *Barlow's Journal of His Life at Sea in King's Ships, East and West Indiamen and Other Merchantmen from 1659-1703*, transcribed by Basil Lubbock (London: Hurst and Blackett, 1934), p. 28.

* Robert Latham, ed., *The Shorter Pepys* (Berkeley: University of California Press, 1985), pp. 119, 125.

† Latham, *Pepys*, p. 993.

‡ Latham, *Pepys*, p. 1006.

§ Latham, *Pepys*, p. 522.

‖ P. E. H. Hair, Adam Jones, and Robin Law, eds., *Barbot on Guinea* (London: Hakluyt Society, 1992), p. 30.

Chapter 3
The Slave Coast of Africa

1. Ouladah Equiano, *An Interesting Account*, in Arna Bontemps, ed., *Great Slave Narratives* (Boston: Beacon Press, 1969), p. 11.

2. Herbert M. Cole and Chike C. Aniakor, *Igbo Arts: Community and Cosmos* (Los Angeles: Museum of Cultural History, 1984), p. 1.

3. Chinua Achebe, Foreword in Cole and Aniakor, *Igbo Arts*, p. ix.

4. Cole and Aniakor, *Igbo Arts*, p. 15.

5. Chinua Achebe, *Things Fall Apart* (Greenwich, Conn.: Fawcett Crest Books, Fawcett Publications, 1959), pp. 114–15.

6. P. E. H. Hair, Adam Jones, and Robin Law, eds., *Barbot on Guinea* (London: Hakluyt Society, 1992), p. 709.

7. Hair, Jones, and Law, *Barbot on Guinea*, p. 696.

8. Hair, Jones, and Law, *Barbot on Guinea*, p. 701.

9. Cole and Aniakor, *Igbo Arts*, p. 4.

10. Equiano, *An Interesting Account*, in Bontemps, *Great Slave Narratives*, makes a special mention of the ritual of handwashing before meals, p. 8.

11. John Thornton, *The African Background of the Slave Cargo of the* Henrietta Marie (unpublished manuscript, 1994), p. 8.

12. For a discussion of the lives of slave women, see Patrick Manning, *Slavery and African Life* (New York: Cambridge University Press, 1990), pp. 118–19.

13. John Thornton, *Africa and Africans in the Making of the Atlantic World: 1400–1680* (New York: Cambridge University Press, 1992), p. 86.

14. Equiano, *An Interesting Account*, in Bontemps, *Great Slave Narratives*, p. 7.

15. Ekpo Eyo and Frank Willett, *Treasures of Ancient Nigeria* (New York: Alfred Knopf, 1980), p. 29.

16. Eyo and Willett, *Treasures*, p. 9.

17. Equiano, *An Interesting Account*, in Bontemps, *Great Slave Narratives*, p. 14.

18. Thornton, *African Background*, p. 12.

19. Captain Thomas Phillips, *Journal*, from John and Awnsham Churchill, *Collection of Voyages*, Vol. 4 (London, 1746), excerpted in George Francis Dow, *Slave Ships and Slaving* (Brattleboro, Vt.: The Marine Research Society, 1927), p. 55.

20. Enzio Bassani and William Fagg, *Africa and the Renaissance: Art in Ivory* (Munich, Ger.: The Center for African Art and Prestel Verlag, 1988), p. 199.

21. Bassani and Fagg, *Africa and the Renaissance*, p. 218.

22. Equiano, *An Interesting Account*, in Bontemps, *Great Slave Narratives*, p. 12.

23. Manning, *Slavery*, pp. 114–15.

* Enzio Bassani and William Fagg, *Africa and the Renaissance: Art in Ivory* (Munich, Ger.: The Center for African Art and Prestel Verlag, 1988), p. 203.

24. Thornton, *Africa*, pp. 77–78.

25. Thornton, *Africa*, p. 93.

26. Equiano, *An Interesting Account*, in Bontemps, *Great Slave Narratives*, p. 10.

27. Equiano, *An Interesting Account*, in Bontemps, *Great Slave Narratives*, p. 11.

28. Phillips, *Journal*, in Dow, *Slave Ships*, p. 69.

29. Phillips, *Journal*, in Dow, *Slave Ships*, p. 63.

30. Hair, Jones, and Law, *Barbot on Guinea*, p. 645.

31. Hair, Jones, and Law, *Barbot on Guinea*, p. 656.

32. Phillips, *Journal*, in Dow, *Slave Ships*, p. 64.

33. Phillips, *Journal*, in Dow, *Slave Ships*, p. 67.

34. Phillips, *Journal*, in Dow, *Slave Ships*, p. 63.

35. Hair, Jones, and Law, *Barbot on Guinea*, p. 400.

36. Hair, Jones, and Law, *Barbot on Guinea*, p. 392.

37. Hair, Jones, and Law, *Barbot on Guinea*, p. 658.

38. Manning, *Slavery*, p. 132.

1. P. E. H. Hair, Adam Jones, and Robin Law, eds., *Barbot on Guinea* (London: Hakluyt Society, 1992), p. 672.

2. Hair, Jones, and Law, *Barbot on Guinea*, p. 675.

3. Captain Thomas Phillips, *Journal*, from John and Awnsham Churchill, *Collection of Voyages*, Vol. 4 (London, 1746), excerpted in George Francis Dow, *Slave Ships and Slaving* (Brattleboro, Vt.: The Marine Research Society, 1927), p. 67.

4. Phillips, *Journal*, in Dow, *Slave Ships*, p. 67.

5. Hair, Jones, and Law, *Barbot on Guinea*, p. 696.

6. Hair, Jones, and Law, *Barbot on Guinea*, pp. 672, 694.

7. Hair, Jones, and Law, *Barbot on Guinea*, p. 695.

8. Patrick Manning, *Slavery and African Life* (New York: Cambridge University Press, 1992), p. 130.

9. Manning, *Slavery*, p. 132.

10. Hair, Jones, and Law, *Barbot on Guinea*, p. 493.

11. Hair, Jones, and Law, *Barbot on Guinea*, pp. 559–60.

12. Hair, Jones, and Law, *Barbot on Guinea*, p. 689.

13. Hair, Jones, and Law, *Barbot on Guinea*, p. 774.

14. Hair, Jones, and Law, *Barbot on Guinea*, pp. 550–51.

15. Hair, Jones, and Law, *Barbot on Guinea*, p. 689.

16. Phillips, *Journal*, in Dow, *Slave Ships*, p. 71.

17. Hair, Jones, and Law, *Barbot on Guinea*, p. 700.

18. Hair, Jones, and Law, *Barbot on Guinea*, p. 700. "All the ships that loaded slaves at New Calabar...lost, some half and others two thirds of them, before they reached Barbadoes: and such as were alive, died there, as soon as landed or else turned to a very bad market: which rendered the so hopeful voyage of the *Albion* abortive, and above sixty percent of the capital was lost, chiefly occasioned by the want of proper food and water to subsist them, as well as the ill-management of the principals aboard." This description of the disastrous voyage of the *Albion Frigate* is included in Barbot's journal, but he credits the account to John Grazilhier who sailed to West Africa in 1704.

19. Hair, Jones, and Law, *Barbot on Guinea*, p. 689.

20. Hair, Jones, and Law, *Barbot on Guinea*, p. 687.

21. Hair, Jones, and Law, *Barbot on Guinea*, p. 689.

22. Ouladah Equiano, *An Interesting Account*, in Arna Bontemps, ed., *Great Slave Narratives* (Boston: Beacon Press, 1969), p. 24.

23. Equiano, *An Interesting Account*, in Bontemps, *Great Slave Narratives*, pp. 25–26.

24. Equiano, *An Interesting Account*, in Bontemps, *Great Slave Narratives*, p. 27.

25. James Walvin, *Black Ivory* (New York: HarperCollins, 1992), p. 46.

26. Equiano, *An Interesting Account*, in Bontemps, *Great Slave Narratives*, p. 28.

27. Phillips, *Journal*, in Dow, *Slave Ships*, p. 74.

28. Captain William Snelgrave, excerpted in Dow, *Slave Ships*, p. 134.

29. Snelgrave in Dow, *Slave Ships*, p. 143.

30. From James Arnold's testimony before the Parliamentary Committee, printed in the *Report to the House of Lords on the Abolition of the Slave Trade* (London, 1789), excerpted in Dow, *Slave Ships*, p. 194.

31. Phillips in Dow, *Slave Ships*, p. 76.

32. William McNeill, *Plagues and Peoples* (New York: Monticello Editions, 1976), pp. 213–14.

33. Herbert Klein, *The Middle Passage* (Princeton, N.J.: Princeton University Press, 1978), p. 166, n. 41.

34. Equiano, *An Interesting Account*, in Bontemps, *Great Slave Narratives*, p. 30.

35. Alexander Falconbridge, *The Ship Doctor's Narrative*, in Dow, *Slave Ships*, p. 166.

36. Arnold, in Dow, *Slave Ships*, p. 195.

37. Equiano, *An Interesting Account*, in Bontemps, *Great Slave Narratives*, p. 29.

38. Walvin, *Black Ivory*, p. 57.

39. Barbot, quoted in Dow, *Slave Ships*, p. 94.

40. Hair, Jones, and Law, *Barbot on Guinea*, p. 775.

CHAPTER 4
The Middle Passage

CHAPTER 4 (continued)

41. Equiano, *An Interesting Account*, in Bontemps, *Great Slave Narratives*, p. 74.

42. Arnold, in Dow, *Slave Ships*, p. 191.

43. Falconbridge, in Dow, *Slave Ships*, pp. 164–65.

44. Snelgrave, in Dow, *Slave Ships*, p. 129.

45. Hair, Jones, and Law, *Barbot on Guinea*, p. 550.

46. Hair, Jones, and Law, *Barbot on Guinea*, p. 774.

47. Hair, Jones, and Law, *Barbot on Guinea*, p. 775.

48. Richard Drake, *Revelations of a Slave Smuggler: Being the Autobiography of Capt. Richard Drake, an African Trader for Fifty Years: From 1807–1857*, in Dow, *Slave Ships*, p. 194.

49. Kenneth F. Kiple and Brian T. Higgins, *Mortality During the Middle Passage*, in Joseph E. Inikori and Stanley L. Engerman, eds., *The Atlantic Slave Trade* (Durham, N.C.: Duke University Press, 1992), p. 323.

* John Newton, *Memoirs of His Life*, quoted in Daniel P. Mannix and Malcolm Cowley, *Black Cargoes* (New York: Viking Press, 1962), p. 136.

50. Kiple and Higgins, *Mortality*, in Inikori and Engerman, *The Atlantic Slave Trade*, p. 325.

51. Suzanne Everett, *The History of Slavery* (Secaucus, N.J.: Chartwell Books, 1991), pp. 58–61.

52. Phillips, *Journal*, in Dow, *Slave Ships*, p. 71.

53. Phillips, *Journal*, in Dow, *Slave Ships*, p. 77.

54. Hair, Jones, and Law, *Barbot on Guinea*, p. 77.

55. John Newton, quoted in Walvin, *Black Ivory*, p. 42.

56. Nigel Tattersfield, *An Account of the Slave Ship* Henrietta Marie *of London: 1697–1700* (unpublished manuscript), p. 20.

57. Phillips, *Journal*, in Dow, *Slave Ships*, p. 78.

CHAPTER 5
The Americas

1. Richard Drake, *Revelations of a Slave Smuggler: Being the Autobiography of Capt. Richard Drake, an African Trader for Fifty Years: From 1807–1857*, in George Francis Dow, *Slave Ships and Slaving* (Brattleboro, Vt.: The Marine Research Society, 1927), p. 227.

2. Ouladah Equiano, *An Interesting Account*, in Arna Bontemps, ed., *Great Slave Narratives* (Boston: Beacon Press, 1969), p. 32.

3. Alexander Falconbridge, *An Account of the Slave Trade on the Coast of Africa* (London, 1788), in Dow, *Slave Ships*, p. 156.

4. Equiano, *An Interesting Account*, in Bontemps, *Great Slave Narratives*, p. 76.

5. Equiano, *An Interesting Account*, in Bontemps, *Great Slave Narratives*, p. 76.

6. Equiano, *An Interesting Account*, in Bontemps, *Great Slave Narratives*, p. 34.

7. Equiano, *An Interesting Account*, in Bontemps, *Great Slave Narratives*, p. 70.

8. Equiano, *An Interesting Account*, in Bontemps, *Great Slave Narratives*, p. 79.

9. Equiano, *An Interesting Account*, in Bontemps, *Great Slave Narratives*, p. 73.

10. Equiano, *An Interesting Account*, in Bontemps, *Great Slave Narratives*, p. 71.

11. Equiano, *An Interesting Account*, in Bontemps, *Great Slave Narratives*, p. 74.

12. Richard S. Dunn, *Sugar and Slaves* (Chapel Hill: University of North Carolina Press, 1972), p. 87.

13. Equiano, *An Interesting Account*, in Bontemps, *Great Slave Narratives*, pp. 74–75.

14. Dunn, *Sugar*, p. 70.

15. Dunn, *Sugar*, p. 69.

16. Quoted in Dunn, *Sugar*, p. 77.

17. Equiano, *An Interesting Account*, in Bontemps, *Great Slave Narratives*, p. 74.

18. Tom Cowan and Jack Maguire, *Timelines of African-American History* (New York: Perigee Books, 1994), p. 13.

* First published in *Essence* magazine, October 1995, p. 60.

19. Dunn, *Sugar*, p. 228.

20. Dunn, *Sugar*, p. 229.

21. Dunn, *Sugar*, p. 70.

22. Dunn, *Sugar*, pp. 110–16.

23. Dunn, *Sugar*, pp. 222–23.

24. Equiano, *An Interesting Account*, in Bontemps, *Great Slave Narratives*, p. 75.

25. Equiano, *An Interesting Account*, in Bontemps, *Great Slave Narratives*, p. 77.

26. Josette Fallope, *Les Racines Africaines aux Antilles*, in *Les Anneaux de la Mémoire* (Nantes, Fr.: Centre International de la Mer, Corderie Royale, 1992), p. 139.

27. James Walvin, *Black Ivory* (New York: HarperCollins, 1992), p. 134.

28. Dunn, *Sugar*, p. 228.

29. Cowan and Maguire, *Timeline*, pp. 17, 228.

30. Dunn, *Sugar*, p. 254.

31. Equiano, *An Interesting Account*, in Bontemps, *Great Slave Narratives*, p. 134.

32. Richard Price, *Maroon Societies* (Baltimore: Johns Hopkins University Press, 1979), p. 39.

33. Price, *Maroon Societies*, p. 38.

34. Price, *Maroon Societies*, p. 149.

35. Herbert Aptheker, *Maroons Within the Present Limits of the United States*, quoted in Price, *Maroon Societies*, p. 150.

36. Aptheker, *Maroons Within*, quoted in Price, *Maroon Societies*, p. 165.

37. Barbados Shipping Returns (London: Public Records Office), CO 33/13, fol. 35.s.

38. Nigel Tattersfield, *An Account of the Slave Ship* Henrietta Marie *of London: 1697–1700* (unpublished manuscript), p. 19.

39. Charles May, *An Account of the Wonderful Preservation of the Ship* Terra Nova *of London, Peter Daniel Commander, Homeward Bound from Virginia* (London, 1688), p. 43.

† The ancestral stools on which Ghana's tribal chiefs sit for ceremonial occasions have come to symbolize resistance to colonialism and the survival of chieftaincies in modern Ghana.

Acknowledgments

No one lent a helping hand to those who traveled aboard the *Henrietta Marie*, neither to the hundreds of Africans transported to the Americas under duress, nor to the few Europeans who sank with her in the Florida Straits. The revelation of their story, however, has been helped by innumerable persons, all of whom were inspired by the tale of those who lived and died aboard this one ship during the course of the transatlantic trade. It is my good fortune to be able to thank them.

First and foremost, I am grateful to Rosemarie Robotham, whose contribution to this book has been far beyond that of editor and who has become a dear friend in the process. My profound thanks also go to the other members of the book team: Katherine Cowles, who held us all together; Craig Bernhardt, whose vision dominates the book's look and feel; and Constance Herndon, Gillian Sowell, Isolde Sauer, and Peter McCulloch at Simon & Schuster. The contribution of Cornel West, whose work I have long admired, shows as always his remarkable clarity of thought and his ability to make sense of the relationships between the past and the present.

Long before anyone became involved in this project, the *Henrietta Marie* site was discovered by Mel Fisher. Mel and his wife, Deb, have given this project every encouragement and without them, none of it could have happened. To them I owe profound appreciation.

I would like to offer my sincere thanks to the John S. and James L. Knight Foundation, which provided initial funding for the research and development of this project. I would also like to thank the staff of the State of Florida's department of historical resources, particularly James Miller of the bureau of the state archaeology department, for the hours he spent discussing the *Henrietta Marie* project. George Percy, Michael Brothers, and Holly Beasely were immensely helpful as well.

Outside input was vital in order to realize this book in a relatively short period. Many scholars contributed, among them Nigel Tattersfield, who completed much of the research into the *Henrietta Marie*'s record in English archives. Additionally, Russell Adams, Jane Landers, Colin Palmer, and James Rawley were with the *Henrietta Marie* project from the beginning. Much information gleaned from their original material appears in these pages. Kate Ezra kindly lent her insight on African art. John Thornton and Linda Heywood provided not only a wealth of background information to the book but also became two of its first readers, finding many of the mistakes and helping to correct them. Only I can assume responsibility for those that remain.

Ozzie and Marion Sykes came to Key West as members of the National Association of Black Scuba Divers (NABS) and found themselves lending a great deal of their energy to the project. Ozzie's patience, resilient humor, tact, and eagle eye remain unchallenged. Michael Cottman, also a member of NABS, brought heartfelt intensity and journalistic integrity to the project. All have given selflessly of their time, as have many other NABS members including José Jones, the club's president.

David Moore's relentless enthusiasm for the *Henrietta Marie* has been a true inspiration, and the generosity with which he supplied me with the fruits of his many years of research is unheralded. Corey Malcom not only led the field expedition to the *Henrietta Marie* but he com-

Madeleine Burnside

pleted almost all the conservation of the ship's artifacts. Angus Konstam came all the way from the Tower of London to Key West to consult on the *Henrietta Marie*'s cannons and stayed in constant touch with the project, sharing his vast knowledge of maritime arms and ordinance. All the staff of the Mel Fisher Maritime Heritage Society worked on this project in one way or another, particularly Melissa Smith, Dylan Kibler, and Robert Cummings; also Carol Shaunessy, Sandi Dalton, and Sandy McKinney.

Tonia Barringer organized the exhibition, and together we sorted out many of the ideas that have found their way into this book. Before Tonia arrived on the scene, Andrew Kelly gathered the circle of scholars and his remarkable energy brought the project from a weak flame to its present vitality.

Last and best, I would like to thank Melissa Kendrick, my partner in so many ventures. Not only did she contribute her tireless energy to the exhibition but she assumed many of my professional obligations under the strict understanding that I would get this book finished on schedule. The level of her support, in this as in so much else, has been beyond anything I would have imagined for myself.

Rosemarie Robotham

In addition to the book team, many benevolent spirits sustained me through the making of this book. My deepest love and gratitude to my husband, my zen beacon, Radford Arrindell, and our children, Radford III and Kai, for their constancy, faith, and laughter, which keep me grounded yet give me flight. Also to my parents, Lascelles and Gloria Robotham, who taught me to seek the details rigorously and never to flinch from the truth. Their example has been one of my life's richest blessings. I am grateful also to Cornel West, for graciously signing on, adding balance, and boldly framing the paradox, and to Renée Kemp and Ione, for sharing their unique perspectives. And thank you to my dear friends Robert Fleming, Lisa Redd, and Joy Duckett Cain, for their wise words and patient listening. Finally, deep appreciation to my colleagues and friends at *Essence* magazine, for always encouraging my growth.

Craig Bernhardt

Like everyone else involved with this project, I was inexorably drawn to the story of the *Henrietta Marie*. The archaeology involved in the discovery and excavation of the wreck site and the history of adventure and despair that were revealed when the findings were assembled all combined to magnify the intrigue of an incredible epoch.

I would like to acknowledge the efforts of those at my firm who helped turn the facts and the artifacts into the object you are now holding in your hands. The talented design and production team, especially Larry Wampler, Nancy Caldwell, and Joy Kilpatrick, for their knowledge of electronic publishing, their graphic aesthetic, and their attention to the endless details. Our associate, Iris Brown, for impartial critique and for keeping our firm's other clients happy during the hundreds of hours that this book required. The photo research of Natalie Goldstein, who can find a picture of anything. And, finally, my partner in work and in life, Janice Fudyma, for inspiring the haunting cover image that instantly captured the emotion of the story and helped focus everyone's vision from the start.

Index

Picture Credits

A Note on the Typography

The display lettering in *Spirits of the Passage* was created especially for this book by Paul Shaw. His calligraphy is directly based on the hand used in the ship's manifest from the *Henrietta Marie* as well as other seventeenth-century documents.

—

Aries, the book's main text face, was designed in 1932 by the legendary English type designer Eric Gill. This typeface, specially commissioned to reflect the shapes of Chinese inscriptions in an elaborate catalog of Chinese ceramics, remained in private ownership for sixty years and fell into obscurity. In recent years it was revived and converted into digital form by the type designer Dave Farey.

—

The typeface used for the captions, designed by Californian Robert Slimbach in 1989, is known as ITC Giovanni. Modeled on classic letterforms but updated to reflect contemporary proportions, Giovanni was also created to accommodate the requirements of modern electronic imaging devices.